A Widening Field

A Widening Field

Journeys in Body and Imagination

Miranda Tufnell and Chris Crickmay

Triarchy
Press

Published in this edition in 2023 by:
Triarchy Press
Axminster, UK
www.triarchypress.net

A catalogue record for this book is available from the British Library.

ISBN:
Print: 978-1-913743-73-4
Ebook: 978-1-913743-74-1

First published in 2004 by Dance Books

Language

The First Father of the Guaranis rose in darkness lit by reflections from his own heart and created flames and thin mist. He created love and had nobody to give it to. He created language and had no one to listen to him.

Then he recommended to the gods that they should construct the world and take charge of fire, mist, rain, and wind. And he turned over to them the music and words of the sacred hymn so that they would give life to women and to men.
So love became communion, language took on life, and the First Father redeemed his solitude. Now he accompanies men and women who sing as they go:

We're walking this earth
We're walking this shining earth.

Eduardo Galeano, *Genesis.*

Contents

About this Book

It is difficult
to get the news from poems
    yet men die miserably every day
        for lack
of what is found there.

from: William Carlos Williams, *Asphodel, That Greeny Flower.*

A Widening Field

The activities and ideas explored in this book are concerned with widening the field in which we perceive and experience our lives, a waking up to the sensing body, moving out of our heads and into the present moment of what is within and around us. To live 'well' is an art that grows from how fully we perceive and inhabit our worlds, and our ability to respond creatively to what we find. Imagination is an integral and essential part of our being. Our sense of being alive in each moment depends on our capacity to play and imagine with what is there and to meet events with flexibility, curiosity, wonder, humour and passion. Yet all too often we live with a sense of being cut off from our bodies – our immediate sense of things is muffled, narrowed and distanced, and how we feel lies hidden, inaccessible to us, our everyday words unable to reach what we deeply and instinctively know. Through creating and through reflecting upon what we make, we can inhabit our lives more fully. In making, we discover the poetic language of metaphor that opens us out from the necessary narrowing of our everyday purposive thinking and seeing into a wider field of awareness. It is this search to find a richer and more personal connection to what is around us that underlies all that follows.

Using the Text

The book is designed to be used a bit at a time, to stimulate one's own processes of working. It is not intended to be read straight through from cover to cover, nor to be followed to the letter as a comprehensive guide. With this in view, the text is arranged as an assemblage of material of different kinds around its various themes. This material includes practical approaches to working and explorations of the imaginative landscape of our lives. We begin with the body and waking up to our immediate surroundings.

The work of this book constantly shifts between one medium and another – from moving to writing, from writing to making with materials, from making to conversation and story. We have found that shifting between different modes and media in this way stimulates the imagination and gives rise to imagery that could not as easily be found within a single art form. As we continue to explore from different points of view and through different forms of expression, a world of images and meanings begins to open for us. Working in several different media may feel a barrier to people with little or no experience in one art form or another (or perhaps with no arts experience at all). But this need not be a problem, since the improvisational approach adopted calls upon our innate skills and abilities rather than specialised training and experience. Paradoxically we often feel freer in an unfamiliar medium than one in which we are skilled, once we have taken the plunge of having a go.

Although the work described in this book can mostly be done alone, it is always more satisfying to do with others or at least one other. Much of the work therefore includes some element of partnering – taking turns watching or listening to each other. A partner provides a supportive framework and a context within which what we do or make is received and explored.

The intention of this work is to gain a richer and wider sense of what is happening in our lives. We discover more of who we are and what is happening to us as we move out from ourselves and into an engagement with what is other than us. Whatever draws us out of ourselves always reflects back in. To draw connections between our lives and what we create is often seen as therapy – a practice that needs a dance, drama, art... therapist to help elicit material and interpret what is produced. Instead, we believe in the potency of the creative process and the images produced *themselves* to heal, speak for and enrich us.

A practical problem will arise in how simultaneously to work and to follow descriptions of an activity on the page. The reader will discover their own preferred way of tackling this, but possibilities include: working only from fragments that stick in your memory (after reading the relevant section); recording sections onto tape (with large pauses interspersed); or doing the equivalent with a partner reading aloud from the text.

In suggesting activities we have constantly referred the reader to their own sense of what feels necessary and appropriate. One's own sense of what is needed at a particular moment is far more important than any amount of written advice.

It is hard to convey, without actually doing it, the involving, lively, often humorous, and passionate nature of this work – how it changes from moment to moment in mood or tone - how it frequently leaves one with a sense of something understood, without necessarily being able to spell this out. Always, our wonder has been in the extraordinary ability of the intuitive mind to invent the necessary image or expression for itself.

How the Text is Arranged

The first chapter, Arriving, is concerned with preparing to work by tuning in to the body, and waking up to what is around us – becoming 'present' both to our physical bodies and to our surroundings. From there onwards, the text is divided into two parts.

Part 1: Creating as Conversation (Chapters 2-4), introduces an improvisational approach to moving, writing, and making things with materials. Through what we create in these various media, we bring into existence images – in story, picture, gesture, etc. – that are unique and particular to our own experience. Through reflecting upon what we have made, in getting to know our images, we develop a fuller, deeper and wider sense of meaning and connection in our lives. Approaches introduced in Part 1 are then applied within certain themes in Part 2.

Part 2: The Unfolding Image (Chapters 5-10), offers starting points for creative exploration, rooted in the body, our immediate surroundings, and in the stories we tell of our lives. It is the multi-layered nature of our relationships to body and surroundings – at once, physical and sensory, emotional and imaginative, metaphorical and cultural – that we explore in these chapters, both through the text and the activities introduced. Chapters on the skin, the bones, and the heart develop a felt sense of the anatomy and physiology of the body, interweaving material on the physical body with ideas and activities that explore what the body means to us imaginatively. How we perceive and understand the body shifts our experience and use of it. Chapters on materials and on places explore both the physical experience of our surroundings and the personal and cultural meanings that we derive from them. A chapter on stories draws attention to narrative as a metaphorical way of mapping our lives. None of these chapters attempts a comprehensive treatment of its theme. Their purpose, and that of the whole book, is to support and encourage the development of one's own sources for working, from which any subject matter and any form of work can then develop.

The most authentic thing about us
Is our capacity to create, to overcome
To endure, to transform, to love
And to be greater than our suffering.
We are best defined by the mystery
That we are still here, and can still rise
Upwards,....

from: Ben Okri, *Mental Fight.*

Autobiographical notes – how we came to this work

This book has grown out of a long series of conversations between the two of us which began in the mid 1970s with the making of a TV programme for the Open University called *Dance Without Steps*. In all these years we have continued to explore the connections between living and making and to think about the relationships between body, language and imagination. Throughout this time we have been able to share the various perspectives that reflect our different backgrounds, one in dance and therapeutic body work (Miranda Tufnell), and the other in art and art education (Chris Crickmay). Over the years we have also continued working creatively in the arts (both together and apart), and to run courses and workshops with others, and these practical experiences have been a constant reference point for our writing. Our previous book: *Body, Space, Image: Notes Towards Improvisation and Performance* (first published in 1990), drew upon our knowledge and experience of contemporary work in experimental performance. This present book, which turns more towards one's own personal sources for working in any medium, has drawn upon our more recent work, alone and with others, exploring strategies for creative work that lead to a greater sense of personal meaning and fulfilment. What brought us individually to this point is described below.

Chris Crickmay

Here I am splayed against a wall, my feet in the air, paying attention to my left ankle which is wanting to travel sideways and my head which is currently pressed against a wooden floor and seeking some other option. How have I, who grew up in a respectable middle class family, and have pursued a professional career in colleges and universities for the last 30 years, ended up feeling that such antics are among the most worthwhile activities in my life?

I never had any formal arts training, unless you count a degree in Architecture, which, to my mind, is more in the field of design than the arts. Art was difficult for me at boarding school – for one thing I found that the pupils who specialised in art were mostly sophisticates from London who would lock the art room door so that they could smoke. This state of being 'locked out' of the arts is, I think, common to many people, since most of us would like to do something creative but can't always find a route in. At school I collected butterflies and moths because I loved their patterns and colours and also enjoyed being a kind of Sunday painter, following my father who was a keen amateur watercolourist. This same feeling of being on the outside inspired me in my Open University years to help create an arts course for 'non-artists', called Art and Environment. Summer schools linked to this were an extraordinary experience with everyone from retired coal miners, to magistrates and bar maids bursting out with creative and avant-garde ideas in every possible form. I remember one person, an ex fighter pilot establishing a 'formation walking team' with half a dozen of the other (adult) male students. Was this art? Who cared? It was an expressive form out on its own and it worked. Around this time I met and interviewed a writer called Marion Milner, a well known psychoanalyst, whose book, *On Not Being Able to Paint,* clarified for me an approach to art through improvisation and an idea of art as an exploration of one's emotional life. What she called her 'free drawings' also reflected a common interest in spontaneity and the unconscious that had been prevalent in art of the late 1950s (e.g. in the work of Jackson Pollock). This encounter has informed my own thinking about the arts ever since and made sense of what I was trying to do in encouraging anyone and everyone to make and create things.

In this same period (the mid 1970s), I discovered improvised dance, and met Miranda Tufnell, Rosemary Butcher, Mary Fulkerson and others who were pioneering the development of improvised dance in Britain at the time. Whilst growing up, dance had never really entered my field of awareness, unless you count some rather stiff and self conscious attempts at ballroom dancing that became a passport to social events and meeting girls, or my sisters twirling wildly around to a scratchy old 78 record of the Nutcracker Suite – sports, yes, but dance in any artistic sense, no. Perhaps I really enjoyed active sports because they also provided a subliminal kind of dance. Anyway, in later years, finding I could take part in a form of improvised dance without needing to learn steps and without years of training was a revelation. To simply roll on the floor and feel my own shifting weight and the flow of sensations in my body was a sudden fascination and discovery. And to not try to do anything, but rather to let things happen of their own accord, opened up a vast realm of possibility and got round the formidable obstacle of needing some sort of idea before you could begin. Later I was introduced to Alexander Technique, a discipline of body awareness that drew me further into the realm of the body and how we experience it and made me realise how closely linked are our emotional worlds and our physical, bodily states.

Over the years I have found various avenues for making work in and across the arts, working especially between visual art and movement. I have recently been engaged in a project by correspondence with Eva Karczag (the choreographer, dancer, and dance teacher), exchanging work through the post – me sending her things I had made (which could be unpacked to form 'installations'), she sending me tapes of her movement work, each one in response to the other. The idea of making things in response within a conversational framework appeals to me and is taken up as an approach to working in this book. In one sense I never left architecture behind, because I have always loved to make spaces and places and to explore qualities of light (all architectural concerns), but I wanted to do this in a more transient and wilful way than architecture allows. In my teaching at Dartington on a course called Art and Social Context, and subsequently at the University of the West of England in Bristol, I have tried to approach art as a form of expressive playfulness open to all and applicable in any setting. I continue to be intrigued and excited by those moments when someone manages to find their own original form for something that is felt and real to them.

Miranda Tufnell

I have always loved movement. The particular way a person sits, or talks and moves in their daily life is a 'dance' that continually fascinates and absorbs my attention. As far back as I can remember I loved watching movement – the wild turning waters of the millrace, the shimmer of sunlight on wet grasses, the flight of birds across the sky or the insistent chatter of rain on the window. All touched and moved my own body. I wanted to metamorphose and move with each of them – particularly the hidden 'night movers', the owls and foxes calling out through the darkness. As a child everything was movement, and my own body felt silenced and somehow numbed when I came indoors and entered a grown up world of words. I remember my mother emerging from her writing at the end of a day and asking what we had been doing and finding myself unable to convey anything of the living world outdoors. Whatever words emerged seemed thin and empty, creating a sudden distance between myself and the experience.

In those early years I danced passionately, it was a way of 'speaking' the flood of stories, people and events that had moved me. In the glorious moments when music played in our house, it entered my body and awoke all the aliveness I felt outside in the rivers and streams and the winds of our garden. In moving I seemed to find a way in which every part of me was able to see and feel – my fingers, hair, spine, all came alive and had a voice. And not just my familiar known body but some other mercurial and invisible body appeared – a body that constantly transformed itself – now bird, now twig, now old woman, now water – a permeable, changing body that seemed to join and connect me to everything around.

Looking back it shocks me how quickly that world faded, and with it my capacity to hear and enter into things, as if as we grow the body closes in on itself, silenced. My parents were both dedicated writers and our house full of books. And as I grew up I discovered in reading a comradeship that I had previously only known outdoors. In the language of poetry I found again a sense of connection and meaning bright and mysterious as a rainbow. Words like spells or goblins calling up other numinous worlds; each poem a box of delights drawing me into the writer's own particular passion. "Tread softly lest the blind mole hear your footfall".... "The house has been far out at sea all night"...."We were bound on the wheel of an endless conversation...."

So I took a degree in English literature, but as the three years went by, I felt I was living behind a talking mask – and one summer afternoon a sudden impulse made me audition for a dance training. I see it now as the beginning of a long journey to recover something vital in the quality of my relationship to myself and to the world around me. I turned back to dancing because there were no words – and in those first months of classes I felt deliriously excited, like a child learning to walk again. My right foot seemed to have no idea what my left foot was up to, and for a while I did not speak, my familiar language fell away as I listened to a body awkward and unpredictable as a stranger.

Yet after the initial delight of having successfully catapulted myself from one world into another, I was quickly dissatisfied by the military drill of a traditional dance training. I was not interested in parroting another's movement, only in discovering my own source of moving. One day, disheartened and bored, I wandered into a performance at the Royal College of Music in which Eva Karczag was dancing. Watching her move, I felt the solid world melting and becoming transparent, I could see beneath the surfaces of her body to the moment by moment flow of impulse and thought within her tissues.

I left the dance training and through Eva went to meet Bill Williams, a legendary Alexander teacher, who had trained with F.M. Alexander himself. Bill Williams worked with his eyes closed, his hands moving delicately yet swiftly over the body as if reading Braille. It was in the stillness of working with Bill that I finally began to learn about movement and to hear the life and intelligence of the body. He taught me to listen to the subtle, inner music of the body, and to the delicate fluctuations of its response to everything within and around. In the quiet touch of his hand I began to notice the many simultaneous, often conflicting, layers of thought, emotion, memory, and how swiftly the body transforms in response to a thought or image.

I invited another dancer, Martha Grogan, who was also studying with Bill Williams to work with me and explore in movement these principles of Alexander teaching. I was surprised in those early days how hard it was to find a spontaneous movement, as if my body could not hear itself and instead spoke only in other's words or movements. Initially we felt we had to rinse ourselves of all the conditioning of our dance training. For a year Martha and I immersed ourselves in the quality and detail of walking, sitting, running, rolling and we were enchanted by the wit and synchronicities of what grew from such simple beginnings. We were interested, not in the grand movements of a Dancer, but in the particular and personal gestures of the ordinary (extraordinary) body.

Since then I have collaborated with many other people, creating performances that often also make use of sound, light, shadow and projection. Notable among these collaborations have been a long-standing working relationship with the mercurial and magical dancer, Dennis Greenwood. I have also worked extensively with the musician, Sylvia Hallet, whose intricate sound worlds, combining pre-recorded and live sound continue to thrill me. Starting to work with Sylvia coincided with a move to Cumbria, and a shift out of the art world of performance into the community. Among other things, I began working within the NHS, teaching skills of body awareness in a local GP surgery.

Over the years I have moved in and out of performing, dancing and teaching – training as an Alexander Teacher and in Craniosacral Therapy. Through both Don Burton and Franklin Sills I learnt to listen more deeply to the body and its subtleties of movement. Also, through these inspirational teachers, I learnt that in body work only by widening one's perceptual field and accepting a person's body exactly as it is – not trying to fix or change it – then, in that widened field, a sea-change in the body begins to occur of its own accord. For me there has never been one way. I have always needed to explore between writing, moving, music, and visual images; between working with others in bodywork or movement, and working creatively in my own work; shifting between the poetry of language, the sensuousness of making, and the experience of the body, in order to touch into the illusive yet tangible riches of the unfolding moment.

Sources

A book of this nature inevitably draws from a huge range of sources, some of them idiosyncratic. However, there are a number of primary sources and streams of thought from which we have drawn that are mentioned below and further detailed references are given in the bibliography.

Sources on the body

The anatomy and physiology presented in this book have been arrived at through a personal synthesis drawn from many different approaches. Its starting point is in the first hand experience of a dancer – a felt sense of the effect of movement in the body, an attempt to notice and feel what is going on. Some of the information is drawn from ancient sources including T'ai Chi and Chinese medicine, where the body is perceived in terms of flows of energy. Experience of studying and teaching Alexander Technique over many years has also been a significant source, including the influence of Don Burton concerning the details of anatomy, physiology and embryology. Attending to the body directly, through the hands (in Alexander Technique and Craniosacral practice), has been an ongoing way of understanding its nature and functioning. Specific parts of the book have drawn from particular writers. The chapter on Skin has drawn on the work of Ashley Montagu and of Deane Juhan. We are indebted to the visionary perception of Hugh Milne (also to Deane Juhan) for much of the information on the quality and nature of Bone. Hugh Milne's understanding (as a cranial osteopath), of the link between diaphragm and tentorium and the moving relationship between heart, diaphragm and brain has been especially useful. We also owe a debt to the craniosacral work of Franklyn Sills and his understanding of the Breath of Life and the Long Tide. Hugh Molne also pointed us towards the work of Robert Becker and Gary Selden. Their book, *The Body Electric*, looks at the effect of electromagnetic fields on cell functioning. Michael Shea was also helpful in understanding the embryological development of the heart. In coming to understand more of the nature of the heart, we were encouraged by Malcolm Riggler to read the work of Paul Pearsall, whose study of heart transplants provided fascinating information on the heart's biophysical energy. In his book, *The Heart's Code*, Paul Pearsall draws on pioneering research of the body's shifting chemistries and the relationship of the heart to the brain, nervous system and cellular organisation.

The nature of the body and what affects its functioning is a huge and changing field of inquiry. The current passionate debate on the effect of cloning and the nature of cell integrity reveals many of the splits that separate current attitudes and approaches. The world of the body is subtle and complex. Current scientific research is daily providing surprising, ever more fascinating and challenging information. We have drawn both from mainstream anatomical and physiological sources and from various specialised fields in dance/ movement and alternative medicine. We have attempted to bring these different fields of enquiry together within the frame of what we ourselves find stimulating and useful. Given this endeavour, some readers may find material that goes against their own understanding of the body and its functioning. In anticipation of this, we have done our best to make our own sources apparent. Our approach here has a specific intent: to give greater precision and breadth to the way one experiences one's own body from within, to free and energise the body in movement, and to stimulate the imagination.

Sources in movement and improvisation

Improvised dance, rooted in an awareness in the body, must be the most ancient of human impulses, but in modern times it can be traced to the explorations of such figures as Isadora Duncan and Loie Fuller at the beginning of the 20th century. Detailed links between anatomical knowledge, body awareness and movement work were developed during the 20th century by many writers and practitioners such as: Mabel Todd, Barbara Clark, Bonnie Bainbridge Cohen and John Roland. Improvised dance/ movement, drawing upon the work of these and other (mainly American) practitioners, took off in Britain during the 1970s. Simone Forti, Nancy Topf, Lisa Nelson, Eva Karczag, Steve Paxton, Mary Fulkerson, Nancy Stark Smith and Anna Halprin, were among them, and all have influenced our thinking. Besides these, a number of Japanese dancers have influenced us who focus upon movement improvisation and the senses. Prominent among these is the work of Min Tanaka, also the Sankai Juku company. In addition to the writers and dancers mentioned above, David Abram's writings on sensory awareness and language were an invaluable source, as were Lusseyran's writings on the heightened sensory world of a blind person.

Sources on creativity, image and imagination

For our approach to the above themes we have drawn especially on the ideas of James Hillman, Marion Milner and Ted Hughes. A number of well known writers and poets, who have also dwelt on these topics have been stimulating including Eduardo Galeano, Hélène Cixous, Adrienne Rich, and Pablo Neruda. In addition to the above, we have been influenced by the writings on imagination of: Thomas Moore, Marion Woodman, Robert Sardello, Bani Shorter, Miller Mair, Arnold Mindell, Christopher Bollas, and D.W.Winnicott. Although ours is not a book about arts therapy, we have drawn both generally from the world of arts therapies and specifically from certain practitioners, including Alida Gersie's interesting work on therapeutic story telling. Brenda Mallon's books on dreaming have also been useful.

Sources on place and identity

On questions of place and our experiencing of it, writings by Lucy Lippard, John Berger and Gaston Bachelard have been especially useful. Our ideas about making places and responding to places have drawn upon the work of the many contemporary artists who create 'installation' art and 'site-specific' art. The works of Joseph Beuys, Bill Viola, Rebecca Horne, Illia Kabakov, Ian Hamilton Finlay, Edward Kienholz, James Turrel, Janet Cardiff (a musician), Dennis Oppenheim, Walter de Maria, Christian Boltanski, Louise Bourgeois and Miroslaw Balka, have all informed our text. Many of their works feature in illustrations throughout the book.

Other sources in visual art

Marion Milner and James Hillman have both influenced the chapters on making and on looking at images. Shaun McNiff has also influenced us in his approach to images. Our thoughts on the cultural aspects of materials have drawn from such writers as Primo Levi, whose books on the human aspects of industrial chemistry make such good reading. Numerous sculptors have influenced our thoughts on materials. Those who particularly use (or used) everyday or 'found' materials such as Marcel Duchamp, Joseph Beuys, Eva Hesse, and the 'Art Povera' artists of the 1970s and sculptors such as Bill Woodrow, Cornelia Parker or Andy Goldsworthy, in Britain today, have all influenced our thinking. Vast amounts have been written on the subject of colour. We have drawn especially from the works and notes of artists Ken Kiff and Winifred Nicholson. Derek Jarman's text *Chroma,* on the associative aspects of colour has also been of interest. Certain groups involved in visual performance have also influenced us, including the British groups, Horse and Bamboo, I.O.U., and Theatre de Complicite, and the Russian theatre group AKHE.

Acknowledgements

For their invaluable advice on the text at particular stages we are indebted to Tony Burch, Jennie Crickmay, Jane Fitzgerald, Penny Greenland, John Hall, Vicky Hamilton Tufnell, Brenda Mallon, and Gentian Rahtz. We would like to thank Northern Arts (and particularly Mark Mulqueen) for the Encore Bursary awarded to Miranda Tufnell in the final stages of our work. Thanks are also due to Hazel Barrett for her work on text copyright and a very special thanks to Pippa McNee for her untiring work on picture copyrights. Lastly we are much indebted to our respective families for their moral support throughout.

It was always our intention to include in this book many other voices besides our own. This is reflected both in the numerous illustrations – particularly examples of creative work - and in the quotations from other people's writings (as well as those we have specially commissioned). We would like to thank the many visual artists, dancers, theatre companies and photographers who have provided us with pictures of their work (or work on which they have expert knowledge), and in many cases contributed explanatory text – their contributions are listed at the back of the book. We would also particularly like to thank the following who have contributed more extended pieces of text: Niamh Dowling, Eva Karczag, Lucinda Jarret, Ruth Jones, Annea Lockwood, Annie Menter, Lisa Nelson, and Steve Paxton.

1. Arriving – preparing to work

Arriving contents

arriving into the body, into the world

stirring up the body

weight

breath

space

what calls?

Winifred Nicholson, *Gate to the Isles*, 1980
Oil on canvas 18 x 24 ins

Fern

Here is the fern's frond, unfurling a gesture,
Like a conductor whose music will now be a pause
And the one note of silence
To which the whole earth dances gravely.

The mouse's ear unfurls its trust,
The spider takes up her bequest,
And the retina
Reins the creation with a bridle of water.

And, among them, the fern
Dances gravely, like the plume
Of a warrior returning, under the low hills,

Into his own kingdom.

from: Ted Hughes, *Wodwo.*

Arriving into the body, into the world
becoming present

It is through the sensuous world of the body, through our eyes, ears, skin, muscles, and organs, that we see, feel and respond to all that happens. The body is the ground from which all our knowing of the world begins. It is within our bodies, in our instinctual and sensory responses, that we discover the changing field of what is happening to us. In the rush and pressure of our everyday lives we easily become numbed, cut off from our bodies. Without a sense of the body, of sensation and feeling, we lose connection to what is around and within us, to the immediate and present moment of our lives. To move out of our heads and into the sensory world of the body awakens us not only to sensation but also to a slower, deeper landscape beneath the surface of everyday awareness, a landscape of feeling, memory, impulse and dream.

arrive....river F. *rive* stream, Ital. *riviera* shore bank, L. *arripare* to come to shore, to land
prepare....pare, to shave off, to trim, L. *parare* to prepare

Preparing to work takes time – time to slow down and catch up with ourselves, steer ourselves out of the currents in which we have been borne along, out of the swiftness of the noisy and often tumultuous river that is our lives, and make our way towards a shore. At first we may feel clumsy, stiff and numbed, as if from travelling in cramped conditions. Who and where have we been? What have we been doing? We may need to rub our eyes, loosen faces and shake out limbs and simply rest. And at first we may feel nothing, as if our skins have hardened, closing us in. It takes time to come back to ourselves – to breathe, and feel the touch of air around us, time to feel the living, sensing presence of our bodies, and the ground beneath our feet – to notice where we are now. Our preoccupation with of all we have been doing recedes only slowly as we settle and wake up both to ourselves as body and to the living world about us.

Miranda Tufnell, study for *Wing*. Photo: Caroline Lee

Rub down

Give another (or yourself) an all-over rub down
a light dusting.... a brisk car wash
Let the hands be open.... skim.... scour.... scrub.... stir up.... slap
wake up.... the outside of the body

Feel the skin.... and what is beneath the skin.... layers of muscle and bone, blood and breath
Notice what is tight.... bruised.... tired – where feels numb.... forgotten
breathe.... lengthen.... widen.... make room inside the body
Let the outside of your body wake up and.... soften.... loosen.... brighten
let the inside of the body expand.... fill out

Feel.... what is there.... today?

What time is it, I mean to say where am I, I mean to say where have I gone – I don't know anymore, in this instant when I call out to myself, where I'm passing or where I'm going.
Hélène Cixous, *Stigmata*

Landing.... time to be still

Lie comfortably on the ground
Feel the shape and form of your body
from the soles of the feet to the crown of the head.... let the length of the spine open
Let go of the need.... to do.... anything
Let go the chatter of your thoughts.... be empty
Rest.... take time to breathe

Let the weight of each part of the body give way.... settling.... gentle as snowfall
feel the support of the earth rising under you
Let the whole body.... rest and fall
small world of the body.... resting on great world of the earth
feel the resonance of the body with the earth
mountains...valleys... deserts... rivers... pools... seas

What is soft.... fluid?.... What is hard.... dense?
What is fragile?.... What holds pain?

Let the field of your attention.... soften and spread out
Sense the temperature of the ground.... of the air
Sense the time of day.... season of the year.... weather
Open.... your ears.... listen.... let in the sounds around
Let each eye soften and rest.... sensing light.... shadow

Let the breath come in.... opening space.... inside the body.... opening inside to out

Body map

Make.... a map of the inside of your own body
as you feel it today

Brancusi, *Head*. Photo: John Haselgrove

Stillness....... of a quiet room.... of a ship at anchor

What appears?

When we first enter a wood the noise of our arrival drives everything into hiding. Only as we are still and wait silently do we begin to see its inhabitants, the myriad worlds existing within it. A spider swings itself up through the air on an invisible thread... a shadow of a crow passes above... the leaves brighten as the sun comes out... a rustling as a squirrel darts along a branch.

So the sensing, perceiving world of the body awakens only slowly as we are still. The more I sink into the physical presence of my own body, the more the fullness of being and particularity of what is outside and around me becomes apparent. As I breathe and wake up into the detail – my body seems to soften and become permeable. And the concerns and worries that filled my mind loosen and give way, opening me into another more fluid and vital 'world', of textures, colours, sounds – layer upon layer of living detail that touches me in each moment – a sudden illumination of sunlight on my skin, the warmth or chill of the ground under me, the rise of my breath joining the movement of a breeze. As the field of my attention spreads out I begin to notice a sense of response moving within me – responses which my body continually makes but of which I am usually unaware.*

***Footnote:** It may happen that as I soften and come into awareness I begin to notice feelings that I have suppressed in my everyday life. Grief, anger, pain may rise like genies from a bottle, threatening to overwhelm me. Yet if I stay with the present moment in my body, and continue to feel its weight, breath and the movement of sensation, what threatened to overwhelm me may slowly begin to change, transformed by tides of a richer and wider field than I had been able to see.

What is moving? – following sensation and impulse

Be still.......... rest
Sense your weight.... let each part of your body breathe.... listen
What do you feel?.... Notice a particular sensation
Watch and follow as it rises into movement
awakening.... impulse

Let the rest of the body.... follow and support
Discovering a pathway.... through.... and out

Blow gently.... on the embers of each impulse to move
Be generous.... give way into your responses

Feel the beat of your heart
feel the movement of breath.... of thoughts and impulses.... of dreams and memories within the body
listen.... feel how the body is moved moment by moment.... even as you are still
opening... closing... turning... returning
there is no moment that is ever the same

Let each movement.... take its own time through the body

Slowly let movement inside.... stir.... waken and brighten.... the outside of the body.

Let sensation from outside.... enter in

LISTEN DREAM MOVE FOLLOW

When in spring a fern develops with the unrolling of its fronds, the unfolding, seen with the naked eye, is apparently a growth through unrolling from the inside out, increasingly toward the light, upward. But, submicroscopically, it is demonstrably an intimate uptake of particles from the soil and from the air, thus, inversely, the growth is the expression of molecular movements and of movements of microscopical minuscule particles through the cellular membranes from the outside to the interior. Erich Blechschmidt, *Beginnings of Human Life.*

Steve Paxton, Improvisation, Bratislava, 2002.
Photo: Chris Crickmay

Stirring up the body
find.... warmth, energy, momentum

Javier Hinojosa, *Borrachas de sol* (wind in palms),1989.

The Forest People, the Pygmies, sing... to awaken their forest world... and to thank it for sustaining their lives. If misfortune strikes it is because the forest has forgotten them and has gone to sleep.
Colin Turnbull, *The Forest People*

Run.... race.... roar.... expand
let the body fill up.... fill out
stir up... shake out... rumple... jostle... disturb
loosen.... shake up.... whatever shape the body holds

let go your name
loosen shoulders and arms.... shake out the wrists and hands
scour and loosen the face
greet and move.... every part.... of the body.... of the room
stir up.... the air around you.

move in every direction.... to the sky... sea... city... wind

Wake up.... each part of the body

Wake up.... wherever you are

settle... tip... erupt... collapse... melt down... keel over... rise... float... fly... balance... lean... sink... dump... fall down... break up... freeze... turn around... change colour... explode... soften... melt... grow... reassemble... merge... multiply

Kirstie Simson, *solo improvisation, following the flow of weight and momentum.*
Photo: Chris Nash

Moving refreshes all the parts of our selves, stirring up what feels dulled by lack of movement or awareness, quickening the flow of blood and enlivening circulation. Movement stimulates sensation within the limbs and joints, shakes up postural and perceptual habits, awakening the senses – scent, taste, hearing.... Moving clears the windows of our senses, to let the world in and to let us 'see' out. I notice what moves me, and I notice what I have held unmoving, and sense the need to shake up, shake down, be very still, clown, put on a mask, be 'other' than everyday – impulses to which I am usually blind, but which, once sensed, enliven my whole being.

Movement stimulates circulation and the flow of intercellular information throughout the body. The arterial blood is propelled by the heart outwards through the body. And the movement of muscles speeds the return of blood to the heart for re-oxygenation. The vitality of the body depends on the movement of blood. Forgetting to move causes stagnation, a backing up of fluids and hence information within the body.

The movement of the embryo within the womb is vital for the development of the musculo-skeletal system – crucial not only for the muscles themselves, but also in aligning the trabeculae (filaments) within the bones, the correct attachment of ligaments, and the coiling of collagen fibres into the tendons. Movement begins as early as the seventh week of embryonic life – slow, asymmetric, twisting and stretching movements of the trunk and limbs. Movement stimulates normal skin growth and flexibility as well as helping the musculo-skeletal system to mature.

Walking together

Take a walk with a partner.... fall into the rhythm of a shared walk
let the backs of your hands touch.... meet
Give way into the momentum and rhythm of your shared walking
follow.... allow changes of direction.... circling.... reverses
let the whole body follow the pulse of your shared walk
Let arms and legs swing.... let the length of the spine open
Let go of any attempt to control direction
walking.... as falling
get lost.... in changing pathways

Explore - one person with eyes closed
stay awake to the pulse of your shared walking
let your whole body respond to the movement received through your arms.... to the swings of direction
Allow yourself to ride and be moved.... on the waves of momentum.... arising between you

Working with a group of refugees in Gotera, El Salvador
Having returned to build a village four years earlier and only in the previous week located a place for a well to give the village water, I was playing with the children before the workshop began. They were running through a skipping rope with a partner looking to find the moment, the impulse to run together without counting each other in. Others joined and soon partners became small groups and eventually the whole village of 20 people were poised together as one breath awaiting the moment they could pass together under the turning rope. They waited building a sense of direction, a sense of purpose, carrying the babies, supporting the elders, keeping the goal in mind and not putting their attention to the rope, the obstacle, just as they had kept their attention on surviving fleeing their country and the massacre of their young men, years in exile and returning to begin to literally rebuild their lives and knowing they have built new homes and now a well, through this unity, this ensemble. Knowing that they will survive and succeed in finding water, food, work, they wait, listening to the breath, to the group breath, breathing in together and out together, in as one and out as one and waiting as one until the moment arrived and eventually in exhilaration, in glee, in ecstasy running as one through the turning rope...... Niamh Dowling

Walk about

Move everywhere through the room.... between windows.... walls.... people
Travel.... breathe.... changing pace.... direction.... swing out arms and legs
let yourself be drawn.... now here.... now there
Let each part of the body see.... and respond
let in... and ride the flow of breath.... letting what is outside come in
What is closed.... unmoving?... What in the body needs to move.... loosen.... and wash out?
let the body greet and welcome what is around

One hundred voices

As you move around the room
Call out.... to others.... to yourself.... and move
"head" ......"elbow" ...."chin"...."ear" ...."heel"...................."knee"
"from behind"....... "up above"........"belly"...."inside out"..........."tip of the nose"
Shift attention.... move that part.... finding other.... different parts

Being moved

Invite another person.... two people.... to move you
let the moving.... grow slowly
through the contact.... sense your edges
Slowly.... find your own movement in response
Allow time: to be still.... to resist.... to surprise.... to merge.... to question

Mark Wallinger, *Oh No He's Not, Oh Yes He Is.*
Pantomime costume in fibreglass resin,1995.

Disrupting habit

Go 'backwards'
be upside down... inside out... oppose... reverse... provoke
(in whatever way it occurs to you)
Wake up your senses.... what animal speaks to you today?

When the Crow Indians feel stuck in some habit
they do everything in reverse – ride their
horses backwards, eat breakfast at suppertime

The Kalahari bushmen called the Whites, "heavy people".
Move...... to lighten up

A sense of your own weight

weigh Anglo Saxon, *wegan* to carry, move, raise (as in weigh anchor) lift balance in the scales..... have heaviness or weight

Releasing downwards

As I begin to loosen and feel my body, I discover a sense of its weight, mass, and fullness, which in turn opens me more into the present moment. As each part of the body finds a sense of its own particular weight, it lets go of the parts around it, and this allows a softening and spreading out – weight of the head giving way and letting go of neck; weight of pelvis letting go of legs; shoulders falling from ribcage and spine; hands falling from wrists. What may have felt inert or dense begins to flow and move, and paradoxically to lighten. And as we find our own living, breathing weight, we also discover our own rhythm and pace.

Images from a Contact Improvisation workshop led by Nancy Stark Smith at Moving East, London 2003

Eva Karczag, improvisation. Photo: Nienke Terpsma.
A river of internal movement flows constantly in me and is the underlying generator of the form that is then perceived by the viewer. Eva Karczag

Leverage.... moving with the ground

Explore.... moving close to the ground

Feel how your bones give leverage.... and make room within the body

Feel the directions of the bones within you.... feel their hard edges.... let them meet the ground

Travel the ground... creep... crawl... raise... straddle... slither... lift

Let each bone discover and use the ground

Move.... as an animal.... leaving traces.... footprints.... signs

It is the meeting of ground and bone... that allows the body to lighten, rise and move

Edward Hopper, *The Martha McKeen of Wellfleet,* 1944.
Oil on canvas 32 x 50 ins.
(© Colleccion Thyssen-Bornemisza. 1980.32)

Ironing out - using weight to roll out tension and compression

(derived from Contact Improvisation)

With a partner –
one person lies.... on the ground
the other.... lies over
alternate rolling

person underneath

Breathe....... take time to receive/ let in.... your partner's weight
let it fall through you....and through to the ground beneath you
Give way.... notice resistance.... hard edges.... density.... fragility
Slowly roll.... sense how each of your bodies softens and spreads out

"As pillars crumble in an earthquake
ground tremor... everything tumbles... shatters, all that I carried within me but did not see"

person on top

Let your weight settle.... accept support
let your whole body spread out.... as a star.... in all directions
moment by moment.... cell by cell.... falling.... giving way.... breathe
sense your partner's breath rising under you.... share the movement of breath

slowly... shift positions.... roll.... slowly.... over the landscape of your partner's mass
allow your body to be changed.... softened
widen.... lengthen....deepen

"She was tight as electric cable pressed out... pressed together... the wires longing to unwind listen to the rain falling... softly... sinking... she was falling through layers through stiff and closed rooms... shells... encrustations... she had not noticed somewhere deep below the surface a river flowed... far underground.."

Finding movement in the flow of weight

Rest against.... walls.... doors.... another person
take time.... let the body receive support.... at the edges.... and deep within
Feel how your weight flows.... breathe.... follow it
slip... slide... flow... ripple... flare... pulsate... shimmer... pour... hover... fly... spring... leap

What does the weight.... give.... allow.... invite.... within your body?
Follow momentum.... allow changes of direction
Explore falling.... upwards.... outwards.... downwards
Sense the rebound.... at the bottom of a fall

Let the floor.... or another.... be your living partner
play.... in.... and out.... of balance.... Be extreme, take risks
Let the body brighten as it moves.... stirring weight.... with breath

Giving weight, finding support

Find a partner.... lean against them
Rest.... listen.... feel the dialogue of your breath.... small shifts of weight.... as you meet

Explore.... each pushing at the other
Play in the meeting of forces.... energies
Take time.... to feel the 'animal' of your living weight
discover.... support

Commit yourself.... expand.... be enormous
change shape.... be two headed.... four legged
share.... balance.... off balance.... bridges.... blockades
merge... disagree... echo... be deaf to... suggest... tell a joke... surprise

Slow down.... change gear.... listen more deeply
Find.... your own centre of gravity

Make a dance that grows in the fluctuations of your shared weight
Follow a conversation of movement.... between you
Explore moving in contact.... with one... two... three... a crowd... of others

We become heavy when we carry.... take on.... too much.
Take time.... to lighten up.... shed burdens.... fall apart
feel the support of the ground
We can let go.... only as we find support.

A widening breath

Gk. *psyche,* soul, breath, wind

Werner Bischof, *Kyoto* – Japan, photograph,1952.

The wind, one brilliant day, called
to my soul with an odor of jasmine.
Antonio Machado

Breath of life

In many creation stories the world begins in the movement of wind over water, the breath of life stirring the darkness. And as we prepare to make or create, it is the breath that brings us back into life, loosening and awakening what has forgotten to breathe. We are born into breath, and as we live each moment, the breath nourishes our life, connecting us with all else that breathes. Our breath depends upon the leaves of the world's forests and the plankton of the deep oceans – we breathe in what they breathe out, an invisible exchange throughout the earth's atmosphere. Our lives depend on the invisible air as the creatures of the sea depend on the waters of the ocean. Without renewing oxygen, each cell of the body is quickly poisoned in its own waste – we suffocate and die. To breathe is the means by which we open, cleanse, nourish the body. Every aspect of our lives depends on our capacity to breathe. Without the winds of breath, the body becomes heavy and dense, closed in on itself, as a plant that withers without light or water; without breath we lose connection to an essential rhythm within ourselves, of inspiration and letting in... of softening and exhalation. And as the winds of the world come in many forms and from many directions, so the inspiration of each breath opens, lightens and helps us to move on.

breeze.... gust.... gale.... sigh

Wind

Open your skin
Invite the winds to come from all directions
and fill.... the body's breath
from north.... south.... east.... and west
let the breath turn the body.... inside out

Listen.... what is carried on the wind?
distant voices.... scents.... flying seeds
Let the body follow

Travelling in the breath

Listen.... be still.... feel the movement of air.... on your skin

Open... nose... mouth... skin... breathe in
watch how the breath fills.... turns.... empties in the body
as a wave rising.... and turning over within the body.... falling away
Let in the movement of the breath.... throughout the body
let the breath.... go everywhere

Breathe in.... see how far the breath reaches into the body.... now deep.... now shallow
See how the breath softens hard edges.... fills and nourishes.... what is inside
each breath taking its own time.... twisting and turning as a river within the body
see.... each is different

Open the skin
the whole body.... permeable to the air

Notice the coolness of air as it enters the nose
Open the passage of the throat.... let the trees of the lungs expand
the shoulders resting on the rise and fall of breath.... ribs and spine softening
Let the movement of breath create spaciousness inside the body
Breathe out.... *the air is warmed by its circulation within the body*

Let the body welcome.... each new breath
rising.... settling.... veering.... hovering
Each breath calls up.... movement within the body
washing through.... as water.... as light
around you.... within you.... beyond you
breath opening.... what is closed

Let the body.... become the breath

For nine months the child lives and grows in the liquid dark of the womb,
weightless and floating, nourished through the umbilicus.
At birth we enter 'the breath of the world' as the cord is cut;
the lungs begin to function and support our separate life.

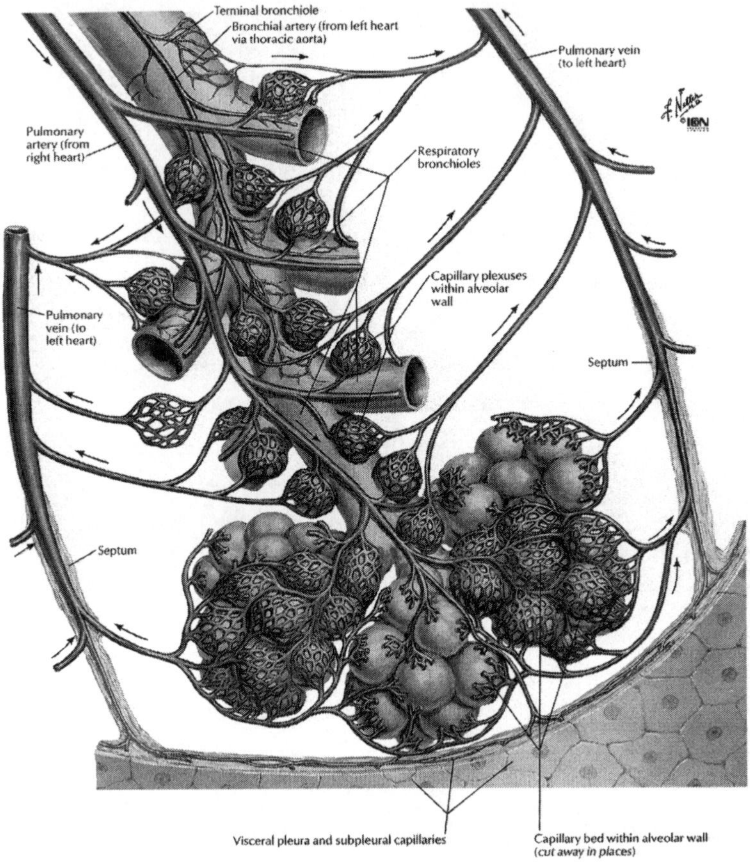

Diagram of lungs showing alveoli and take up of oxygen into the blood
diagram: F. Netter, from a colour original

The granny's house by the sea

A week before she died I asked her what she thought happened after you die. She said it was like going to a granny's house and she would let you in and say "There you are". As the time of her death drew near I spoke to her of the sea which she loved. I described the width, the depth, the colour, the peace and calm on this warm, sunny day. Her breath had been laboured and rasping all day and as I spoke it became natural and regular. No longer the laboured gulps of intaking breath but now breathing out and intaking breath as the natural part of living. I reminded her of the granny house and the realisation that the house was by the sea. She had a room in that house with a balcony overlooking the sea and on the balcony were flowers and plants. I told her that when she was ready she could go and reminded her that I would not be coming with her but that I would stay here with her as long a she wanted to stay. And we turned to look at the granny house and began to head up the path. I told her Granny would be waiting when ever she wanted to go. She gave a small cry, like a child or a bird, hawklike, then she breathed in and out and in and out and did not intake another breath. I felt a swoosh of energy running from her head to her feet and I knew she was gone...... Niamh Dowling

Breathing

Air enters the body through spaces in the ethmoid bone, which lies behind the nose and just between the eyes, a bone formed as delicately as a piece of coral or honeycomb and threaded with passages, or air sinuses, which in turn connects with sinuses that run throughout the bones of the face and forehead. The movement of the ethmoid is crucial in the everyday draining of mucous from the air passages of the head. The ethmoid flares, compresses and rotates, constantly adapting to movement and strains within the rest of the cranium.

The bones of a bird are also hollow
to lighten its skeleton and permit flight.

Air is filtered, moistened and warmed within the conchae (protuberances) of the ethmoid before descending to the lungs. To breathe lightens and refreshes the face, and cools the brain where it lies behind the face. The air descends through the trachea or windpipe into the two trees of the lungs, the right and left bronchus. Each cell of the body communicates with the atmosphere by way of the lungs. The lungs are formed as a forest of some 700 million alveoli, which together create a surface area the size of a tennis court – their capillary walls so thin that, in the movement of breathing, oxygen and carbon dioxide constantly fall through, like flour through a sieve. As the lungs expand, the whole length of the spine is delicately moved. Resting, we breathe 7-8 litres of air per minute; when active this increases five fold.

The domed muscle of the diaphragm, the muscle which most deeply affects the movement of breath within the body, forms a strong midline interface between upper and lower parts of the torso. The diaphragm creates a floor to the heart and lungs and a roof to the stomach, liver, and gut – hence its movements directly affect every structure and system within the torso. The fibres of the diaphragm span throughout the width and depth of the torso attaching to sternum, lower ribs, bodies of the vertebrae, and blends with the fibres of the psoas muscle running downwards to the pelvis and legs. The rhythm of breathing expands and moves the depth and volume of the rib cage, moves the sacrum and whole length of the spine. The left portion of the diaphragm blends with the pericardium (outer covering of the heart) – hence the movement and electrical field of the heart affects, and is itself changed, by the movement of our breathing.

What stops your breath?

The movement of the diaphragm is governed by the *phrenic nerve* (which branches from the spinal cord at the 3rd, 4th and 5th cervical vertebrae), and the respiratory centre in the *medulla* at the base of the brain. If the neck is free, we sense more easily the need to breathe.

Let the neck be free.... breathe in.... let the breath lighten the bones of the face
Let in the air.... let the breath open and move the body
Let the body belong.... in the air of the world

Unknown American Artist, *Meditation by the Sea*, mid 19th century.
Oil on canvas, 34.61 x 49.85 cms (13⅝ x 19⅝ ins).
Photograph © 2003 Museum of Fine Arts, Boston

What is inside the body.... awakening.... to what is outside?

Open your eyes.... travel out.... take a walk
Let the body.... greet.... whatever it finds
walls.... people.... colours.... noises.... views

Let the body spread open
Sense.... what calls on the body from without
Open the ears..... scent the air.... feel the touch of sound.... texture
Open your eyes,
what do you see?
Move, spread out.... into the spaces around you.... close or distant
Explore.... upwards.... inwards.... outwards.... across
through and between
Spread open.... the field of the body.... of the senses.... widen
Make room inside
both for what is already there
and for what is as yet unknown.... unseen.... arriving

Small spaces

Between sitting.... standing.... lying
Begin moving into the small spaces in and around the body
Breathe.... and sense the changing need
to open.... outwards.... regather and return.... inwards
Let ears.... eyes.... fingers.... skin.... awaken.... as antennae
uncurling.... as the tendrils of a vine
Find the small stretches.... unfamiliar.... between one part and another

Wall-Lizard, photo: H.G.F. Spurrell

intend L. *in-tendere* to stretch, to apply the mind to; **tend** to aim towards
attend... attention F. *attendre* to wait, L. *a-tendere* to stretch toward, give heed to

As we become ready to work, stretching (in whatever way seems comfortable), brightens what has dulled in our attention. In stretching, our breath, posture, thoughts loosen. If we sense and explore into the detail and small spaces in and around our bodies we inevitably discover a need to expand and open out, a lengthening, widening and deepening of our physical bodies, echoed in the expansion of our breath and the generosity of the movements we find. We can only move as we make room to move.

What opens us..... outwards?
expanding... curious... wondering... meeting
drawing us out... of inertia, collapse and compression.

Connective tissue

Every part of the body is woven together through a branching lattice of connective tissue which connects, wraps and anchors each and every part of us. Connective tissue forms a continuous weave, wrapping and uniting every tissue in the body – suspending, gathering, anchoring, separating, tying together, every organ, muscle, bone, nerve and blood vessel. Without the stimulus of regular stretch and the friction of movement, connective tissue becomes dense, and over time its fibrils tend to pack more tightly, forming adhesions, gluing the body together. Hence, our vitality and freedom to move depends on warming, softening and stretching the very tissue that binds us together.

Miranda Tufnell, Study for *Wing*. Photo: Caroline Lee

Making room inside... yawning and stretching

Lie down.... Take time to spread out
let the mouth... throat soften.... open and taste the breath
Let the hard palate.... roof of the mouth.... widen and open upwards.... as a dome
Let jaw.... tongue.... soften.... let the breath fill.... into the spaces of the mouth
As wind.... filling the sail of a boat

Let the whole face dissolve and loosen.... finding a new face

Each yawn reaching.... into the interior of the body
spreading out.... opening.... the length of the spine

Let the whole body expand and yawn
heels... shoulders... hands... knees
welcoming.... letting the outside in
Let the yawns stretch and fill the whole body.... to its full size

Working with nuns in Gotera, El Salvador

Doing partner work and working to connect the arms into the back, visualising the trapezius and latissimus and working with the image of the arms as wings, big, expansive wingspans stretching from the whole of the spine to the fingertips, dancing with this open, wide image, opening the ribcage, the heart, creating space and freedom. And when they had completed the exercise the group came to rest, bringing the wings to rest. And as the group of eighteen nuns stood with their wings I noticed they had each been working with the image of angels wings and they each had a glorious, huge pair of Angel Gabriel wings bursting high out of their backs!........ Niamh Dowling

If you mould a cup you have to make a hollow
it is the emptiness that makes it useful

In a house or room it is the empty spaces
the doors and windows – that make it usable
Tao Te Ching 1

picture above: Neolithic Stone Bowl, h.10cm

Creating space

Be still....... breathe
let go.... the need to do anything
Sense the stillness.... emptiness.... at the bottom of the breath
Pause in the turning moment.... between.... one breath and another
wait
Open the inside of the body.... open the pathways of bone
open the skin
let the body spread open as a sail to the wind

Move in the spaces in and around the body
Sense endings.... beginnings
the space between.... one bone and another

Feel the play and delicacy of the joints in the body
Pause... in the moment before.... an action........ at the edge
Sense the possibilities.... of movement.... changes of direction

interval silence emptiness

Listen.... to the space between one moment.... and another
Let the body breathe.... make room......... inside.... and out
Sense the body.... sense the horizon
let the present spread out.... into past.... into future

What calls?

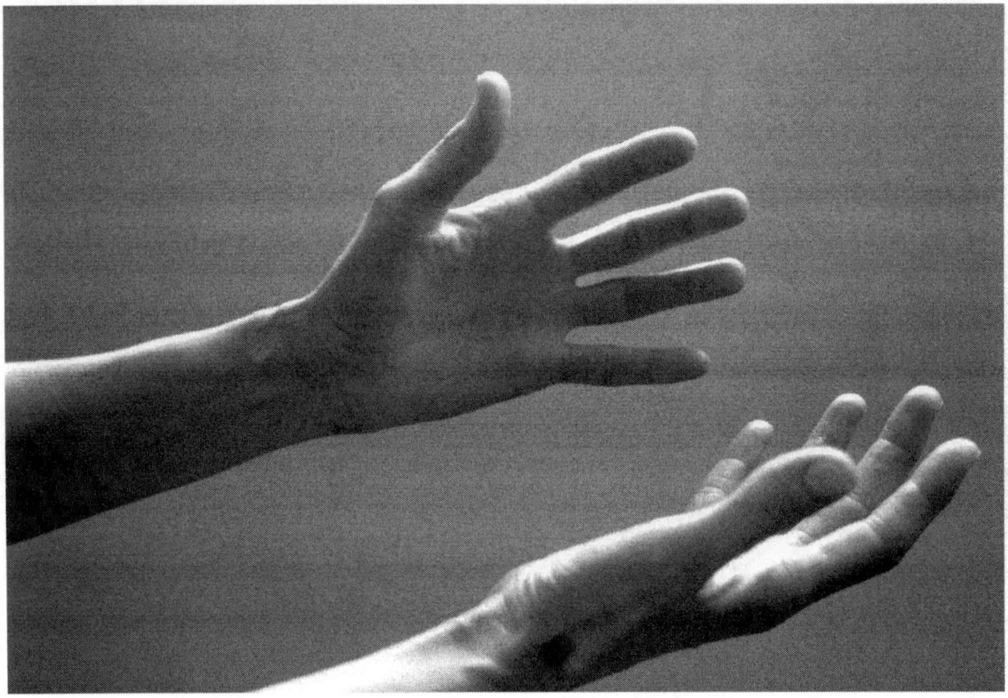

interest L. *inter esse,* lit. to be among

As I widen and settle my attention – simply receiving... not trying to notice anything in particular... just seeing what comes – certain details in what is around me or in my sensing body begin to call out to my attention. In letting go of my own desires and needs and simply remaining open to whatever comes, parts or aspects of the world around me (or of my body) suddenly seem to come alive and sing out in all their particularity. At such moments, details in what I am seeing or sensing find resonance with my internal, feeling world. These are moments when our sensing comes into connection with the wider field of who and where we are, and we seem to move out of ourselves - we begin to imaginatively participate in the world around us. It is through this felt connection that we find sources for our own creating.

I only went out for a walk
and finally concluded to stay out
until sundown
for going out,
I found
was really going in.

John Muir (1838-1914)
American naturalist.

Callings

The moon calls to the sea and the sea calls to the humble stream, which flows on and on from wherever it springs in search of the sea, no matter how far away it may lie, and growing as it flows, the stream rushes on until no mountain can hold back its surge. The sun calls the grapevine, which spreads and rises in its hunger for sunlight. The early morning air calls forth the smells of the awakening city, the aroma of newly baked bread, of newly brewed coffee, and the aromas fill the air and possess it. Night calls to the water lily, and at the stroke of midnight those white points of light burst open in the river, opening the darkness, penetrating it, breaking it apart and swallowing it up.

Eduardo Galeano, *The Book of Embraces.*

Part 1 Creating as Conversation

Part 1 - Contents

Introductory notes to Part 1

create L. *creatus,* pp. of *creare,* to make, bring forth, cause to grow
creature L. *creatura,* Old French *creatur,* a living being created
crescent L. *luna cresces,* the waxing moon, L. *crescere,* to grow, increase
recreate L. *recreare,* to play, to revive, to refresh, nourish, restore to a good condition
concrete L. *con-crescere,* to grow together
accrue L. *accrescere,* to come to by way of increase

Carving from Les Rochers Sculptés, Saint Malo, completed early 1900s. Part of an extensive work depicting local legendary figures carved into the granite rocks by the hermit priest, Abbé Fouré, and his assistant over a period of thirty years. Photo: Brenda Mallon

"To be in conversation is surely to live in the open...

To be in conversation is to think and feel 'on your feet' and not to speak only from prepared positions...

To be in conversation is to be in who you aren't as well as who you are
It is to live in what is not yet – in the other
and what they are leading you to...

It is when centres meet that the world is changed...

To live in serious conversation is to live with the converse
to live with and in contradiction
with opposites
with the other than we are
To be a place of meeting
not a place of judgment...

To be in conversation is to enter into what flows
in and amongst and between you
To be present in conversation is to speak of and speak to
the world
now..."

Excerpts from Miller Mair, *Between thee and me*
in: *Between Psychology and Psychotherapy: A Poetics of Experience.*

Creating as conversation

To create is to make, to bring forth. Creating, or making, is an integral part of our daily lives – as we make a cake, make an excuse, make friends, 'make a mountain out of a molehill'... all the time we are forming and interacting with our surroundings.

Creating in touch with sensation and feeling in the body awakens us to the sensuous detail of the material world – the opening of a hand, the coolness of a stone, the flow of a pigment... and paradoxically it is this attention to detail that opens and loosens the field in which we perceive things. Creating, in whatever way is available to us, moves us out of the abstractions and generalisations of our everyday seeing and language into the particular qualities and feel of the world about us. What we love; what is beautiful or delights us; the aesthetics of our lives; strengthen our sense of who we are. Forming or creating things that move us changes and expands our perception. What we create is always in some way speaking into being a part of ourselves which is as yet hidden and unspoken, unexpressed even to ourselves.

aesthetic Gk. *aestheticos* – things perceptible by the senses
anaesthetic Gk. *anaisthaetos* – numb, without feeling

We come to know more of what matters in our lives, less through an in-turned search for self, than in 'conversation', in relationship to what is around us. We rarely know what currents flow beneath what we are doing and feeling. The impulses, instincts and intuitions that impel our thoughts or actions are as animals moving in the shadows of our everyday awareness. As we create we discover events, characters, places, sights and sounds, whose significance we cannot quite define, yet whose presence makes more visible what is moving through our lives. Creating is a way of listening and of trying to speak more personally from within the various worlds we inhabit. It is a way of discovering our own stories, refreshing and reawakening our language and giving form to the way we feel things.

Creating becomes a conversation when we enter a dialogue with whatever we are doing. In this conversing we are drawn along in the moment by moment flow of sensation, interchange and choice, rather than following a predetermined intention or idea. Conversations grow as we listen and explore – a constantly shifting process of discovery that changes in momentum, rhythm, clarity or chaos as we work.

Conversation connects us to what is other, lets in the converse, the opposite – we allow the solid walls between things and events of our lives to melt; we step to the side of positions we habitually hold, we explore, fall silent, hesitate. Conversation loosens and re-forms us in the questions that arise, in incompleteness, differences, beginnings, contradictions, new possibilities – a surrendering of what we know towards what is as yet unknown – sensed perhaps, but as yet unformed. In conversation everything is movement, our boundaries loosen, even break, and some of what we are spreads out and changes. A conversation dies the moment we forget to listen.

converse F. *converser* to associate with, L. *conversari* to live with, *versari* to dwell – literally to turn oneself about, to take a turn with, become familiar with.
conversion, to be changed
verso, the other side

In creating through conversation we get to know more both of ourselves and of what is other than us – a dialogue, where listening, questioning, dreaming, becomes a way of discovering form. We let whatever we are making gather to itself what it needs in order to grow. These needs seem to arise, not within ourselves, but between us and whatever we are doing – the need for a certain quality or ingredient... need to run... need for the colour blue... need for water... need to oppose... need for space or silence. As we sense and follow the impulse of each moment, we let go of any drive towards an intended result. And this very loosening of intention allows up from the depths of ourselves forms and images that give voice to the currents in which we are moving. In creating, in whatever medium, we begin to sense and gradually make visible the rich and changing landscapes of our lives. Through finding form in materials, in moving, in writing, we glimpse the unformed or yet-to-be-formed in ourselves. From these conversations of creating emerge images, forms, gestures of unexpected potency, for they have grown outside of our usual frame of reference, and they surprise us as they appear.

Sharing with a partner – a companion

Creating or making springs from a need within all of us to communicate and to share with others. Without expression, our sense of ourselves shrinks and contracts. The presence of a partner who goes with us in our journeys of imagination, making alongside of us, watching, looking at and sharing in what we create, enables us to get to know the life and significance of our images more deeply. What we make, or do, or say, grows and comes more alive for us as it is heard, received by another. To enter another's imagery is to get to know the feel of their world, to sense them much more fully than we can in everyday life. And we discover a world that is shared, no longer simply inside ourselves, but coming alive and growing between ourselves and another.

company L. *companiem* taking of meals together
(*cum* together, *panis* bread)
companion, one who accompanies, 'walks with you'

Gathering sense – a conversation between media

As a general working strategy, this book encourages the use of various art forms in combination, as part of an ongoing working process that constantly shifts between one medium and another. Ideas and perceptions are thus explored from varying points of view and amplified and extended as the work proceeds – a circling and recircling, that lets in the many, often conflicting, facets of our experience. No conscious or deliberate attempt is made to carry ideas forward from one medium to another. Rather, we trust that this will take care of itself within the flow of working provided that, stage by stage, we take the time to absorb what we have done. It is because of this need to assimilate that, in what follows, writing is suggested in connection with moving, why reading back to (and talking with) a partner is an important part of the writing and why making is coupled with a process of getting to know what one has made. This process of moving between phases of making, looking back, absorbing, and making again, gives time for a slow gathering and deepening of sense. In our successive choices of media, it is crucial to follow the flow of one's own needs, interests and impulses, rather than any prescribed sequence.

Note

The following chapter develops a thread of ideas begun in the previous chapter, "Arriving". There the focus was upon waking up the physical body into sensation. Here it is upon the development of one's own personal language and imagination in movement and a sense of its connection to the wider field of one's life. In the next chapter moving is coupled with writing – writing as a way of discovering and gathering up imagery latent within moving. And throughout the book, moving is seen as part of a continuum of working that includes writing and making. In moving we come back to the body – it helps us to feel through our senses again. This sense of embodiment profoundly affects how we enter and explore whatever we do or make.

2. Moving and Writing

Looking in a Mirror

It was as if I woke
after a sleep of seven years

to find stiff lace, religious
black rotted
off by earth and the strong waters

and instead my skin thickened
with bark and the white hairs of roots

My heirloom face I brought
with me as a crushed eggshell
among other debris:
the china plate shattered
on the forest road, the shawl
from India decayed, pieces of letters

and the sun here stained
me its barbarous colour

Werner Bischof, *Sardaigne – Italy,* 1976

Hands grown stiff, the fingers
brittle as twigs
eyes bewildered after
seven years, and almost
blind/buds, which can see
only the wind

the mouth cracking
open like a rock in fire
trying to say

What is this

(you find only
the shape you already are
but what
if you have forgotten that
or discover you
have never known)

Margaret Atwood,
from: *The Journals of Susanna Moodie*

Long long before we knew how to talk, we knew how to sing. Long before we knew how to sing we knew how to make sounds. Older than sounds, we knew how to gesture and before gesture we knew how to posture. All these are our languages, we can speak all four or five. Hugh Milne, *The Heart of Listening.*

All life is movement. 3.5 billion years ago life began in a pulsation of single celled creatures – a fluctuating tidal movement of expansion and contraction that continues within us today in the hidden movement of our own cells. In each moment we are moved by a myriad of impulses and stimuli which the body registers and responds to, whether we notice or not – our bodies are the meeting place of messages, every cell within us awake and responding to signals from outside and within. We constantly move and are moved towards or away from what is around us. We move as a plant moves, following the light of the sun, opening and closing in relation to what attracts or repels us – what feels light or dark. The movement of thoughts, dreams, feelings, conversations.... rise and fall away within us. As we become aware of the feel of the body, its weight, breath and the flux of sensation moving on its surface or welling from its core, we may begin to sense the small 'dance' within our tissues – the silent language of the body's voice.

The movements of growth

At conception, the beginning of new life, the fertilised egg hangs motionless,
then gradually begins to turn – as the stars in the cosmos turn – as it begins a journey down the length of a fallopian tube to implant in the walls of the uterus.
Once rooted, a wave of movement travels up through its centre, establishing an axis between head and tail,
a dynamic midline around which the embryo develops.
The growth of the embryo is expressed in a continuous, slow, flux of movements
up, down, and around this axis,
curling, uncurling, opening and folding, around the developing limbs.
Its movement travels upwards to the developing brain and downwards towards the tail –
movements of growth that begin under the beat of the mother's heart
expressing the flow and impulse of life within us.
These early movement patterns remain within the body
echoing invisibly within each part of us throughout the days of our lives.

Fountain - Madrid, 2002

The womb is all the world. The child is made from all sides.
Throughout months, years. It is not me,
it is at the crossing of my thinking body and the flux of living events
that the thing is secreted.

Hélène Cixous, *Stigmata.*

Between inside and out – moving from sensation and impulse

As I turn my attention away from the preoccupations of my daily life and begin to settle into the feel and detail of my physical body, it is as if I begin to put out small roots that extend both down into the detailed sensations of my body, and also outwards into the particular feel of wherever I am. In this silencing of my daily concerns, the shape of my self begins to change, to soften, and I enter a quieter space, where the scattered and disparate parts of my life begin to cohere in new ways.

As I move out of my head and into my body, I begin to notice not only the details around me and my physical state, but also, impulses to move, as my body responds to feeling and sensation. In breathing, I allow the passage of air in my body, giving up control of my ordinary everyday posture and movement, letting myself 'be breathed', and the breath itself awakens impulses that stir up a sense of movement. These impulses to move, in turn, call up other movements, and I discover the flow of my weight rising or falling and the gathering of energy and momentum – the swing of an arm leads into the delight of a spin or turn, or a surprising balance. These are movements that come, not from any intention or idea, but from the body's own response to what is in and around me.

improvise L. *improvisus* the unforeseen

I let my attention rest in the present moment, following moment by moment wherever it is drawn. I allow any impulse or direction to come from some part of me that wants to move and follow it as long as it lasts. All the time I am moving, I do not force the pace, or feel I have to keep going. When my body wants to stop, to hesitate, simply to listen, I allow it.... accepting the rhythm and impulse of whatever comes - even waves of boredom and emptiness will in their own way move me. I listen to the body's need to hover, hesitate, be still — or to go wild, rush, race, roll, swing out. Whatever the need, I let myself go with it, not knowing where it will take me, knowing only that if I keep my attention wide and awake to the present moment both within and around me, my movements will begin, as it were, to tell a story, a story beyond words. And whatever I notice or feel, stimulates an answering impulse that shifts and changes the inner world of my feelings and emotions.

We are all programmed to think of dance as essentially elegant, graceful, flowing, rhythmic. It is essential for now to set these associations aside and to avoid looking at or judging how one's movements may appear from the outside. This way of moving is not concerned with style, reflecting instead the particular and subtle intelligence of an individual body. It may not be interesting or dramatic in the conventional sense and yet from within, what is found is always a surprise. At times movement may be slight, almost imperceptible; at times prosaic and simple, as a walk; at times less familiar. Frequently, by some subtle shift in awareness, what I do will seem strangely alive for me. It is as if my inner world breathes and comes out to meet the present world around. In this loosening of myself into the moment of moving, I become aware of other selves, other qualities, or states of being, masked by my usual preoccupations. Often I have a sense that these are more real, more true than what I usually think of as me. They somehow reconnect and transform the different aspects of my world. Between the moment by moment shifts of sensation and movement inside me and what I notice and respond to outside, the phrases of a 'dance' emerge, in which I sense more of who, where, and what I am. As I move, the state of both my mind and body transforms, finding expression in ways I could never have planned or intended.

Kinaesthesia Gk. *kinein* move, plus *aeisthesis* sensation

Min Tanaka, Outdoor performance, 1980
photo: Masato Okada

When the whites defeated the Sioux Indians, massacred the buffalo on which their lives and culture depended, and penned them into reservations – in this time when the Indian world was systematically erased, a leader emerged who called on the people to dance and so call back the spirits of their world, calling back what was being destroyed, obliterated. These dances were called the Ghost Dances, and they were prayers for life. (derived from Ted Hughes)

Calling back the body.... calling back the world

*Begin.... resting.... in stillness**
Let your attention settle.... spread throughout your whole body
Sense your weight.... let the breath come in and move through you

Let go the chatter of thoughts.... let go the need.... to do anything

How does your body feel?..... What do you notice?
What in your body draws attention to itself.... shoulder... ear... finger... throat... heel?

What is touching you from the outside.... sound... air... shadow... ground?

Watch.... as response rises.... a wave moving through you
Listen.... let your body breathe.... what needs to move?
give way.... towards even small movement impulses........
opening of a hand... turn of an arm... tilt of the head...
follow wherever they go.... and let the rest of your body travel with them

Sense each part of the body.... listen and follow as connections appear....
face to throat... shoulder to spine
How does each part feel?.... speak.... to the other?
Go under the surfaces.... feel the bones.... the beat of your heart
sense the depths of your body
like a river.... sense what needs to move from within

Moment by moment.... move as your body needs
Hear the small voices of impulse.... let them echo through you

Sense how far.... a movement travels within your body
What answers it? What does it call up elsewhere?
As one movement ends.... pause.... let another wash in

drift like a bird... turn over... disappear... sleep with dogs... consider... take a chance... be hungry... make a black hole... come from water

Open the skin.... let your attention spread wide.... into what is around you
as a bird spreads its wings feeling the moving air

Move.... into the shadows.... into the ground.... into the spaces between one thing and another
Notice.... what comes to you from outside.... as a visitor.... welcome its presence

Listen to the changing rhythm of impulse.... as weather and seasons moving through

shimmer... darken... surrender... dart... fumble... spin out... skim... toss... stagger... withdraw... creak... menace... light up

Letting in.... what has been forgotten.... lost
Let associations.... memories.... feelings.... float through the body
Answering.... what comes

The body has many voices.... many characters
What are you becoming?
Sense the need.... to change shape.... change direction.... change voice

Moving.... in conversation.... with whatever appears

***Footnote to prevous page – eyes open, or closed:**
Sometimes it can help to close your eyes as you begin to move in order to settle and focus attention. As I close my eyes, I feel more clearly where I am, and notice more particularly what is touching me. With eyes closed, I wake up in other senses, letting go the familiar ways in which I sense things, compelled to listen to the present moment of what is happening within me and around me – the feel of what touches me from outside and from within, the movement of thoughts, memories, emotions. Each calls to and changes my awareness and my moving.

The temperature of a given space is a very important conductive medium for conveying dance. If a dancer is anxious to merely show dance, then there is no role for the temperature of the space to play. But for me, whether the space be hot or cold, heat must eventually emerge, and the air must circulate, otherwise my dance cannot be born. Min Tanaka, quoted from: Ondřej Hrab and Yoriko Tsuda, Eds., *The Sea Inside the Skin.*

Min Tanaka, performing a solo dance, *Romance 2-3*, 1999. Performed within an installation by the sculptor, Noriuki Haraguchi. The installation consisted of a pool of oil on the floor of the Plan B Theatre, Tokyo. Photo: Toshimi Frusawa.

We think by feeling. What is there to know?
I hear my being dance from ear to ear.
I wake to sleep and take my waking slow.
Theodore Roethke

Finding where you are

I move to feel and inhabit my immediate world and it always surprises me how little I have noticed of what is around me and touching me; I move in order to listen to and notice all that lives and moves within me and to which I become blind in the noise of my everyday life; I move to find what is alive for me, flowing beneath my everyday awareness; I move to re-member who I am; I move to find what I have lost or forgotten, to feel and to recover a sense of rhythm and time that is connected to my own feeling, sensing body; I move to find another kind of language for which I have no words; I move to find the 'music' by which I am moved.

Move.... to tell a story.... discover.... as you move its elements.... characters.... events
Move.... to send a message.... find as you move - what it concerns.... who it is for
Move.... to invite a series of 'accidents'.... How do you respond?... Who do you become?

Images arising while moving

As I move, associations, memories, phrases, pictures... may drop into my mind, and I let them in and out again. They are glimpses of imagery for which I am not yet ready, and which, if I follow at this point, will draw me away from the present moment. Later these images may re-emerge in my writing or making.

Eva Karczag filmed by Chris Crickmay, *improvisation on video* – part of an installation, Dartington, 2002.

This is where I work with long pieces of wood stacked against a wall and my moving is pedestrian, rough and 'clunky'. I have edited it in such a way that the flow of movement is intermittently frozen for periods from a few seconds to a minute.
Eva Karczag

Working with a partner as companion*

One person moves.... the other watches from the side of the space
later, the person who watched moves and/or writes in response (see following pages)

The presence of a partner who is quietly with us as we move, helps settle our attention, thereby deepening how we work. A partner, as companion, who does not judge or interpret, helps us to suspend our own critical voices – their gift of attention affirms our working, an acknowledgement and acceptance of our exploration. A partner's presence gently holds the space in which we work (both physically and emotionally) – creating a sense of safety to travel deeply in the imagination. At the same time they 'stand for' a connection to the everyday world on our behalf, ensuring our subsequent return. Later, in their response (through moving or writing), a partner in reaching into their own imagination miraculously reflects back to us something of the inner universe of what we ourselves have done in a way that always surprises us with its intuitive connectedness.

reflect L. *re-flectere,* lit. to bend back, hence to return the rays etc.,
relates to **flexible** L. *flexus* pp. of *flectere* to bend

> *Wandering along together, wading through the high grasses side by side, is a kind of conversation that needs no tongue, a perfect interchange of perceptions, moods, questions, answers, that is as simple as the weather, is in fact the merest shifting of cloud shadows over a landscape or over the surface of a pool, as thoughts melt out of one mind into another, cloud and shadow, with none of the formal structures of speech.......and knowing in a kind of fore glow, before the thought arrives, what it will be, having already received the shadow of its illumination.*
> David Malouf, *An Imaginary Life.*

***Footnote:** For people familiar with Authentic Movement there may seem to be similarities here in this use of a partner who observes the person moving (referred to as a 'witness' in A.M.). However, despite some similarities, our approach has grown from different sources and has a different intent, as will become apparent in reading the text.

Chris Crickmay in collaboration with Eva Karczag, *Wall drawing of moving figure.* Part of an installation, Dartington 2002. Charcoal, 2m x 1.8m.

Person watching

Find a place to sit at the edge of the space, near the person moving

Take time to settle.... breathe.... make room inside
Let your own thoughts quieten.... wipe your mind clear
Let the focus of your eyes soften and widen
let each cell of your body breathe and see

Be as a bowl of water.... letting your partner's presence fill and reflect within you
receiving each moment of your partner's moving
Don't try to remember or name what you see.... let it wash through and over you
Let go of any thoughts or words that arise – judgments, opinions, fantasies

Let your own body stay awake.... breathing
Be as a window.... simply let in what you see

Looking with 'wide attention' in the way described - seeing with the whole body - enables us to 'feel-with' the mover. It is as if our body becomes permeable and imaginatively participates in the moving. If, on the other hand, we focus our attention narrowly on observing and noting the action, consciously trying to remember it, we distance ourselves, keep ourselves separate, cutting ourselves off from the body's perceptions. We can only see intuitively when our senses are wide open and our controlling purposive minds are at rest.

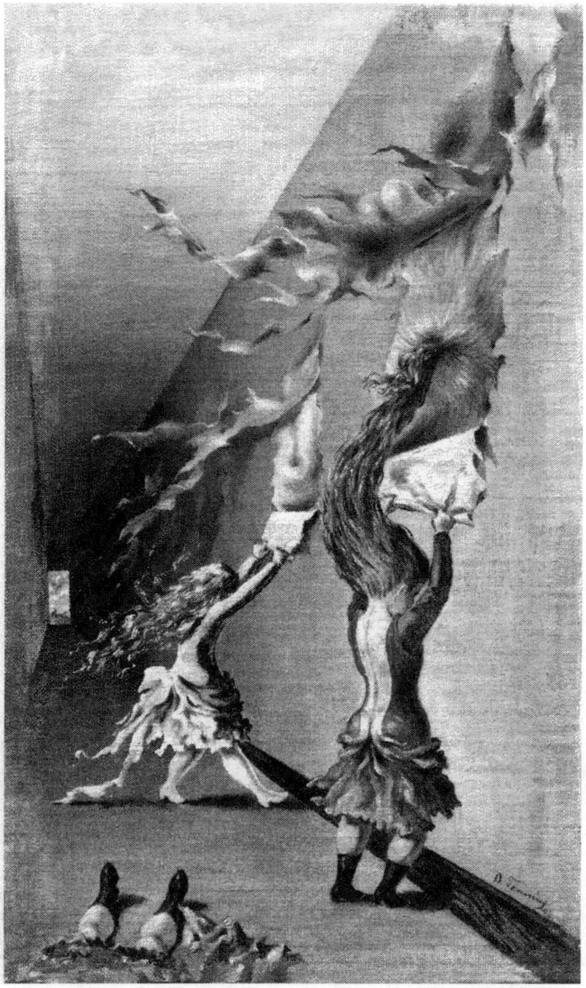

Dorothea Tanning, *Jeux d'enfants* (Children's Games), 1942
Oil on canvas 27.9 x 18 cm. (111/32 x 7 1/32 in.)
Collection Dr. Salomon Grimberg, Dallas

What the body sees

In our lives, we are rarely clear about all that we see and feel about things. Yet as our dreams gather up the unseen fragments of our days, all that has passed before us leaves a trace – we see far more, and more deeply than we ever realise. As we move in response to another's movement, our bodies reveal the depth of our looking without us trying consciously to recall what happened or to condition our response. Our bodies register, respond, and imaginatively communicate what it is we have seen. To move in response opens us into the feel of another's world – as we move we sense and see more of the landscape of their lives.

I know what I think when I see what I say Gertrude Stein

Responding to another's moving

move.... in response to what you have seen,
not knowing how the response may develop.

Be still.... listen.... spread open
Let the sensory memory of your partner's moving body fill through you
breathe.... remember and feel their presence
Sense how your own body responds.... echoing.... answering
As you continue.... let go of memory
wonder.... echo.... question.... counter
Discover in each moment.... what you have seen/ felt within the body
it comes back in its own way.... a landscape.... sense of a story
a flow of responses.... changing as a river
How.... does your own body speak of theirs?

Spontaneous L. *sponte* of (one's) own accord, also unpremeditated, natural

Moving in response (to any chosen starting point)

Whatever the starting point – something we have made, a dream, a concern in our lives – it is always surprising what emerges as we begin to listen to the body and respond. As our attention loosens and spreads out through the living body, gestures, expressions and movements begin to rise into our awareness, giving form to unspoken and unseen parts of what we feel or think. (note: numerous starting points for moving are given throughout the rest of the book).

Respond L. *Respondere* to answer, reply
Sponsor L. *Spondere* to promise
Despond L. *Despondere* to give up, lose (hence to despair)
Correspond L. *cor- (con-, cum)* together (hence, to answer each other)

Discovering response

Be still.... listen.... breathe
Let your body soften
in your mind's eye.... turn towards whatever you are responding to
then.... let it rest within and around you
listen.... sense your own body.

Take time to let an answering impulse rise through you
Let go of naming.... describing.... where you are going

As water.... as wind.... let impulses move you
let the body hear.... question.... explore

Follow the moment by moment movements of response within the body

We imagine the impulse of response as sudden, but it is often slow, almost imperceptibly drifting up from the depths. And we wait, gently welcoming, receiving slowly, as watching cloud shapes form and dissolve, noticing what seems to call, to move us, delicate as the touch of a butterfly's wing... and we follow, not knowing where it is leading us.

Lisa Nelson in concert with David Moss, Brattleboro,Vermont, 1978.
photo (shot with infra red film): © Stephen Petegorsky

David and I met in Bennington in1970 and worked together for some years, often with the voice, sometimes both moving. This concert had all these elements. I'd been working with vision for many years at this point and I like the photo 'cause it captures a moment when the only thing holding me up is my eyes. Lisa Nelson

A page written by Lisa Nelson, 2002:

I look at the senses as attentional tools. Their physical organs are focussing instruments. My body must move to tune each of them in to a desired channel. I'm grateful that their simple instructions give me cause to move.

When my body and eyes are still, I can feel the movement of my attention shifting from sense to sense, and past to future, a sensation of light roving inside me and weaving in and out through my skin. And also a more muscular sensation of tiny shifts inside my eyes.

My dancing, like my imagination in my resting body, arises out of an ocean of sensorial images. I find myself in an active dialogue with both the shocking originality of the details of my local circumstances and the associational imagery—the memory in the body—they almost simultaneously trigger. Caught up in this scintillating adventure I practice moving my attention to focus through one sense at a time. This choreography of shifting attention serves to reposition my imagination and intensify my sense of permeability where the oft-useful boundaries between inside and outside my body dissolve.

> *Close your eyes and imagine yourself dancing. Don't get hung up on what the word dancing means. For one minute.*
>
> *Now, clasp your hands and continue. For one minute.*
>
> *Tell me: What did you imagine?*
>
> *How did the image come into focus? Where were you? Was there a visual image? Color? Were the surroundings familiar? Were you a spectator seeing your dance from outside? From how far? Was it a body you were seeing? Were you alone? Were you inside the dance? Was it you dancing? Were you dancing with your eyes closed? Was there a kinesthetic image? Were you feeling it? Seeing the room or your body parts pass by? What were you wearing? Did you hear something? Music? Did your moving make sound? Was it a dance you've done before? Seen someone else do? Always wished you could do? Done in a dream? Was it physically possible for you to do? For any human to do? Were you having thoughts? What happened after you clasped your hands?*
>
> *What were you doing right before you closed your eyes?*
>
> *Now, from which senses did you build the image?*

Gathering images – writing in response to moving

(much of this section could also apply when responding to something made – see next chapter)

Macolm Green, *Children catching locusts,* Bali Nyonga, Cameroon grasslands, 1980. Photograph

> Why does one write, if not to put one's pieces together? From the moment we enter school or church, education chops us into pieces: it teaches us to divorce soul from body and mind from heart.....
> Eduardo Galeano, *The Book of Embraces.*

Writing from the body

Writing continues the imaginative journey begun in moving, or watching a partner move, dancing the dance on in language. Writing gives us time to absorb the feel of what has just happened. While movement is ephemeral, quickly vanishing from our memory, written language remains, giving us a means of dwelling upon and finding significance in what has occurred. Writing in this way is 'dreaming with' and reflecting imaginatively upon what we have done or seen. The writing calls up images that begin to make visible what has been drifting just beneath consciousness, not by describing, but by letting what has happened act on us and 'move' us as we write. Words and phrases sourced in this way continue to build upon the imaginative field of the moving. If we were literally to describe what we did or saw, this would narrow our focus, cut us off from this more intuitive seeing and knowing. By allowing words and images to spread out in response, we open up an imaginative field that plays upon and around what has occurred, writing as we might write a poem in order to touch into the deeper currents felt within the moving. It is in this imaginative looking and responding that we sense the richness and complexity of what is there.

Writing in the wake of moving (or watching another move) brings the living, sensuous world of the body into our language. Our words change, form and move differently for us when they are drawn from the thinking, feeling body, as in the felt language of poetry, or the fresh and inventive play of a child's naming of things.

Listening through the body brings up words and images we did not know were there. We let them find their own way onto a page, playing with the feel of their resonances and associations. The writing draws images together just as dreams create a world that plays with the familiar syntax of our waking lives. We welcome whatever words and images arrive onto the paper and take time to absorb their presence, as unexpected visitors whose arrival surprises us and whose reason for coming we do not as yet know. The images that emerge gather their own sense as we write. Our writing may be fluent or clumsy, abundant or brief, poetic or plain. We have to assume it will be the necessary expression for this moment. To mumble or stutter may be as eloquent and necessary as to sing.

> *I do not write to keep. I write to feel.*
> *I write to touch the body*
> *of the instant with the tips of the words.*
> Hélène Cixous, *Stigmata.*

Bringing words back in

With a partner, one moves, the other watches, then both write
Read to each other
Listen and dwell on the images that arise
Exchange roles and repeat

Be still.... empty.... as a room
open the doors/ windows.... of your body.... listen
let your attention/ your heart.... soften and spread open
What word.... phrase.... image or sensation.... comes to you?
Let it onto the page

Sense.... what other words or phrases follow it.... one phrase calling up another
feeling for a thread.... of connection between: word... association... story
follow its sense.... until it comes to an end
Breathe.... feel the body again.... listen.... wait
until another thread.... appears

Open your attention wide.... in every direction of your life's experience
Let in whatever comes on the breeze
Let in stories... people...voices... places
let the words live.... as animals.... finding their own way

Let whatever comes take its own time.... have its own pace and momentum
flowing.... hesitant.... fractured.... harmonious
Letting a theme go.... when it becomes empty.... has come to an end of its story

Don't hold the mind tightly
Allow.... other voices: questions, jokes, contradictions, interruptions, provocations, disruptions
Allow what may seem to be breaks.... discontinuities.... swings of direction
What comes may seem irrelevant.... shreds... fragments... diversions
yet trust.... as you listen and follow.... that these will coalesce

Let sense come in its own way.... like the flow of a river
pieces.... slowly gathering together

Another way of remembering

In writing after moving or seeing another move, I do not try simply to remember and record what I have done or witnessed. To do so would prevent me gaining a wider, deeper sense of what has happened. If, as in moving, I continue to improvise, letting words and phrases come of their own accord, a world of imagery appears that, piece by small piece, makes visible an inner, felt sense of what has occurred.

> *"...a pilot... a man so scared he cannot speak... a bell reverberating amongst his ribs..... take a look at the sky... something small in her pocket... whisper... close to an ear"*

As I write in this way, where I have been in my moving (or in watching another move), mysteriously finds its way back to me. It emerges in what may at first seem like unconnected phrases/ thoughts/ images. Each word gathers to itself other words and associations, sense coalescing slowly out of what may appear to be merely scraps and fragments. What I have done, or seen, returns to me with its own connections – the images, stories, metaphors that arrive, amplifying my sense of it.

I sometimes find that writing from my own moving makes visible a different angle, even an opposite state, to the one in which I moved. Also that the feel of my partner's writing contrasts with my own. What does this mean? Perhaps that how we see or feel at any one moment is only a part of a larger weave that is formed of many shifting and even conflicting strands.

Writing and reading, image and metaphor

As I write in response to another's moving, the writing will often produce a shared world of imagery that has grown invisibly between us. Images that appear in the writing offer a sense not just of the moving itself, but also of the wider context of our lives. In their oblique metaphoric language they show us a sense of this with a subtlety and depth that we could not express in literal terms. Words offer us a shared means of expression a common language which always implies speaking to or with another. Sharing what we have written with a partner by reading it back to them and weighing its images together, creates a meeting place between our own inner worlds and the larger world in which we both live. Yet to find a sense and a personal relevance in these writings we need not interpret them – their imagery carries a precision and closeness to feeling which communicates directly. Instead we ponder the images themselves: "prising open a lid"..... "a fish on a hook"...."he was almost a giraffe"... The metaphors through which we express ourselves connect body and mind, they embody the feel of things in our lives, they are the kinetic, bodily dimension of language. Metaphor is more easily experienced unconsciously than consciously understood; it is in a sense our first and earliest language in which a word embodies a felt experience. Metaphor is our first language as children and the language of the body, a concrete language expressing and evoking the feel and hence the layers of meaning embedded in our every experience.

Written by the one who moved:

"You must follow your orders", he said, looking sadly.... a turn of three degrees... white-faced... The knuckle of his hand clicked... a huge weight... it seemed forced... leaning. Blood at his feet... looked down... a broken bottle... breath... bobbing in the water... rounded like a tennis ball, like the body of a seal...The back of his hand held up to catch the drops... whirling... a tunnel view, out of the far end of it, trees in the wet...echo of foot-fall inside... outside, balanced on the top of a pipe, arms stretched out... wobbles now, then steady... takes a step forward, looking towards the horizon... hens scattering in the dust... Some years cold and wet, some so dry, dessicated on the tongue... behind hedges they all walked together, looking... a sharp intake of breath... now straps tightly around arms, round torso... pitched forward, a noose... jumping, jumping up and over the bar... muscular... She says she is not interested in sport, but he, he feels the muscles in his instep as he walks over the grass barefoot... the world spun out in fine gold gently glitters as sun after rain... A tear drop on the end of a leaf, runs down it... Cool, still eye, watching... still face... impassive.

Written by the one who watched:

He looked out over the sea... the walls had become so thin he was not sure if the house would outlast the night... something whispered... pale... murmured... he was not quite sure... ham-fisted, what was intended?... was he meant to turn left or right?... why couldn't they be clearer with the instructions?... Perched on the cliff he remembered the story of Excalibur, the sword offered up out of the lake... Excalibur... unsheathed and pointing... He was too cold, too chill to go on anymore... more than anything he needed to make a fire... perhaps then in the illumination and shadow of its flames... in its embers... he would unlock the bafflement... battlement... that encased him... he imagined wild animals creeping forward out of the darkness, climbing over the palisade... and that somehow these animals would unlock this particular imprisonment... he found himself silently calling out "Mother... don't go, mother"... No father only a gaunt and staring emptiness... Who was he?... had he ever existed?... He had not realised that frown... like the ubiquitous Cheshire Cat... had unnerved him... had somehow had him removed... displeasure and displace... live alongside each other... he decided tonight he would build up the fire.

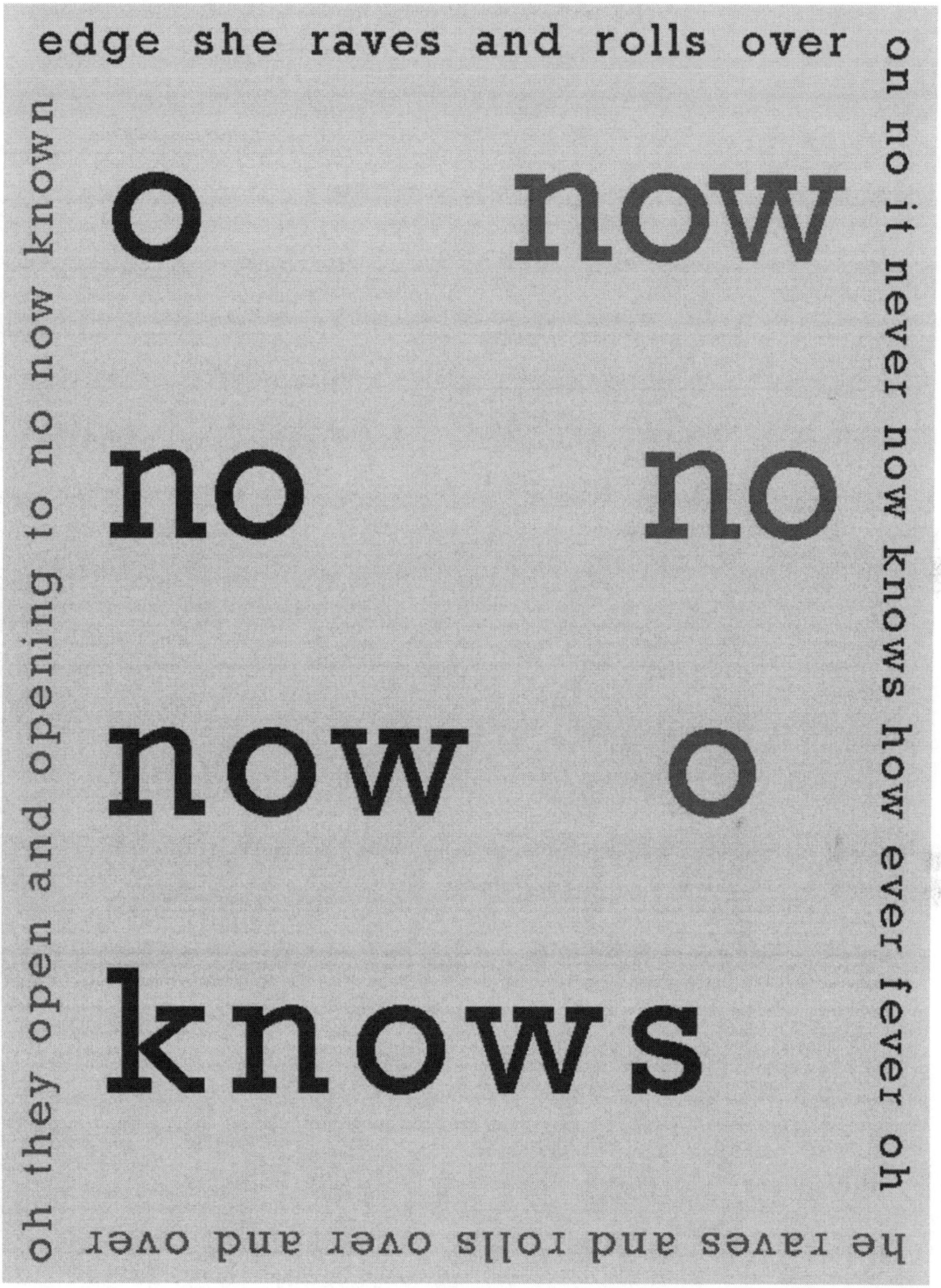

John Hall, visual poem – from: *A Lone Knower's Disavowals*

3. Making

so, when you hold
the hemisphere
of a cut lemon
above your plate
you spill
a universe of gold.

from: Pablo Neruda, *Ode to the Lemon.*

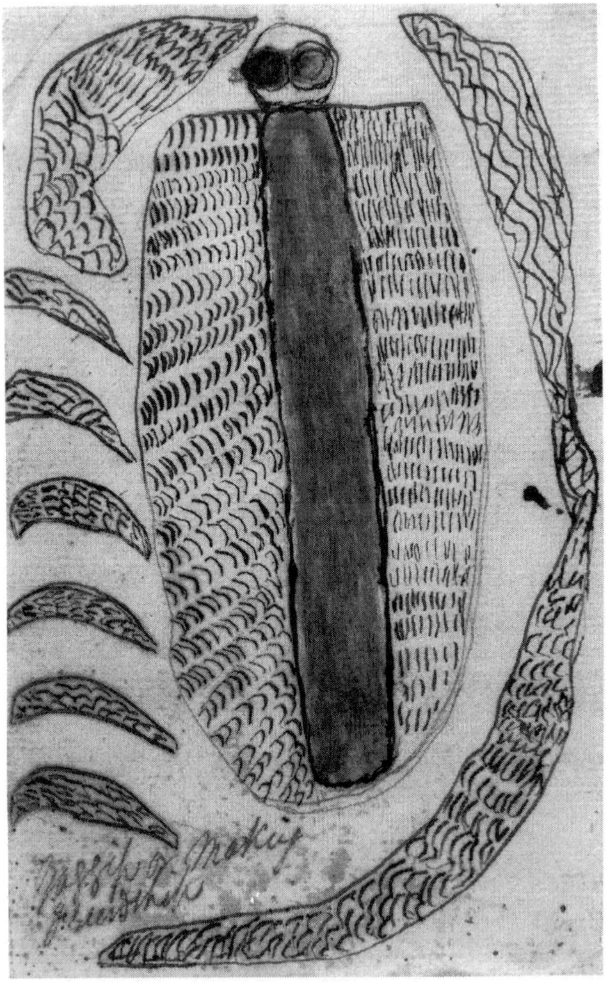

Unknown aboriginal artist, *Yaggip or making friendship*
© State Library of Victoria.

Yaggip refers to a dancing ceremony in which two tribes pledge friendship and suspension of the hostilities which normally prevailed between tribes in traditional aboriginal society.

To the Greeks 'techne' means neither art nor handicraft but rather: to make something appear, within what is present, as this or that, in this way or that way. The Greeks conceive of 'techne' producing, in terms of letting appear. Martin Heidegger, *Building, Dwelling, Thinking.*

Making as 'letting appear'

Making can be a kind of conversation in which we become immersed in something that is other than ourselves, a reverie in which we explore and 'dream into' the materials within our hands. And this in turn wakes up and refreshes how we see things. In the textures and particularities of the materials we choose, we are drawn out of ourselves – through this making we embody experience in material form. As children we all played with the things around us, created stories and dramatic events using even the simplest of objects and materials. As we moved them about and arranged them, we allowed these ordinary and inert things to come alive for us, to become transformed in our imaginations. It is in just this way that as adults we create with materials through improvisation.

Figure F. *figure* a thing made, L. *fingere* to make to fashion (also **fiction** from the same root)

An improvisational approach to making runs counter to the way in which we generally work with materials and objects in daily life, where we visualise something and then make it. In improvising, by contrast, we feel our way into a conversation with our materials and listen out for an emergent form to appear. When we make in touch with the sensing body, we *feel* the movement of our materials, their dynamic, how they flow resist, run or fall; we touch and feel them with our fingers, laying one texture next to another. In each moment of making we are presented with many choices and we need to choose sensuously, just as we taste and adjust ingredients in cooking. The impulse towards what we choose may be very slight, perhaps something our body senses and does before we realise it.

The porridge was.... too hot... too cold... just right! (The Three Bears)

As we follow the journey of making, we discover the subtle distinctions between things and explore how they may come together in their differences. The more we discriminate, the more choices we have available to us – through finding an exact shade of white I realise how many other possible shades there are.

Notes

1) In the continuing flow of ongoing work, making things with materials will often take place in association with movement or writing, and the making will give rise to images and forms which reflect and extend what we do in other media without us consciously attempting to contrive a link.

2) In the pages that follow, three dimensional and two dimensional work are separately described. This is simply for clarity, since slightly different issues arise. In practice, we may well move between two and three dimensions within the same piece of work, extending upwards or outwards as the work demands.

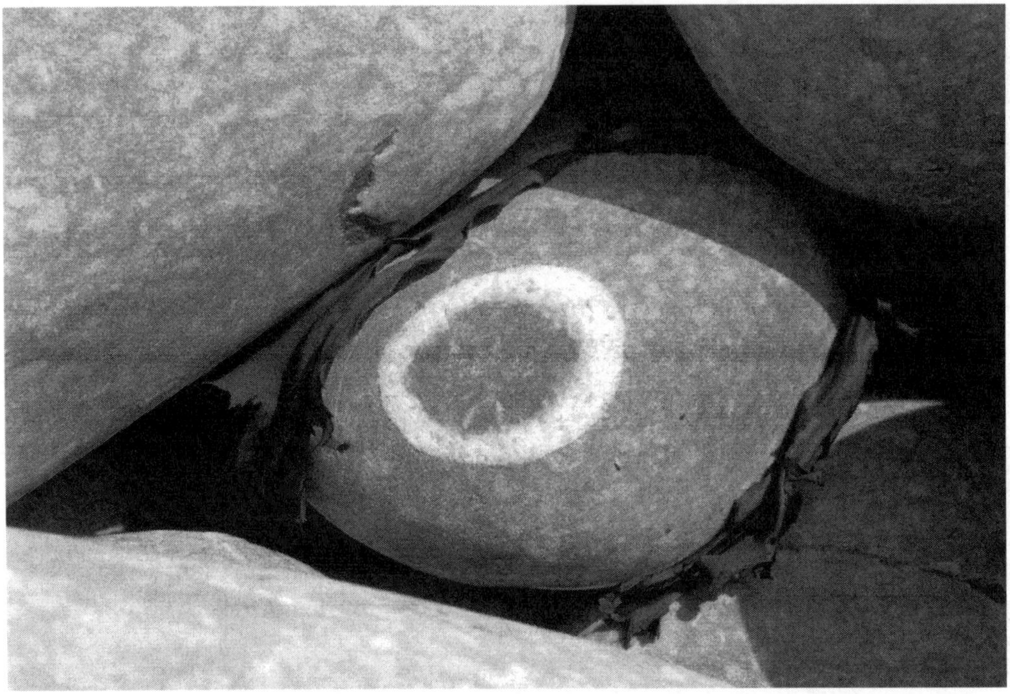

Stocking up the kitchen – assembling a bank of materials to work with

Gustare Spanish. to enjoy to relish L.*Gustare* to taste

In gathering materials, take time... be inventive. Choose materials without knowing what you are going to make with them – just choosing on the basis that they appeal to you. Give yourself as wide a range as possible to select from and combine – various qualities, textures, structural possibilities, resonances... let your choices be aesthetic and sensuous, tasty. As cooking needs: salt, pepper, spices, herbs – savour the quality of each particular substance.

Expense is always an issue with materials, but ultimately, the only principle worth following is that you need to love what you work with, however cheap or expensive it may be. If well loved and cared for, even the most seemingly impoverished material will come to life and sing. Conversely, materials chosen and used in an expedient or neglectful way will always be dead. Starting with materials you in some sense value, or have a feeling for, helps you to value what you do with them.

> *At Nenette's they bring you quantities of little prawns, freshly boiled, with just the right amount of salt, and a most stimulating smell of the sea into the bargain, heaped up in a big yellow bowl; another bowl filled with green olives; good salty bread; and a positive monolith of butter, towering up from a wooden board.*
> Elizabeth David, *French Provincial Cooking.*

Some possible ingredients to select from

A range of everyday materials or objects:

e.g. tin foil, grain, broken furniture, earth, muslin, a torch, salt, feathers, cotton cloth, mirrors, cane, carpet felt, coloured plastic sheeting, willow, bricks, sheet of glass, hay, jam jars, soap, old wooden boxes, velvet, coloured electrical wire.... materials from everyday things dismantled..........
i.e. anything that catches your interest.

Surprising finds:

e.g. broken toy.... sheep's skull.... bugle.... old map

Connectors and basic tools:

e.g. wire, various kinds of sticky tape, string, rope, glue, pins, needle and thread, velcro craft knife, scissors, pliers, stapler, glue gun...

Paint and graphic materials:

e.g. pastels (soft pastels are the most subtle in range), oil sticks, very soft pencils, drawing ink, fabric dyes, food dyes (use as inks), charcoal (compressed charcoal makes a much denser black), graphite sticks, P.V.A. glue, grease chalks, sheets of plain coloured paper (to cut or tear up and paste on)
Colour is one area where it is worth spending money. Subtlety, variety, good consistency and permanence of colour (e.g. of paints, of pastels) generally only come at a price. In addition to art-specific paints (acrylic, oil, water colour, raw pigments), also consider house paints (emulsion/gloss), spray paints, enamels, etc.

Paper and other surfaces to work on:

different sizes, weights, textures, colours to choose from in the moment of making. Beyond the standard papers sold in art shops, there is a huge variety of paper and card used commercially for packaging, for printing on, for wrapping, often available in unusual shapes and sizes... (try the local scrap store).
e.g. brown wrapping paper, cardboard, coloured cellophane, tissue paper, carpet underlay, news print (end of rolls)

Graphic and painting implements:

with different possibilities for preparing, applying, and removing materials,
e.g. dip pens, a quill, thin sticks (for applying ink), brushes (from small to large, e.g. house painting brushes), pieces of sponge, rags, sandpaper, erasers, masking tape.

Woman creating a *Kolam* (threshold design), Kerala, India, 1988. Photo: Bobbie Cox.

These traditional threshold designs, indigenous to certain parts of India, are drawn before sunrise each day by a woman of the house. The maze-like form, normally created with one continuous white line, is intended to appease the god Siva and to entrap evil spirits, thus preventing them from entering the house. In making the design, a small patch of the threshold or road in front of the house is first swept and sprinkled with water. The design is then made by feeding white pigment between the fingers using a small rag to soak up the liquid. The pigment is made with any white material, frequently a small quantity of ground up rice made into a paste. A wooden bowl (often, as here, a coconut shell) contains the paint. No attempt is made to preserve the patterns, which are soon obliterated by the tread of people in and out of the house, scratching chickens, or passing bicycles.

Threshold design, Madras, India,1996. Photo: Bobbie Cox.

Starting with found objects

Things chosen from our surroundings offer a starting point in making – through their particular character they provide something to respond to. And already in choosing these objects or materials a journey of making has begun. What we have found is gradually transformed, and takes on a new identity as it is brought together with other things, partly or entirely letting go of its original use or meaning.

Anne Lefebvre, *Absolutt Vodka*

What is it that we find?

Everything we are drawn to, that we feel for and choose spontaneously (as if it had chosen us), comes to our attention because it somehow resonates within us. The sense of connection between ourselves and what we have chosen deepens as we begin to take in its particular qualities. As we stay quietly with an object and slowly explore it... entering into it in our imagination and allowing it to affect our thoughts and feelings – we embark on a process of discovery, exploring its sensory properties and its capacity to change and transform under our gaze. As we take time to ponder the chosen object, our sense of it expands and becomes more vivid; associations, stories, memories, connections, begin to emerge.

> *I study the shell's ordered fluted edges, at the moment they look like bony grasping fingers ... When I hold it with the hollow side facing me... it seems to expand and become a great bird, eagle-like, its wings outspread to cover the earth – but its head deeply bowed. Also the light coming through the dimly transparent shell gives its outspreading wings a golden glow.*
>
> Marion Milner, reflecting upon a shell in: *Eternity's Sunrise.*

Take a chosen object

touch it.... look at it.... 'listen' to it
speak to a partner about what drew you to it
describe it in detail.... as if your partner cannot see it

> *What qualities or details particularly draw your attention?*
> *What associations or memories do these evoke?*

See it as a landscape, or as an event.... what has just happened?
Discover its stories
Perhaps.... speak from its point of view

Then.... go out and wander to gather more things
that seem to belong or speak to.... your chosen object
Returning.... find a place, and gradually.... make its world
See what the object becomes as part of this new environment

With your partner watching
***move** in response to what you have made*
Together.... reflect on all that happened

A discarded object

Things that have been thrown away, deprived of their everyday context of use and meaning, take on a new existence. We see them, as it were, naked, in their raw state, deprived of their identity, yet somehow more intensely real.

Claes Oldenburg, *Torn Notebook, Three,* 1992, muslin, chicken wire, clothes line, steel, resin, latex paint; on aluminium plate. 24 x 33 x 36in.(61 x 83.8 x 91.4cm.) Private collection, New York. Photo: Ellen Page Wilson

Something had been eaten, discarded, worn away, broken. What you experienced afterwards was a residue. Except for the Torn Notebooks *where you're in the midst of the action and things are flying through the air. But they're headed for the wastebasket* Oldenburg, interviewed by Arne Glimmcher.

Caricature an object

Wander.... to come upon something..... someone else has thrown away
bring it to your work place... get to know it... its parts... its qualities
With the materials and objects you have around you
loosely assemble or arrange them to make a version of what you have collected

Take its features and qualities to any extreme..... caricature it!
work on any scale – smaller? larger? than the original.... perhaps something tiny made huge
Let the materials you are working with influence the form
What has the object become?
If it were a person, what kind of person would it be?
what posture, gesture, facial expression does it seem to be adopting?
***Write** to get to know it further*

Making - 3D
Creating a landscape with found materials

Take a walk to gather materials and objects

Wander.... notice what draws itself to your attention
a pigeon's feather.... a toy boat.... a rope

Follow the slightest impulse
See what comes into your hand

Returning to the work space
linger.... see what part of the space draws you

Choose your spot.... in a patch of light.... beside a wall.... under a window
introduce something to this space.... from what you have collected

Explore how it wants to go
slowly.... bring in others (from what you have just collected, or from your bank of materials)

discover what is needed.... moment by moment

Explore how things meet each other.... merge.... oppose.... echo.... cover.... maintain a distance

Where do I want to put this? What goes with it?... feeling choices

As in a conversation, when things meet they are changed
they come to life.... are diminished.... become overwhelmed.... change size.... brighten

continued over

Sense...... what is emerging

Allow developments, changes, transformations... moment by moment

Take out as well as add
letting go of how things are........ dismantle.... rearrange
Allow a surprise to enter

Let associations come and go
 hint of...... a forest... a ruined city... a person fishing... animals... a rib cage... a huge wind
 Imagine...... different time zones(?).... different scales(?)

Work from sensation - both from the sense of your own body and the feel of the materials...
 the feel of textures/ forms/ spaces

Bring in other media as needed.... perhaps an element of drawing.... colour
Perhaps combining two and three dimensions

What is appearing.... taking form?   landscapes.... events.... beings....?

Sense when it is time to find an ending

With a partner.... reflect on and get to know what you have made (see ch. 4)

We don't want to try to do it, it only works when it just comes out, it's like gardening.
You water it. You don't really make it. You don't know what it's made from. You just water it.
Simone Forti, Contact Quarterly, vol. 22, 1997

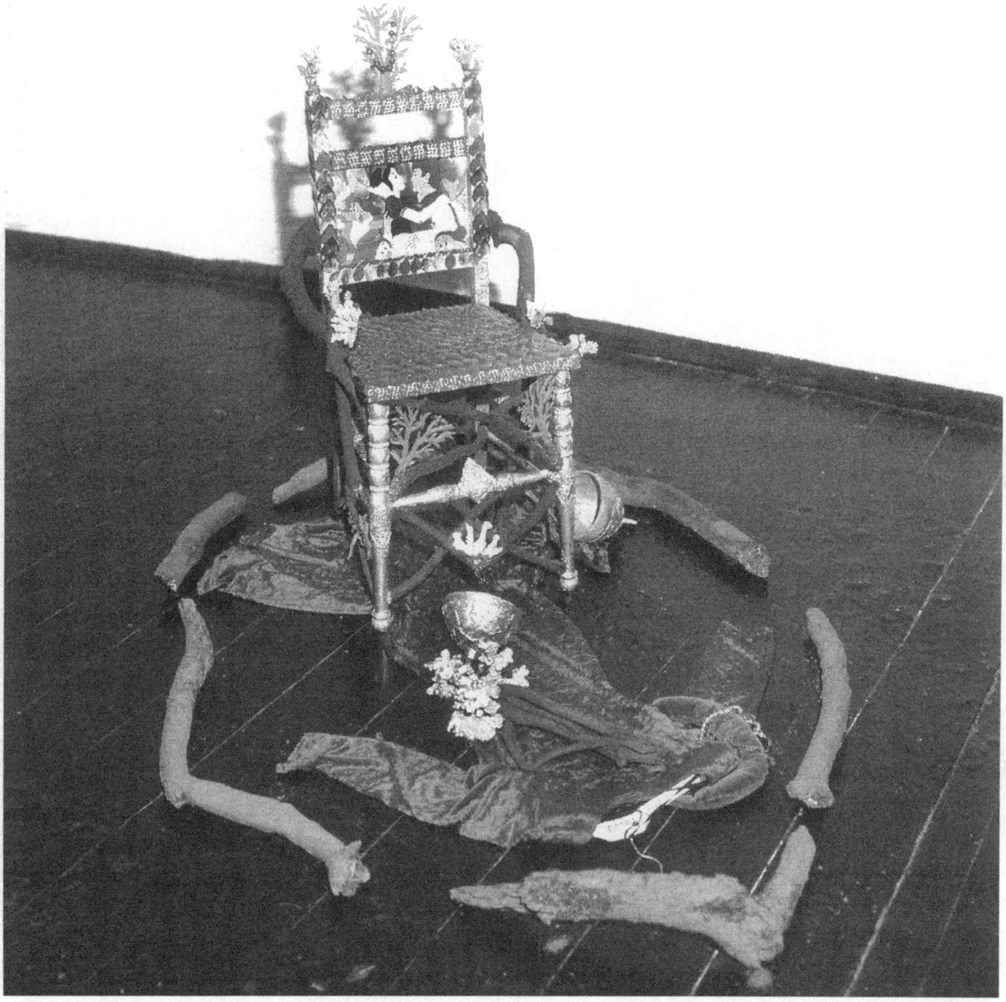

Sheila Clayton, *Snow White's Chair,* 1988.
Nursing chair covered in real and plastic imitation coral, tree branches painted cobalt blue, red velvet dress, aluminium orb (containing plastic jewellery).

This work, which connected to my daughter as a teenager, is a celebration of a female child as a princess. The materials I use are a mix of the valuable and the worthless (fake). Both are carefully crafted, as you would make anything for a person you care about. I work fairly intuitively with only a broad idea of what the work is going to be. Although I know what the sources are, the process usually dictates the outcome.
Sheila Clayton, 2003.

Making - 2D

the movement and transformation of materials (surfaces, textures and colours)

Choose a shape/ size/ colour/ texture of paper, card, wood, etc..... to work on
and a few materials.... colours.... to start with

If possible, work flat on the floor to involve your whole body in the work

Choose for this moment a colour/ texture to apply first
Let the whole body choose.... what draws you?
a particularly dense black.... a watery surface.... a torn edge of paper.... something stuck on

The surface you are working on is one of your materials,
remember its full extent.... how you treat it....
what you do with its edges.... what parts you leave empty

Sense the movement of the material.... how it wants to flow.... resist
Sense your own physical weight and breath as you work and the movements and sensations in your body

Listen.... feel.... as you work
sense when other materials are needed

see how the materials meet.... glue meets powder.... water meets ink
Allow any mix of materials you are drawn to moment by moment

Meet your materials in conversation... listen... suggest... wrestle... introduce another point of view
What is their response?

Work slowly enough to take in and absorb the changes as they happen

Monet's paint must have been very much like what we made: it was shiny and resilient, thicker than cream, more liquid than vaseline, more rubbery than melted candle wax. If it was smeared with the finger, it would leave a ribbed gloss where the lines of the finger print cut tiny furrows; if it was gouged with the tip of a knife, it would lift and stretch like egg whites beaten with sugar. Only paint like that could smear across the canvas for a moment, and then suddenly break into separate marks.
James Elkins attempts to discover Monet's technique by experiment in: *What Painting Is.*

Feel how you want to apply material.... with what energy?.... what sense of touch?

forcefully – scrub on... scribble on... trowel on... scratch into... pour on... stick down... smear... throw
delicately – float on... sprinkle... lightly brush... roll on... rub in... tickle... spray... dab... moisten... dry

Allow a sequence of actions.... each one a response to ones that came before:
paste on, score into, paint over, partially wipe off.... sprinkle on, rub in, draw into....

Let things 'move' on the surface

What is needed?
more space... a division... a figure... another colour... emptying... ?
Spreading attention through the whole.... while working on the parts

Let go plans
let the hands.... whole body.... take the work forward

Stay flexible.... open
Take time.... let the pieces find their own order

images come of their accord
like visitors.... make them welcome

Allow in whatever is coming to form

Leftovers: *Having finished use the leftovers to quickly make a new piece of work*

With a partner.... reflect on and get to know what you have made (see ch. 4)

Painting is stronger than I am. It makes me do what it wants.
Picasso

Karen Challis, *Dance*, 1993. Pastel drawing on paper, 74 x 43.5 cm
Colours: white background with pale blue, dark blue,
and black markings - touches of orange within the enclosed shapes.

This drawing was no. 3 of a short series made in 1993 during a twin pregnancy. The drawings were characterised by my attempts at the time to maintain space within them. Usually my work is over-full, slightly oppressive and engages the eye in a mighty struggle. These were very different. I remember standing looking for so long that when I did approach the paper with the chalk it had a feeling of significance, like a formalised dance. This remains in the drawings now; the space I tried so hard to maintain is vibrant, alive and playful. It is ironic that I felt it necessary to make space in these drawings just before the birth of twins who successfully filled any space/ time or thought that could have existed for some time to come. Karen Challis, 2003.

Further notes on flexibility in working

Keep things loose (as when undoing a knot).... not over defining
add water.... blur the edges
mix... smudge... cover... erase... tear
Play.... allow surprises
Allow the whole thing to fall apart.... to lose all coherence
Find new connections

Drop, let go of an image.... see what comes up from underneath
abstract marks, shapes, lines.... now something you recognise emerging
a figure, a plant, a rock, a building.... let it be there.... not holding onto it too tightly

Allow a sense of space, of depth, of scale
Let your lines/ colours seem to travel.... inwards/ outwards.... defining imaginary spaces

Allow discontinuities.... contradictions
of scale... of distance... of idiom... of subject matter........ in the imaginary spaces of the image
person big as a mountain... biological diagram of an eye... a cartoon rabbit... storm in one corner

Take a risk!
Disturb.... shake up.... what you are doing.... add an alien ingredient

> *I have sometimes self-consciously taken an illogical... decision... gone against the sense of the project, wilfully taken a wrong turn, because I feel that, sometimes, the clearly sign-posted way leads only to known territory.*
> Gerard Davies, from catalogue notes for *Deluge Drawings* ,1996.

Need a change of ingredients? Something no longer fits? Something missing?
Take out.... add.... accordingly

Needing a change of landscape?
Break the edges..... tear, cut, fold, crumple your paper
to get the size/ shape/ surface.... you need
Split up the image and continue parts separately.

Change your own position in relation to the work

Extend outwards or upwards – beyond the surface on which you are working
Add more paper.... spread onto the surrounding floor

Let the image become three dimensional
add objects.... string, sticks, a bucket...

Finished one image for the time being?....stuck?
Start another, come back to this image later

Doing more with less

While the lists at the start of this chapter may suggest working with an abundance of materials, mixing and merging them freely, it can also be an advantage to deliberately restrict one's materials, putting energy into seeing how far one can push the possibilities of very little.

Every Monday morning Wolfli is given a new pencil and two large sheets of unprinted newsprint. The pencil is used up in two days; then he has to make do with the stubs he has saved or with whatever he can beg off someone else. He often writes with pieces only five to seven millimetres long or even with the broken off points of lead, which he handles deftly, holding them between his fingernails. He carefully collects packing paper and any other paper he can get from the guards and the patients in his area; otherwise he would run out of paper well before the next Sunday night. At Christmas the house gives him a box of coloured pencils, which lasts him two or three weeks at the most. Walter Morgenthaler, *Madness and Art*

Adolf Wolfli, detail from: *Great Great Highness Imperial Princess Olga at the Throne of Saint Adolf in Poland,* 1916. Coloured pencil on paper.

Getting to know a material

Take just one graphic material you like the feel of.... and one kind of surface

a cream coloured chalk and brown paper

tissue paper and a very soft pencil

red paint on cardboard

Spend time not trying to make anything particular.... just experimenting with what you can do

What can happen with this surface?.... What different ways can you apply the medium to it?

Gradually shift.... from experimenting with the material

into allowing something to take form

Colour

> *Iris (the flower, and also the part of the human eye), together with the beautiful word iridescent, have come to us from the Greek goddess Iris, whose outer form was the rainbow.*
> Owen Barfield, *History in English Words.*

Colour is akin to music, close to our emotions and our appetite for living. The word 'colourful' suggests liveliness and pleasure, 'colourless' a draining away of life, disengagement, despair. Look for a while at a colour, then close your eyes or look at a blank sheet of paper – as after-image you see the complementary colour to the one you were looking at. Thus the physiology of the eye, the wavelengths of light and the reflective properties of different surfaces and substances give the way we see colour a basis of predictability. Add to this the fact that pigments mix according to known colour combinations (as yellow and blue makes green) and it would seem that the world of colour works entirely within known principles. Yet, beyond these physical and physiological facts, almost everything in colour depends on context, on circumstances. Black as a colour (or rather a range of colours, for there are many blacks), may seem funereal or smart, drab or vibrant. In a painting or drawing black may suggest despair, or represent a shadow, or simply arise from the medium used, as with ink or charcoal. Our perceptions of colour are never constant. It is a familiar fact to any gardener, that the same colour blue looks different, actually seems to change colour, according to whether we see it against orange or green, it changes again as the colour of light changes from morning to evening. While, as with music, rules and principles exist – of harmony and contrast, of combination and juxtaposition – that can predict these effects, in practice we are bound to rely less on rules and more on our immediate sensations and feelings. For it is the mutability and complexity of colour that constitutes its magic, and just as a given note in music may create a million different impressions depending upon how it sits within a song or a symphony, so any colour is infinitely various in its manifestations. And beyond its optical effects, colour is also tangible, it has a material existence – as chemistry, as consistency, as surface, as stuff. When we apply colour it makes a huge difference to the feel of it whether that colour is oily, watery, powdery, greasy... lies on a surface or sinks into it. Not just its particular hue, but also its thinness or thickness, its density of colour, its dullness of surface or its sheen, all go towards the experience we have of it.

Explore painting a spectrum of colours:
rainbow...peacock's wing...reflection of oil on water
What is the spectrum, the colour range for today?
cold/ warm... light/ dark... pale/ saturated... earthy... ethereal... watery... fiery... sharp... soft?

Grey cannot be found in Cezanne's pictures. To his immensely painterly eye it didn't hold up as a colour. He went to the core of it and found that it was violet or blue or reddish or green. He particularly likes to recognise violet (a colour has never been opened up so exhaustively and variously) where we only expect and would be contented with grey; but he doesn't relent and pulls out all the violet hues that had been tucked inside, as it were; the way certain evenings especially, will come right up to the greying facades and address them as if they were violet, and receive every possible shade for an answer, from a light floating lilac to the heavy violet of Finnish granite. Rilke, *Letters on Cezanne.*

Ken Kiff, *Green Man with Dog,* 1964.
Oil on canvas 183 x 152.5 cm (72 x 60 in.)

Colour notes: This painting has a mottled yellow background. The upper, fragmented figure is green, with a light blue and green head. The lower figure with a raised arm is painted in pinks, greys, and ochres. The dog is a dark brownish grey with a violet nose and a red eye. Kiff is said to have begun his paintings with choices of colour, the imagery only emerging as the work progressed.

Exploring colour

Use colour selectively.... not all colours at once
Make your choices of colour particular, mix the one you really want.

Have ready several sheets of paper....varying colours, sizes, shapes, textures, weights
and paints (a range of colours to mix)
Choose for now a particular colour of paper to work on

***1 colour** – mix/ choose.... a single colour to apply*
use your fingers and whole hand
to move with colour over the surface.... thicken.... thin
work on with fingers.... or any implement.... scratch into.... draw.... paint over

Colour as tactile material:
a play with consistency
Make a surface with the colour.

***2 colours** – in dialogue.... let them mingle, smear, conflict*
lie against each other's edges........ flow... mix... merge

Conversation of colours:
lively, clashing, rowdy, heated
in harmony, cool, quiet,
subdued.

Deliberately steer close to the wind.... two colours that clash or nearly clash.... work with them, explore an edge of disaster.... what happens?

***3 colours** – invite them in, see how they want to move*

Vary proportions.... a sea of red, a touch of blue
Colours are activated or dulled
by how they meet or mix
glowing or muddy.

Let colour create a sense of movement

sparkling... shimmering... shrinking away... shining from within... bursting up from below

Call in colour.... unseen colour
colour of a song.... of a dream.... of the wind
moments of light
illumination of a second.... long grey stretches.... sudden darkness

Use colour to discover form
not just 'colouring in' .

Begin on a base of red.... of black
veils of colour.... layerings.

Colour as music – harmonies... cadences... rhythms... melodies... orchestration

Coloured things

What is pink? A rose is pink
By the fountain's brink.
What is red? A poppy's red
In its barley bed
What is blue? The sky is blue
Where the clouds float through.
What is white? A swan is white
Sailing in the light.
What is yellow? Pears are yellow
Rich and ripe and mellow.
What is green? The grass is green,
With small flowers between.
What is violet? Clouds are violet
In the Summer twilight.
What is orange? Why, an orange,
Just an orange!

Christina Georgina Rossetti,
What is Pink? From: *Sing-Song.*

We rarely see colours in isolation, purely as themselves. More often we see them as part of the identity of the things around us – of creatures, objects, materials, plants, buildings, the land. Colours also occupy a world of metaphor: white lies, rose tinted spectacles, green fingers. And to name the colour of a thing is often to evoke its wider cultural meaning or associations – black belt, red alert, blue pencil.

colours of: water.... pebbles.... an anxious face.... tiled roofs.... flames.... shadows in snow

Nothing exists as single flat colour. Each element is transfused with an incandescence of colours invisible under the surface and changing as the weather....colours within colours Winifred Nicholson

Background colour

Find an everyday object that you can paint on
place it on a surface that has been marked and coloured by time or use:
a rusty sheet of metal... an old garage floor... a lichen-covered rock...
Paint the object to exactly merge with its immediate surroundings in every detail.... make it disappear
In the process.... discover the complexity of colours and patina of the surface you have chosen
Later.... perhaps try the reverse: paint an object in extreme contrast to its surroundings – to really stand out!

white: snow-capped, bleached, albino, milk white, lily white, white as a sheet, polar bear, cabbage white, white horse, white skinned, white haired, bone, ivory, white stick, white coat, white lines, white flag, white sails, white cliffs, surf, seagulls, daisies, white china, white apron, whitewash, white emulsion, white bread, white sugar...

red: blood-shot, red-hot, see red, go red-as-a-beetroot, flushed with excitement, red lips, red dress, red roses, red wine, red brick, red flag, warning light, red-light-district, red-herring, red-handed, red-carpet, cherry, tomato, pillar box, fire engine...

blue blue eyes, blue-with-cold, bruised, wide-blue-yonder, blue moon, blue-eyed-boy, blue distance, blue shadows, the blues, blue-collar, bluebells, cornflowers, forget-me-nots, blueprint, duck egg, turquoise, azure, lapis-lazuli, sapphire, indigo...

yellow: evening sunlight, egg yolk, blond, straw, sulphur, brimstone butterfly, mustard, lemon, honey, sallow-skin, yellow river, wasp, earth moving machinery, primrose, buttercup, dandelion, brass, gold...

brown: winter woods, ploughed fields, a drought, mud, shit, browned with age, browned off, brown eyes, brunette, camel, leather, a hen, Mr and Mrs Brown, brown skin, chocolate, coffee, walnut, hazel, toast, biscuit, chestnut, mahogany...

black: in-the-dark, burnt, Indian Ink, soot, black sheep, black bird, raven, mourning, black market, black mark, blackmail, black eye, Negro, ebony, pitch, blackberry, black-out, black-look, black tie, blackboard...

green: green shoots, green house, green fields, sea-green,The Greens, 'green' (of inexperience), green belt, green light, green slime, little green men, grasshopper, lime, jade, emerald...

grey: ashes, ghost, cloudy, lead, a grey area, grey beard, ashen, wood pigeon, grey suit, concrete, slate, smoke, steel grey, silver, putty...

absence of colour: drained, shaded, mousy, bloodless, washed-out, faded dim, toned-down, under-exposed...

Who does not know the magnificent Moth, the largest in Europe, clad in maroon velvet with a necktie of white fur? The wings, with their sprinkling of grey and brown, crossed by a faint zigzag and edged with smoky white, have in the centre a round patch, a great eye with a black pupil and a variegated iris containing successive black, white, chestnut and purple arcs. Jean Henri Fabre, describing The Great Peacock in: *The Life and Love of the Insect,* 1911.

A colour memory
Choose a colour
In what ways has it entered your life?
Take one instance
move to explore it further
make something from the feel of the moving

I would stare for ages at the coloured spines of books: one, in my parents room was peacock blue with tiny gold stars. Even now I find book spines beautiful and arrange my bookshelves into blocks of colour. Jane Millar

Once, travelling in Scotland when I was twelve or thirteen, I remember being astonished to find white raspberries that tasted just the same as the normal dark red ones. I was really struck by the intensity of their whiteness. Iain Biggs

I remember as a child buying some red patent leather boots. In my memory all I see are these flashes of bright red as I walk along looking down at my new boots – all the surrounding colours have become washed out. Rachel Miles

I once had a dream in whch I was being chased by two guys in black suits. As I ran up the steps of a large classical building I felt something in my pocket. Taking it out, I discovered it was a green bracelet. I had never before seen a colour like it – a combination of bronze and phosphorescent green. It suddenly dawned on me that this is what they were after. Rachel Miles

In Marin County, California, where we once lived, the days often began misty, the colours muted or silvery grey. As the mist cleared and the bright blue sky became visible overhead, everything dramatically changed into a brilliant Technicolor. Claudia Ascott

Pigments – the murals of the Amandebele

Statements by Francina Ndimande, compiled and introduced by Annie Menter,1998.

To paint is to express joy

The lives of the Amandebele are a celebration of colour, searching, experimenting, seeking images that will co-exist in harmony as they place colours and shapes side by side. Today they juggle shades that the twentieth century has delivered to their door, but for many years women only worked with 'found' colours, pigments from the earth, colours conjured from the ground. Chalk and cow dung supplied them with quantities of white, with which to prepare their canvas... the walls of their houses. The only additional colour available was a brilliant blue, taken from the 'blue bags' found in the local store. Francina Ndimande speaks of her early experiences with these ground colours:

Sand, clay and cow dung were our staple colours. There were four types of sands, that can be firm, almost like cement. Umthambothi, which gives deep black like umthambothi the perfumed wood; usowasmabada, which is light brown and rough like river sand; emhlophe, that is fine, white and muddy; and uswayi, that is white like sand and grainy. We would mix these colours carefully to achieve the colours we needed. There was a black mud, igidi, strong red ochre and red ochre and black mixed to give isahilani.

Later the white and Indian shops began selling lime powder, calcium oxide. Women would experiment secretly to find ways of using the oxides to make their colours brighter and more durable. There was enormous excitement when the rains came and some of the colours remained unspoilt and women would ask for the recipe but you never told them, you simply laughed....He....he....he!

The best black was obtained by burning wet green grass; singeing it over a flame very slowly until you were left with a very fine sooty substance which you then mixed with mealie pap, 'umratha' into a fine paste, ready to apply the black outlines so important to our Ndebele designs. An easier way was to grind firewood charcoal or use soot from the chimney where there had been a coal fire and some women even used old radio batteries.

Our colours are deep within us. Painting shows that we are alive, it gives energy and order to our lives... people will know when we are old, because we will not be able to paint any more.

Amandebele murals – Ndimanda house and family compound, painted in yellow, blue, red, white, pink, brown and purple patterns, Kwandebele, South Africa, 1998
Photos: Annie Menter (from the original colour prints)

Seeing and response

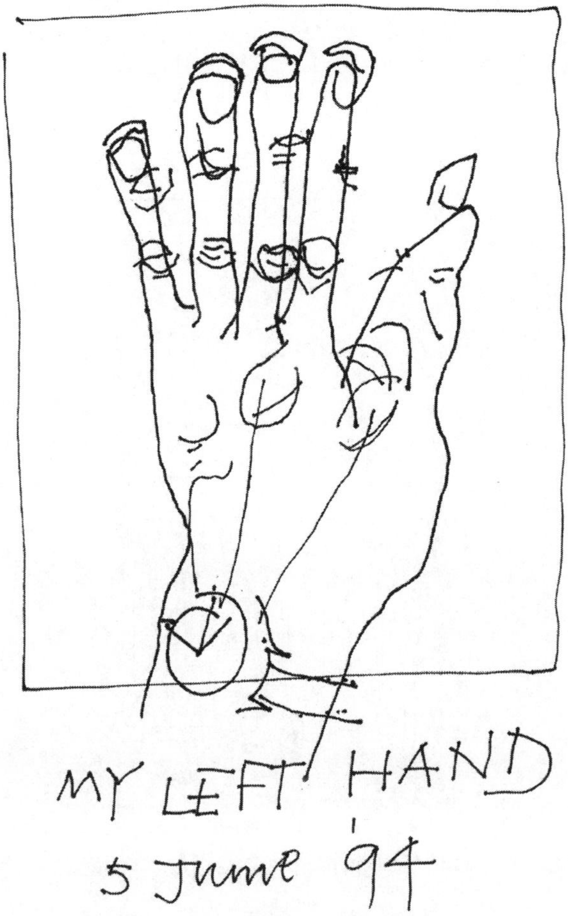

Ivor Weeks, *My Left Hand, 5th June '94* ,
Drawing in black felt tip on paper (one of 365) 29.5 x 20.9 cms

He did one drawing each day for a year using a fine felt tip and always the same sized sheet of paper. He worked mainly from observation, and occasionally from memory. As subject matter he chose whatever had come to his attention that day – subjects included: household objects, toys, works by famous artists, children's drawings, self portraits, etc. In drawing the lines he did not look down at the paper, except from time to time to locate the pen. Written titles were done in the same manner.

Opening your eyes – drawing to see

Drawing is a way of settling our attention and noticing what calls to us in our surroundings. Through drawing or painting we explore our seeing – the act of drawing slows us down.... we look again, and again, and what we are seeing begins to fill out and change before us. As line or colour thickens or thins, sweeps forward or hesitates, we register our response to seeing.... leaving a trace, as monitoring a heart beat.

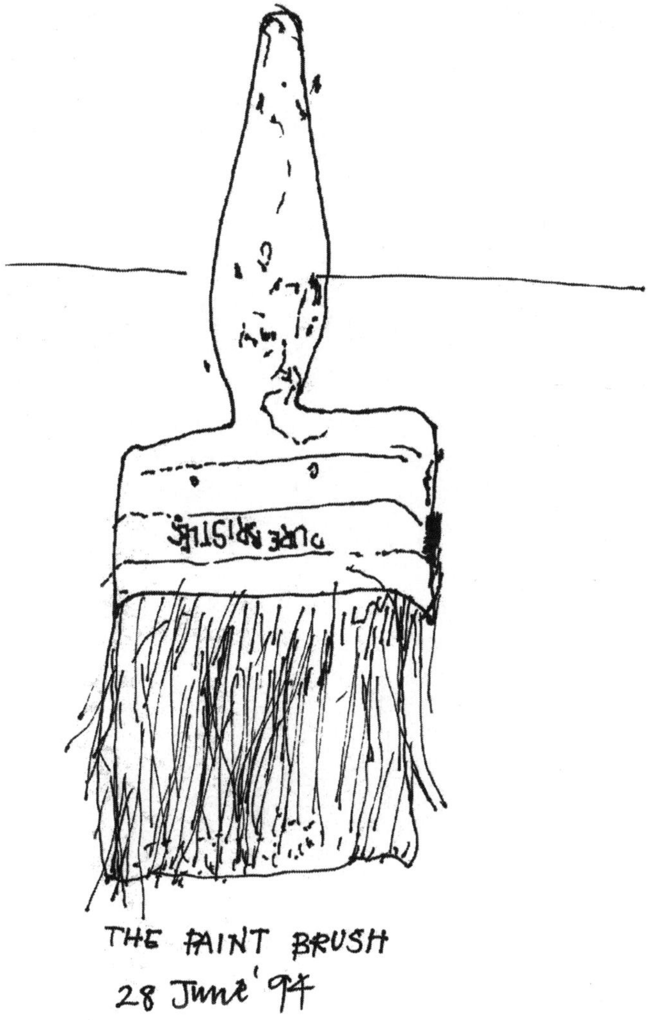

Ivor Weeks, *The Paint Brush, 28th June '94*
(details and approach as previous page)

Following your interest

What we think we are interested in, or might generally in our lives regard as beautiful or significant, is often not what turns out to be interesting once we let our attention drift and settle on its own. In fact the reverse is more often the case – what we are drawn to, as we open our eyes and widen our attention, is more than likely to be something we would disregard in our daily lives. Also, what comes to us may not be an isolated object, quite possibly it will be something in between – a part of one thing seen against another, an edge and a shadow or patch of light. Following our interest means to select, to choose what we attend to, and in choosing we have already, in a sense, begun to make a response.

Seeing is forgetting the name of the thing one sees
from Weschler on Robert Irwin

In order to really see what is in front of us, to take in its uniqueness, we need to let go of our everyday reflex, which is to identify and name. For in the act of naming, we place what we see into a pre-formed category, and behind this naming reflex are all our assumptions about what something is. This is useful in everyday circumstances, to recognise and respond quickly, but it limits what we notice. So, I cease to label what is in front of me as: plant, stick, key... and allow myself to become open to the immediate presence of it. As I settle into the detail, the familiar identity of what I am looking at begins to dissolve, and features that are always there, but don't usually catch my attention, now begin to emerge. I am led forward on an adventure of seeing and of registering my seeing in making, not attempting necessarily to achieve a likeness, but to make a response – in whatever medium I choose – that follows the adventure of my eyes and other senses. I begin to see a fuller presence of the object, more than I had previously assumed. Let it fill out and become an image, slowly discovering it and my connection with it.

Go for a very slow walk

View the world as if it were a show or exhibit,
uniquely arranged in every detail, just for you at huge expense!
each particular shadow... each broken blade of grass.... each movement or sound
open your eyes and all your other senses
listen.... what things (or aspects of things) in particular come to your attention?

A surrender to seeing

Sit, outdoors or in, with drawing/ painting materials to hand
Close your eyes, be still.... quiet

Then, open your eyes.... let your attention settle on an aspect or detail of what is before you

Surrender.... to what you see
Let your hand move on the paper in response.... let the line follow your seeing
Continue to follow the movement of your shifting attention as it explores around where your eye fell
Let your drawing hand follow this journey of your interest.... exploring the feel of what you see
Watch what is emerging on the paper.... without trying too hard to control or correct it
(If you feel it is getting over controlled, try using your less familiar hand)

Revisit your first responses.... adjusting, elaborating as your attention deepens
At any point.... let what is before you suggest other things –
a fish, a bird, a mouth not quite open..
Let these associations help to bring out the qualities of what you are seeing
(a broken plate suggests a moon and becomes a moon-like plate)
Let other images.... memories.... thoughts.... drift through as they will
Keep returning to what is in front of you.... its particular character and uniqueness
Draw/ paint whatever you are seeing

Everyone thinks he knows what a lettuce looks like. Frederick Franck, *The Way of Seeing*

Movement and form

All things arise from process A.N. Whitehead

However static they may seem, things are invariably changing or are part of some larger moving pattern of life. Even rocks are formed in movement and sooner or later will erode or split, or roll – a pen releases ink, a window may slide or swing open and will let through light and air. Within appearances we can sense these present movements, past movements or inclinations to move, in which everything participates. And beyond these proclivities to move that we know but cannot always see, there are movements that we may sense or feel only by looking and empathising... a book spreading open, a lamp dipping forward, a chair crouching low.

Form is the reflection of energy moving –
Look at any thing and see the activity within or around it

The life within

Draw/ paint/ work with clay....in response to an object
work from your body's sense of it
feel its interior movement, its lines of energy and structure
Which parts of the object are heavy/ light.... hard/ soft.... rigid/ flexible...?
feel these qualities in your body, through your hand, arm, shoulder, spine... as you draw/ paint/ make
imagine the object coming to life,
What is its posture, its expression? What is it doing?
breathe with the working.

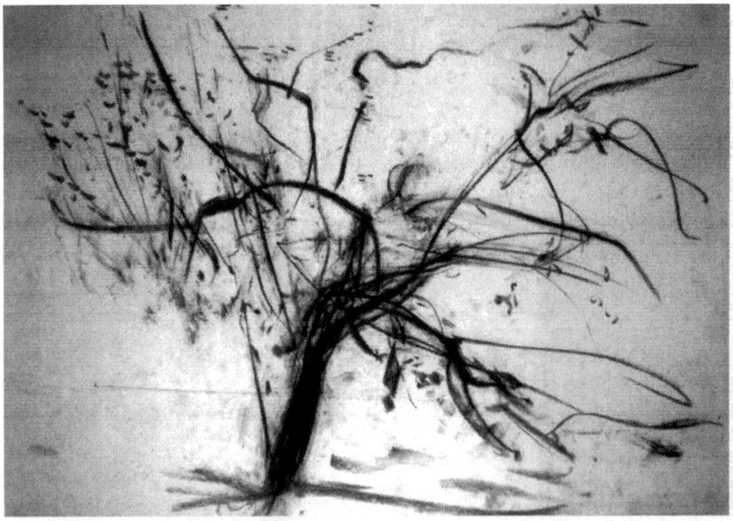

Chris Crickmay, *Apple tree, Devon,* 1997, Charcoal on paper. *As I drew the tree I imagined the growth of its branches as bursts of energy, like a firework display*

Seeing light

Winifred Nicholson, *Cyclamen and Primula,* c.1922-3.
Oil on paper/ board 49.2 x 54.6 cms

Perhaps, I thought, he liked the gloom, as I liked sunlight, because both put objects into a relationship with each other
Winifred Nicholson, Unknown Colour

Objects connected in light or darkness

Light strikes the detail of things, it illuminates and changes how we see, or have assumed to know something, altering our familiar world. In the play of shadows, reflections, ambiguities of shade, of mist and glare, of twilight and moonlight, things may adopt mysterious, unfamiliar shapes and relationships. By looking only at light and shade we can allow the things around us to float free of their usual boundaries, to merge with each other, with their shadows or backgrounds. Light falls on everything regardless of its significance, and connects one thing to another within a total field of illumination – light, dark, shade, shadow. Things thus revealed in relationship come to life and interact with each other, taking on ambiguous and changing identities.

George Rodger, *The Wool Suq*, Tunis,1958. Photograph.

Drawing/ painting light

Let your eye fall on some part of the space around you
see how, in terms of light and shade, things meet/ overlap/ merge.... with each other
or partially merge with their backgrounds.... shadows
Respond in drawing or painting as much as possible to what you see.... rather than what you know
Avoid using outlines.... only using lines where you can actually see a line

Thus the outline represented the world of fact, of separate touchable solid objects; to cling to it was therefore surely to protect oneself against the other world, the world of imagination.

Marion Milner, *On not Being Able to Paint.*

Get up in the night

Move, write, make or draw.... to explore what you see in the darkness.... the moonlight
What takes shape?

Dennis Greenwood in *Urban Weather,* Riverside Studios, 1985 (rehearsal photo)

4. Getting to know what you have made

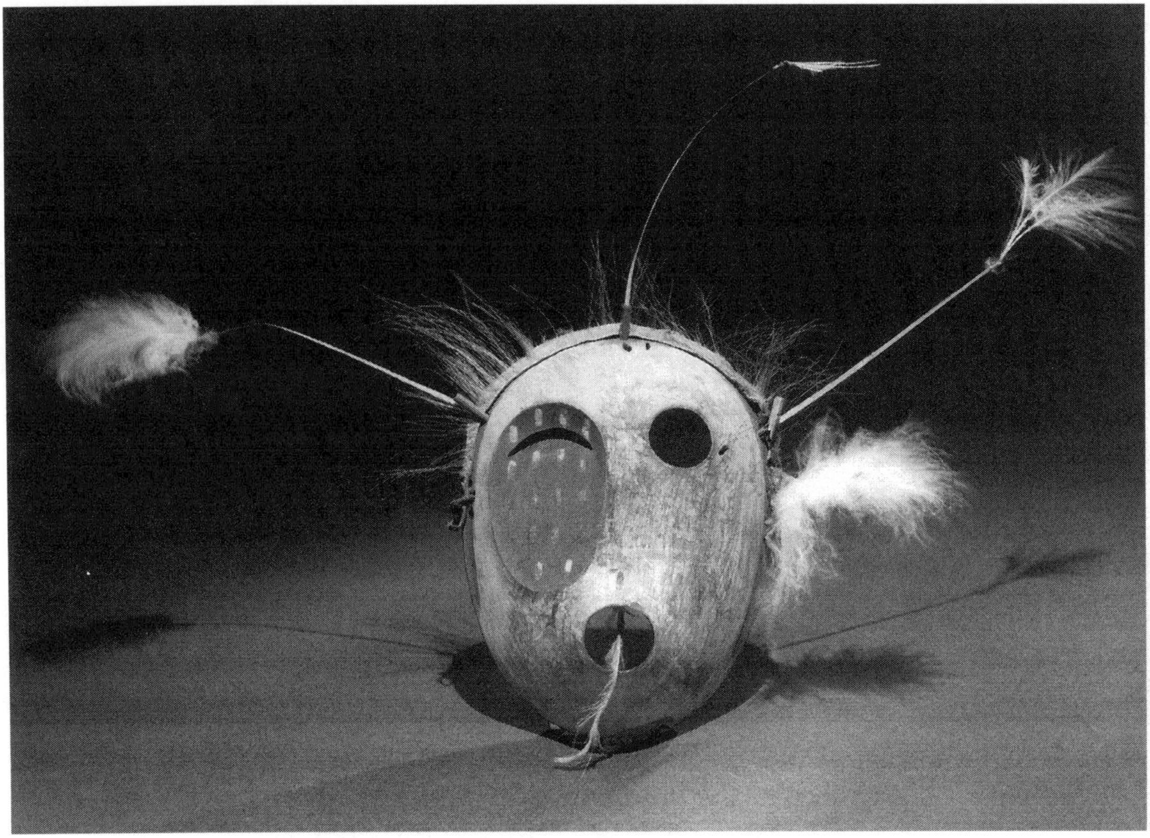

Eskimo Mask, Lower Yukon River or Nelson Island.
Wood with red and white pigment, jaeger feathers and baleen strips with eagledown, sealskin and rawhide strap.
© Coll. Sheldon Jackson Museum. Collected late 19C. Photo: Eberhard Otto.

In a way, I suppose, I think of poems as a sort of animal.
They have their own life, like animals, by which I mean that
they seem quite separate from any person, even from their author...
Ted Hughes, *Poetry in the Making*

Entering the territory of an image

When a piece of work feels finished, we need time to look, to meditate on, and to absorb what has been done. Every image holds a mystery, something outside or beyond the intentions we had for it. A thing once made has an autonomy, a life of its own – we need to get to know it as we would get to know another person; otherwise we will most likely have missed what it contains or speaks of. The power of an image is that it embodies the complexity of what we see, feel and think but cannot literally describe in words. The things we ourselves make reflect our lives, as do our dreams, and to discover what they hold for us, we need to enter their territory. There is a difference here between *looking at* an image, where we retain a certain distance, and *entering into* an image, where we engage with it imaginatively. Entering into an image is as active and creative in its own way as making it. An image invites us to feel things differently, to see other qualities, other aspects of our lives – the familiar transfigured. The images we make and subsequently come to know, do not so much centre around us, as draw us out of ourselves into a wider field of connections and meanings.

Everything we make is in a sense a living world – we explore it as with a new place we arrive in, asking: "What is here?".... "What is happening?" As in the process of making, we follow whatever comes up, and what we find will never be entirely what we expect. Exploring the world of an image takes time – time to let it in, to get to know it.

Our first account of an image will always be only a tiny fragment of what is there, sometimes even at odds with what we eventually see. But it is always difficult not to get stuck with our original thoughts and intentions and instead to allow the image to have its own voice, to surprise us with what it holds. When we start to look, the image may well appear static, fixed. The process of looking is one of letting the life of the image unfold - a sense of movement and interaction within and between its parts.

In looking we need to follow the slightest hunch, let in the faintest impression, accepting wherever our attention is drawn, allowing any fleeting thought or association to take its place within an emerging picture of what is present. We need to 'see lightly', trying not to impose an account of the image artificially, letting a sense of its presence arise and grow in the looking. As we look, we move to and fro between the physical presence of the image (its sensory impact), and the associations, thoughts, feelings, memories, stories, that arise from it; every aspect of our experience is potentially a support for our looking.

Our sense of the image develops gradually, a settling together of elements discovered. As we look, the image fills out and deepens, it begins to resonate within us. Any too vigorous attempt to interpret, to define a literal meaning, tends to divest the image of its concrete existence and metaphoric power. An image is different from a sign. A sign holds just one meaning - this stands for that... as a red traffic light means stop... you just need to know the code. In contrast, an image holds within it a galaxy of related meanings which cannot literally be de-coded. As we look we are not seeking any complete or final account of the image, it will always continue to reveal new dimensions.

Although this work can be done alone, it is much easier to do with a partner who listens and contributes as the person who has made the work meditates on the image aloud. Working with a partner is therefore assumed in what follows. The journey of making allows what is inside of us to take form outside. Getting to know it with a partner is a way of re-absorbing its presence into ourselves, of letting it inhabit and change us.

Rip Cronk, *Venus on the Half Shell*, 1981, acrylic on plywood, 10′ x 15′
Venice Boardwalk Pavilion, Venice, California,
temporary mural produced for the Social & Public Art Resource Center

nature from L. *natus* born, past participle of *nasci* to be born.
Also related to nascent, innate

Looking.... together with a partner

To start: *briefly, tell your partner the story of the making process, the physical steps you took... any thoughts and feelings that came up while you worked. This helps to focus both people's attention on the physical ingredients of the work and enables a partner to tune in to its imagery.*

After this: *make a deliberate shift into the present moment of your looking. Work as described on the following pages, allowing the image to come alive, become active. The maker meditates on the image aloud, tracking what they are noticing/ feeling/ thinking, moment by moment. A partner looks, listens, and responds, accompanying the maker in their meditation upon what they have made.*

The maker: sets out to explore and get to know the image, not to explain it. With this in mind the maker takes the initiative in sharing their process of looking and their shifting understanding of the image. But there is no pressure for them to keep talking; simply to spend time with the image is enough to bring it to life -

a time to look.... to take things in.... to feel things.... to be silent.... to speak in response

The partner: listens and periodically contributes what they themselves notice or feel about what has been made or said, as feels appropriate. The partner follows the maker in what is to be the focus of attention at any moment and how this is perceived, but they may also at times feel the need to question or counter what is said or point to other things, when some aspect of the image seems to be different to the maker's account of it. In asking questions, the partner dwells on the world of the image and the present moment of looking, not seeking explanation for the work in terms of original intentions. Questions and comments need not be clearly formulated; simply to wonder aloud, to express an uncertainty, is often enough to stimulate further exploration. Whatever else a partner contributes, their capacity to receive, to listen and look, is the crucial factor that helps a sense of significance and meaning to become clear.

Listening and looking means emptying ourselves of our own preoccupations, and offering an attention that is both imaginative and generous, an open curiosity that enables us to travel and explore with a partner. The nature of the interchange is playful and exploratory, both participants need to work lightly and flexibly, open all the time to changes of perspective which may widen their focus and ultimately lead towards a satisfying account of what is there.

Time to look

Set aside for the time being any ideas you already have about what you have made
(let them re-emerge if they need to as this work develops)
Sit still with it.... be empty

Let your attention spread wide throughout the image
What part or aspect draws your attention? What do you notice?

What is the feel of it?.... accept any words or phrases that arise
What does it suggest to you.... remind you of?
What is it doing? (in itself or in relation to other parts of the image)

Lie fallow, quietly waiting for what might arrive,
for thoughts/ questions/ associations to unfold.... stories to arise
drift.... don't know.... curious

Stay awake, both to the physical presence of what is there.... its colours, lines, forms
and to what these elements may seem to represent or suggest
figures? buildings? implements? animals? plants?

Give time to the looking
where is your attention drawn.... next?

Gradually discover a sense of action and interaction within the image
What is happening.... about to happen.... trying to happen?
can't happen....... what is stopping it?

revealing its qualities.... energies.... narratives

Feel out the form and emotional quality
Is there a sense of need?
What is a particular part calling for?
lack? predicament? longing? waiting?

Could another part of the image help?

Keep returning to the detail of the image itself
let your looking be particular

Allow changes of perception
forming, dissolving and regathering your sense of what is there
not fixing words to the image too strongly
opening up, rather than pinning down

Allow a 'rebel voice'.... a protester.... a question
the facts of the image that may even contradict what you have been saying about it

See the edges,
the insignificant (perhaps even undesirable) parts,
Anything you may have neglected/ discounted

Locate the feeling.... of the whole.... or of any part
Let a story or account of what you have made gradually unfold
Finish when you feel satisfied that enough has been said

20 minutes or so is an average time for this to take. Its important not to rush to a close simply because the conversation has dried up, or because the image has all been 'explained'. Stay with the work for long enough for something unexpected to come. Stay open, accept silences, hesitations, and times when nothing much is happening.

Chris Crickmay, temporary work in a garden, Luxembourg 2000
Assemblage of found materials made on the edge of a rough grassy area, sited at a drop in level.

An example of getting to know an image

When I got to this place I found a log and some metal reinforcing bars already there... I went to find another object and came back with a dead branch that had a bunch of green leaves caught in it. I stuck some of the bars in the ground to support the stick... it seemed a little bit like a figure suspended on its side. I propped up the log on its end and found a nail sticking out, to which I attached a clod of earth. Then I felt the whole arrangement needed something else, so I walked about and found a rusty head of a spade, which I eventually balanced on the rest of the metal bars. This looked a bit severe, so I added a loose bunch of grass where the bars crossed.

To begin with, looking at what I had made and talking with a partner, I had a sense that the branch (now definitely a figure), was flying out over the garden, and the spade was a companion creature flying by its side. There was something quite exciting and majestic in this. A contrary version then occurred to me in which the metal bars, instead of simply supporting the figure, had become a trap which had closed upon it. In this version, the spade, now seemed to be facing the other way, and became the head of a primitive and brainless animal with something in its mouth it had bitten on but couldn't let go of.

In both versions, the log seemed itself to be a figure, and the clod of earth something in its arms or on its back.... something puzzling it had been given to cope with. The grass reminded me of a grass skirt, giving an exotic African flavour to the whole arrangement. The green leaves felt like a hopeful element.... a sign of life even for the version in which I saw the branch/ figure as trapped.

> What is it that I know? When I think I've caught a glimpse of it it's not there anymore. When I come near to touch it, it is already moving away, because I've taken something moving into my hands.
> Jackson Webb, *The Last Lemon Grove.*

Other ways of 'looking'

Moving in response

Look briefly with a partner, then ***move****.... then write.... share the writing.... look again*

In order to get to know the feeling world of the image, we may need to let go of words for a while and explore how an image affects us in our bodies. Our bodies always see more of the feeling sense of an image than we consciously register. From this response in the body we may then begin to find the feeling words for what has been made.

Group response

As a group go round to visit what each person has individually made

For each piece of work, the maker gives a short account of the making process, simply what happened as they worked.

Then, each person in the group offers a short response – something they particularly notice or respond to.

As we hear other people's responses, it frees up our own response and can be a way of beginning to get to know the different layers and meanings around the work for oneself. This shared looking reminds us that there is always more within any piece of work... more than we consciously know at the time of making.

Write a story out of making

Make something, then immediately write a story, whatever comes to you,
(ie. not deliberately giving an account of what you have made).
With a partner, or a group, read the story and look at what was made.
Let this be a point of entry for your looking and speaking with a partner.

Adjusting an image

Sometimes, in the course of looking, we gain a sense of something else needed before the image can really live. We may feel the need to change something of what is there – perhaps taking a piece out and putting it on its own, or taking a fragment of one image and adding it to another.

At the moment of sensing that a change is needed within the details, or in the whole:
Shift something.... see what happens
Speak with a partner about the way this is changing the narrative of the image

Move from a fragment

Choose one element from what you have made and let it be in the space with you
Find a response to it in movement.

Giving the image (or a part of it) a voice – allow it to 'speak'

It can be freeing to let the image itself 'speak' rather than speaking about it (inside and looking out, rather than outside and looking in).

Imagine that images have their own stories to tell –
feelings to express, complaints to make

With a partner develop a dialogue with the image
Maker or witness can ask the image, or its parts, questions
Only the maker can speak as/ on behalf of... the image

Ask the image questions.... encourage it to express itself
Perhaps.... ask the whole image.... "What are you feeling?"

Ask what part of the image wants to speak -
a colour? a line? an empty space? an animal? a tree?
How does it feel?.... What does it need?
Does it speak to you.... or to another part of the picture?

Use your curiosity.... don't make any assumptions.... let the image surprise you

Allow conflict.... let the image, or parts of it, rebel.... be irritable – it might even say, "go away"
See if there are predicaments
If so.... can other parts of the image help to resolve them?

Perhaps.... ask a part of the image.... "why are you here"?
Allow a conversation with the image to unfold.

(derived from McNiff - see, Art as Medicine)

Sorting and grouping images

Once several pieces of work have accumulated, pull all your images together. Arrange them in groups, relate them spatially. Compare for common threads, themes, common qualities or differences. Get to know the set just as you may have done with individual pieces of work, allowing your attention to be drawn from one to another as you look.

Remaking – taking apart, beginning anew with the same ingredients

(after a pause – perhaps the following day)

Start with something you have already made. Spend time looking at it again while making a drawing or diagram of it. It may well appear different now from when you made it.

Afterwards: spend time quietly, letting impressions come in from around you
Then: go back to what you made.... loosen the parts
Take things out.... change.... add a new ingredient....
Gradually, let go of what you had
letting something new grow in its place

***Write**, or again talk, with a partner*
Let a new story emerge

Remaking offers possibilities of clarification or of added complexity.... or may perhaps give rise to an opposite to what was made before

Marge Ziius, drawings of a temporary work made and remade in a garden in two successive workshop sessions, international arts camp for young people, Luxembourg, 2001.

In our first session she made a sort of shrine with a single budha-like figure, a kind of guardian spirit, set on a stone slab. A path of tiny sticks led to it through what seemed like a formal garden, made with four leaves and fragments of green glass. She said that the figure radiated happiness or good energy... In remaking the arrangement, the next day, there appeared a second figure with an arch of leaves and a kind of nest filled with the little pieces of broken glass which she said could be either good or bad. The two figures were engaged in a continuing debate, one representing good things, the other bad. Whoever came out strongest at any moment prevailed in their influence over events and what was in the nest was accordingly made good or bad. In this second version it seemed that she had arrived at an image that felt more real to her, closer to her experience.

Ongoing work

Through our making, and looking at what we have made, a part of what lies hidden inside us has risen to the surface, found form in the external world and come to life in the stories we find as we look. The imagination with which we look and the resulting account of an image makes visible a web of interrelationships connecting what is hidden within us to what we are consciously aware of.

Looking inevitably brings up responses in us which could now be the basis for another phase of creating – an ongoing cycle of work in various media – moving, writing and further making. Aspects of the same image may return to us in some other form. Or perhaps what we have made could be re-worked and therefore deepened, the same or similar images extended or distilled. But it may be time to leave these images for now and let them settle. Work can resume another day when we can see what is needed next.

Record Spanish *recordar* to remember,
L. *recordare* to recall to mind, from L.*cor* (stem *cord*) the heart.
literally: to pass back through the heart.

Each time we work, something of what we need will emerge. But an image may also take a long time and many attempts before it is fully realised – a groping towards what may only arrive after a long struggle. In successive phases of making and re-making, we 'pass things back through the heart' – we may seem to let go of an image then to re-discover it as it re-emerges in another context. Gradually we sift out what it is we were seeking, letting the image we need slowly surface perhaps over many weeks or even years.

For now, the essential thing is that what we have just made has been absorbed and shared – at some level it speaks to and affects us. As we continue, it remains a presence within us – something indefinable understood.

> *There is a gap for me, crucially important in almost every painting and drawing that I do, between the first wave of activity on the individual work and the subsequent wave and between that and the subsequent wave and so on. The development is not just rethinking, its as though another level has to be reached which I tend to describe as respect or acceptance.* Ken Kiff quoted in: Norbert Lynton, *Ken Kiff at the National Gallery*, 1993.

Notes on timing, pacing and getting stuck

Ken Kiff, *Gardener* (Sequence No.62) c.1972-3.
Acrylic on paper, 71x58.5cm (28 x 23 in.)

Taking your own time

In moving, writing or making with materials, we need to find our own rhythm.... proceeding at a pace that works for ourselves and for what we are doing. Working 'in one's own time' also implies doing it on one's own terms. Yet, even without external pressures, it is sometimes hard not to rush.... to remember to take enough time to feel our way forward – time for impressions to sink in; time to sense what impulse is waiting to come through.

Every creative activity has its phases; it proceeds not in one straight line from start to finish but in a series of unexpected twists and turns, stops and starts. As we work we are constantly feeling out what is needed and when it is needed; we may sense a moment to fill a space... to empty it... to press forward or wait... to find a new ingredient. We sense a time to be fallow and empty; a moment to select, perhaps discarding all but a small part of what has been done; a time to stop and digest, when enough has happened for the time being. If we push ahead, disregarding this sense of need and timing we lose the thread of what we are doing. The pauses, stillnesses, standing back from, standing still within... creates the opening into which what we do not as yet know may arrive and expand our working.

In whatever you are doing.... allow a space... between one thing and another
pauses.... silences.... gaps
in making.... pull things a little apart.... so that they may discover a looser form
in moving.... allow stillness

Adjusting your pace

Living rhythms are never regular:-

> *Notice moments in your working when you need to change pace -*
> ***Slow down**, take your time: linger, absorb.... dwell, savour, dream.... return again and again.... perhaps even digress, embroider*
> ***Speed up**: make a bold gesture, dash in energetically, shock/ surprise yourself...*

Any physical task has its own necessary time and rhythm. The steady, chink... chink... of a carving tool on stone gives the task its own measure, its own musical rhythm, and creates an atmosphere of relaxed concentration, the sound and rhythm carrying the work forward and yet seeming to suspend time. And this rhythm in time gradually becomes visible in the emerging form of the work... it creates its own subtle, subliminal order.

Forced pace

Sometimes we need deliberately to break our habit of pace or duration, to go outside the boundary of what we normally do or regard as reasonable (i.e. as the appropriate time for a given task).

Set an extremely short time limit for a chosen task

In two minutes and in any form, make a portrait of today.... everything you have done, felt, noticed, wished, forgotten, said, not said, hoped...

> *These artificial limits create a crisis, which rouses the brain's resources: the compulsion towards haste overthrows the ordinary precautions, flings everything into top gear, and many things that are usually hidden find themselves rushed into the open. Barriers break down, prisoners come out of their cells.*
> Ted Hughes, *Poetry in the Making.*

Time frame

A specific duration, a 'time frame', gives an opening in which to work, a protected interval in which something may emerge.

The time it takes: for an egg to hatch... for the snow to melt... to prepare a meal
to forget... for the wind to drop... for bread to rise
for floodwaters to settle... for the tide to turn

Each day, allow half an hour (with space and materials available)
in which something unknown can happen
Follow whatever comes up

Getting stuck

On my face in the mud.
Becket, *How It Is.*

Getting stuck at some point in working is an uncomfortable, yet probably unavoidable part of any creative work. Something is needed that we have overlooked. Paradoxically, getting stuck can be the only way we begin to find direction, recovering what we have neglected or forgotten in ourselves. Often when feeling stuck, we need to step back, perhaps just for a moment, to widen the field in which we were working and to listen for some suggestion at the edges of our awareness, so that something outside our present way of seeing and working can come in. Our bodies may know a way through, even when our conscious mind feels lost and confused. Often, although we feel stuck, something beneath our awareness is brewing, but it needs time and space to come through. Also, to feel a bit lost, (which may seem like being stuck), is not necessarily a bad thing. It may simply mean that we are working at the edge of what we know and need to continue to grope our way forward.

...frustration, fear, loneliness, and boredom...... all belong to what the alchemists call the 'afflictio animi', the depression and sadness which precede a creative act. Von Franz, *Creation Myths.*

Stuck at zero – Sometimes it is not so much a matter of becoming stuck as of not knowing how to begin – perhaps because we feel lost for an idea. Yet the essence of an improvisational approach is that we start *without an idea* of what we are going to do. Having made a first movement/ chosen a first word/ drawn one line, another will usually suggest itself. Only as we engage do we in fact begin to find our way.

Sometimes this feeling of being unable to start is because the conditions are not yet right for working. Perhaps I haven't prepared myself – taken enough time to 'arrive'. My attention hasn't settled, so I am not yet in touch with my materials or with any impulse within myself.

Becalmed – We may have plunged forward, driven by an idea or intention and suddenly find ourselves empty, directionless, lacking a sense of connection to the work, because we have acted out of touch with ourselves – our moment by moment needs and impulses. A pause, simply receiving what is calling for attention, will allow a fresh impulse to arise.

Bored – We find ourselves working to a formula, repeating, stuck in a familiar habit, locked into one viewpoint.
Our attention has become too vague, glazed over. We may need to let in the outside world again... to return to the detail of what is before us, to pause and reconnect with sensation and specific impulse... dare to ask – "What do I really want?" "What really wants to happen here?"
Within a particular piece of work, we may need to introduce an element of chance or chaos....or to eliminate something.... or to restart with just a fragment of what we have made.... perhaps to work more slowly, to let in a deeper sense of what we need.

Overwhelmed – Emotions overwhelm us and make it hard to focus. If we can manage to stay in touch with the immediate and sensory detail of what we are doing, the working itself may begin to reconfigure the feelings in which we are locked. Working begins to move the emotions within us and loosens the intensity of our feelings. As we let our focus loosen, so our perceptions shift.

Repelled – We produce something that we don't like, it may even frighten or appal us. The work may seem to reflect aspects of our lives that we cannot tolerate. If instead of simply rejecting what we are doing, we try to: turn towards it, engage with it, give it a voice, listen to it, build around it, allow changes... we may cease to feel so repelled by what it presents and what we recoiled from will begin to change its character.

Lifeless – The work feels dead, perhaps because it has been over controlled. Yet, letting something change feels difficult because we may lose track and fall into a directionless chaos. These are ordinary fears, they reflect our need to hold ourselves together in the world. Yet even a slight loosening or reconfiguration of what we are doing, perhaps changing our pace of working, will allow something more vital to grow.

Failed – The work seems empty/ meaningless/ inadequate – we feel we have got nowhere and crushed by our own self critical, and self doubting voices. To recover, we need to let go of aspirations and judgments and pay more attention to what is actually emerging – give it credence, see it as separate from ourselves and our sense of personal worth or worthlessness. If we think of what we have done as independent of us, we can see it as something new emerging, wanting to enter the world and in need of our support. Even when we feel we have achieved little, if we spend time attending to what we have done, it usually turns out there is more to it than we thought. In this it can be helpful to work with a partner, spending time together with what we have written or made with materials, exploring it, rather than judging.

Jean Tinguely, *Self Destroying Sculpture*, Las Vegas, 1962

Cultivate
Find what you regard
as a dry and arid place
Introduce an ingredient
that in some sense
moistens it and
allows things to grow

Part 2 The Unfolding Image

body, imagination, and the immediate world

Part 2 – Contents

Gary Fiegehen, River Stikine

In the time of origins, people lived far under the earth. They had certain reasons for coming up – there were too many of them, they were too crowded and quarrelled too much – so some of the chiefs thought something must be done. By sending birds to explore, they managed to discover an upper world. They climbed up on a fir tree...... and reached another layer.

Part of a Hopi Indian myth, *cited in:* von Franz, *Creation Myths*

Introduction to Part 2

In Praise of Ironing

Poetry is pure white.
It emerges from water covered with drops,
is wrinkled, all in a heap.
It has to be spread out, the skin of this planet,
has to be ironed out, the sea's whiteness;
and the hands keep moving, moving,
the holy surfaces are smoothed out,
and that is how things are accomplished.
Every day, hands are creating the world,
fire is married to steel,
and canvas, linen, and cotton come back
from the skirmishings of the laundries,
and out of light a dove is born –
pure innocence returns out of the swirl.

Pablo Neruda, from: *Fully Empowered.*

The poetry and prose of our lives

It is a strange and paradoxical thing that we live through events, yet often do not feel fully connected to them. What happens in our lives may seem to fly swiftly past us, leaving us wondering what really occurred and what it meant. Unconsciously, our sensing bodies see and feel far more than we ever realise - only a fraction of what we take in ever rises into consciousness. If I retrace a path along which I have previously walked, there is so much I recognise as having seen, yet did not remember. There are gaps, not only in what we consciously register, but also in our ability to speak about or express it. When we try to describe even the most ordinary quality – the feel of a meeting with an old friend, the way a bird flew across the evening sky – our words often seem to falter, to slip and slide over and around what it is that we wanted to say – there is a sense in which literal description with its tendency to generalise, always fails, even dulls our sense of things. Yet the particularity of what we saw or felt becomes surprisingly accessible if we move into the metaphorical world of images, as when in common speech we say, "he felt crushed" or "she swanned into the room" or as in poetry, language is used evocatively: "The river is within us, the sea is all about us".... "It tosses up our losses"..."The shattered lobsterpot, the broken oar" (Elliot). It is the sensuous language of image, of metaphor, that captures the feel and complexity of things. And image is present, not only in the way we express ourselves, but also in the way we perceive and remember things around us. In this imagistic/ metaphoric way of perceiving, apparently neutral aspects of the world take on a personal and particular meaning - they embody a quality or feeling we are unconsciously looking for. We are mysteriously drawn to a place, or attracted to some object, or we find ourselves remembering a phrase of a song... and each of these without our knowing it, embodies a quality we are seeking. An image forms a bridge between what is inside us and and what is outside – it brings us more fully into a felt relationship with the world.

> *Might it not be that I must disregard chronology and simply stare into the cave of memory and just wait? When I tried this it did work; memories began to crystallise out with a gentle incandescence; only at first they were not of the famous buildings and places we had gone to see, the public experiences, the shared sights, but small private moments that came nuzzling into my thoughts and asking for attention.*
> Marion Milner, *Eternity's Sunrise.* On going back over the events of a holiday, part of a quest to find out what mattered in her life.

And as certain things around us draw our attention, something within us is touched and our imagination answers in response. Imagination is constantly at play in all our experiencing. As I begin to notice a table and explore its presence it seems to come alive, drawing to itself a wealth of associations, feelings, memories, thoughts and dreams. Imagination is not a separate faculty - rather it engages all parts of our mind and intelligence – fusing or bringing together often surprising aspects of what we know or feel. imagination expands our seeing.

In a similar way, as we create, with colours, textures, gestures, we discover images and forms whose significance we cannot quite define, yet whose presence somehow speaks to us. As in our dreams, these images arrive naturally and spontaneously so long as we do not consciously interfere by trying to pre-determine what they will be. Once made, an image communicates to us mysteriously, it registers within the tissues rather than the intellect and in doing so shifts our feeling about ourselves and our way of perceiving the world. The sensuous quality of images acts upon us directly without translation or psychological explanation. *

Every image evokes a world, a solar system of connections and meanings – of associations, qualities, textures, and memories. In this world of connections, an image carries the complexity of our feeling, holding together the otherwise fragmented field of our experiencing. In the images we make or find we discover hidden, neglected, and forgotten aspects of our lives. These images give shape and form to what we sense but cannot fully see; as fictions they throw light upon the facts of our lives. Images reflect an intuitive seeing and knowing different from the workings of our everyday purposive mind. As with our dreams, these images always surprise us with the extraordinary wit and precision with which they express our feeling world. Through our images we discover not one, but many (often conflicting), layers of meaning, meanings revealed slowly as we explore the details of what we have made.

*The word 'image' is, of course, widely used in our culture and means different things in different contexts. In advertising and fashion it means one thing, in optics it means another, in visual art it means something else again. In dance and movement it sometimes refers to a schematic mental picture of one's own anatomy that can facilitate and energise movement. In this book it has a broader meaning as explained above. (see also under 'image' in Glossary)

The chapters that follow offer themes and ways in to making images as a way of becoming more in touch with the depths and breadth of our familiar world:

Ch5. Skin: our meeting place with the world through touch, also the physical boundary of self.

Ch6. Materials: the feel and significance of what immediately surrounds us – textures, surfaces, substances.

Ch7. Stories: our world of events, histories, imaginings, and dreams.

Ch8. Bone: our body's resilient physical structure and support, which gives the body shape and definition and carries within it the imprint of the events and circumstances of our lives.

Ch9. Places: the larger physical world in which we dwell and through which we move – the contexts in which we find ourselves.

Ch10. Heart: the energetic centre of our circulation, also the centre of our feelings and impulses.

Each of these themes provides a broad frame within which many starting points for creating are introduced. The intention in working from any of these starting points is to reach towards a personal and particular imagery and through each image to discover a world that in some sense reflects the complex weave of one's life.

5. Skin

Edward Wachtell, *deer hidden in tall grass*

The sights and sounds which speak most deeply to us
move us
move us
where we thought we were sealed over.

Miller Mair, *Between Psychology and Psychotherapy.*

A place of meeting

There is only one world. Things outside only exist if you go to meet them with everything you carry in yourself. As to the things inside, you will never see them well unless you allow those outside to enter in. Lusseyran, *And There Was Light.*

(Lusseyran went blind at eight. As a member of the French Resistance, he was responsible for interviewing and assessing new recruits because of his extraordinary ability to 'see')

Moving beyond our selves

The skin is a place of meeting, a border and surface of exchange between ourselves and all that surrounds us. The skin is a window, letting in, letting through, the touch of the world. And what is within us shifts and changes according to what we meet – only in meeting is there any kind of knowing of ourselves. We become more of who we are as we get to know what is other than us – what is inside opening to and renewed by what is outside us – what is outside drawing us out of ourselves. We grow as we come up against differences, edges, the mystery of the 'other'.

Be still.... listen.... What do you notice around you?
What draws your attention?.... beckoning.... inviting
What do you avoid?.... pass by?.... shut out?

Through the surface of the skin the whole body listens and looks out, moment by moment informing us of where and how we are. Numbed, without sensation from the skin, we quickly become disorientated, losing both a sense of who we are and any feeling of connection to what is around us. What touches us, and what we ourselves reach out to touch, shapes every aspect of who we are. We are formed by touch, our sense of ourselves growing from the feel of contact between our bodies and what is around us. The chemistries of our bodies constantly change in response to the flow of information felt on the skin – the sound of a voice, the scents of cooking, the feel of a conversation – everything that happens around us, even things we have not noticed, touch and leave their trace within the tissues of the body. And within our bodies we sense and respond with feelings, thoughts, and imaginings.

in touch.... out of touch
lose one's touch.... touching.... untouched

To feel the touch of the world on our skins awakens us and puts us 'in touch' with the present and living moment. Perception is never passive; what we feel on our surface is met by a reciprocal flow of information and response coming from the depths of us. The feel of wind and rain on our faces, the sounds of children playing, call up responses within us that are at once physical, sensuous and imaginative. Sensation on the skin awakens us to what is felt beneath the skin, evoking buried layers of memory and emotion. Visibly and invisibly the borders of our selves are always changing. Moment by moment, as we sense and respond, our bodies becoming by turns permeable or impermeable, changing in colour and texture, hardening or softening, flushing or going pale. Without an awareness of touch, and the physicality of our bodies, the myriad and changing world in which we live seems fixed and distant and we ourselves caught within stories that seem to repeat themselves. But as we awaken to the touch of the world on our skins, we discover a sense of dialogue and the possibility of change.

Why must 'deep' be inside people? James Hillman

Close encounters

> *Touching the tomatoes in the garden, and really touching them, touching the walls of the house, the materials of the curtains or a clod of earth is surely seeing them as fully as eyes can see. But it is more than seeing them, it is tuning in on them and allowing the current they hold to connect with one's own, like electricity. To put it differently, this means an end of living in front of things and a beginning of living with them. Never mind if the words sound shocking, for this is love. You cannot keep your hands from loving what they have really felt,...* Lusseyran, *And There Was Light*

The listening skin

The moment we close our eyes, we wake up through the skin, surfacing into a world of proximities in which everything around us seems to touch and speak to us – a world in which empty space no longer exists, a world transformed into a dense and shimmering pattern of textures, vibrations, sounds and scents. With eyes closed, the feel of the ground, of walls, of doorways, of light and shadow – the touch of air, of clothing, of objects – all seem to come to life. These presences, other than ourselves, are mostly hidden to us, yet appear as we become still and listen, as we awaken to the touch of the living world on our skins.

The skin is the largest, oldest, and most sensitive of our organs. The ectoderm, from which brain, nervous system, and all our senses develop, forms an outer surface for the developing embryo, and this vital connection between skin and nervous system continues throughout our lives. The skin plays a crucial role in keeping us informed of what is going on outside us. It is the eyes and ears of the whole body, moment by moment informing us of touch, pressure, pain, vibration, and sound - awake also to the intangible and invisible movement of all that is around us.

The sense of touch is the first of our senses to develop and is our earliest means of communication. Hearing, taste, smell and sight are all in some way a modification of the primordial sense of touch. At six weeks the tiny embryo already responds to the lightest of touches, and throughout early life, the infant relies almost entirely upon the sense of touch. Hellen Keller, deaf and blind from infancy, was taught to speak and communicate by stimulation through her skin. The functioning of every system in our bodies – breathing, circulation, digestion, or immunological resilience, the physical growth of bone, muscle, and organ, as well as our mood and emotion – are all profoundly affected by touch, or lack of touch. In infancy, lack of the sensory stimulus of touch causes a wasting in all the tissues similar to that of malnutrition and an apathy from which a child may even die. * Without stimulation of the skin, we lose an essential and present sense of connection, both to ourselves and to what is around us. Where other senses fail, the sensitivity of the skin deepens, keeping us 'in touch' with the world in which we live and belong.

*footnote: In 1951 James H.M. Knox, Jr. of the Johns Hopkins Hospital noted that: "in spite of adequate physical care, 90% of the infants in Baltimore orphanages and foundling homes died within a year of admission" (Gardner L.I., quoted in Deane Juhan, *Job's Body*) and there have been similar reports from the orphanages of both Rumania and China.

Spread out, the average adult skin covers 15-20 square feet and weighs around 8-12 lb (depending on fat stored). The skin contains some 500 million sensory cells that are connected to the spinal cord by over half a million nerve fibres, which continually provide the brain with information about touch, pressure, cold, heat and pain. Skin cells are sensitive also to vibration, sound and sunlight.

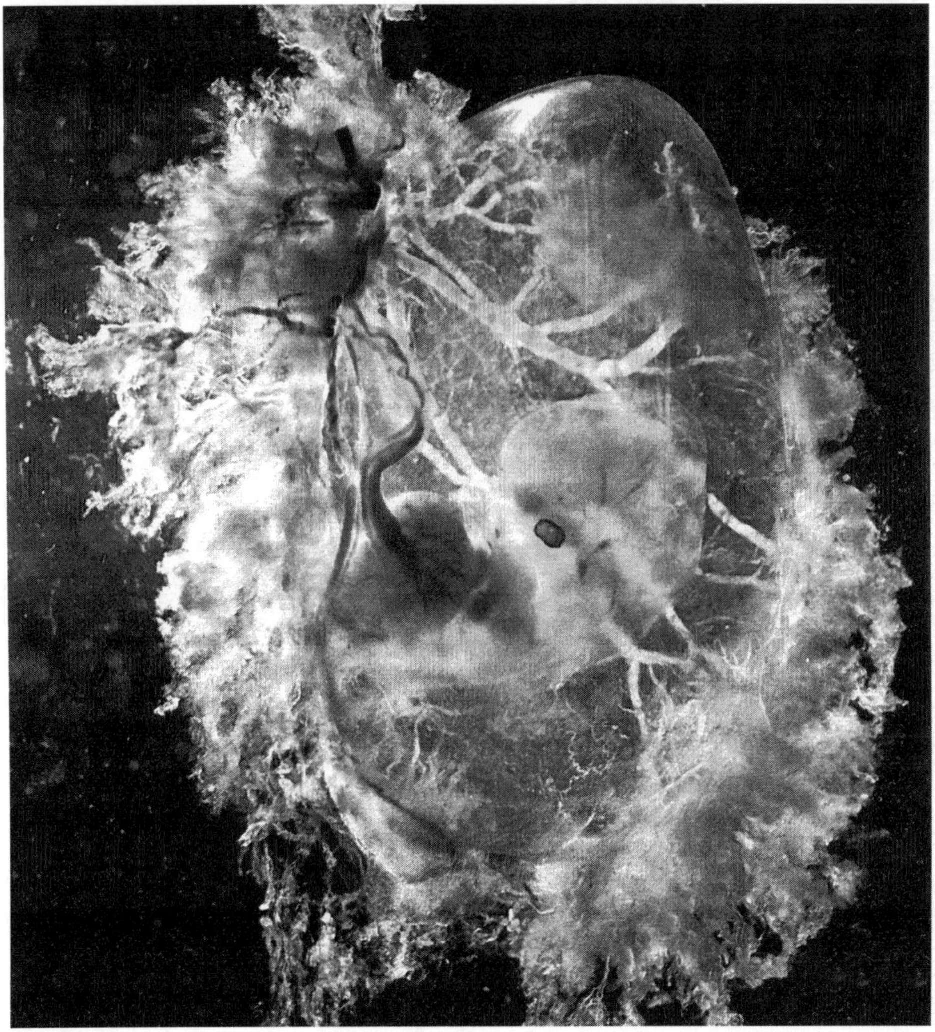

Human Embryo at 6 weeks

The mind is as much in the body as the body is in the world. The body penetrates the mind just as the world penetrates the body. We like to believe, since we see ourselves as enclosed within a shield of skin, that we are demarcated from the world by this envelope of skin, just as a theatre curtain separates the audience from the stage before the performance. But the skin is a porous membrane. Electrically and chemically the world moves right through us as though we were made of mist. John Bleibtreu, *Parable of the Beast.*

Find the skin

Lie or sit.... close your eyes.... be still.... listen.... breathe
let your attention spread out.... to your edges

In your mind's eye.... travel the skin.... the entire outer surface of the body
around your ankles... under your heels... over your fingers
and the back of your neck... into ears and nose... over the crown of your head
sense.... the feel of your surfaces.... let the skin soften and open.... as an ear listening

How does the skin feel?
delicate... thin... warm... full... bruised... hardened... soft... tired...?
sense.... what is covered.... what is exposed
sense the play of light.... of shadow.... on your skin
feel the quality of the body.... resting inside its skin

Sense.... the texture of the skin against the hardness of ground.... sense the touch of air
Open the skin as the surface of a lake.... receiving reflections.... sounds.... impressions
Notice how the skin changes quality.... as it 'meets' whatever is touching it
What reaches beneath the skin?.... stirring the deeper layers of your body

Let the skin soften and spread out.... listening in all directions
sense what is just above you.... just below.... to left.... right.... just behind
Which direction invites you?.... feel how the skin responds
let each surface of the body listen and be moved

Be curious.... move and explore.... all around you
What do you notice?.... What becomes visible?
What is close, foreground?.... What is hidden, background?
What is illuminated?.... What is in the shadows?
Let your attention travel as the air.... over your surfaces.... moving between inside and out

Let sensation on the skin.... invite conversations.... meetings in movement
take time to follow... the movements of response.... a dance of listening
What do you find?.... Who do you become?.... Where do you go?

Afterwards:
Be still.... listen again.... ***write****.... to gather up and give voice to impressions*
Gather materials.... to ***make****.... a map of the skin, find ways to make visible its field of activity*
Share.... and reflect with a partner

The voice of the other

How could I have lived all that time without realising that everything in the world has a voice and speaks? Not just the things that are supposed to speak, but the others, like the gate, the walls of the houses, the shade of trees, the sand, and the silence. Lusseyran, *And There Was Light.*

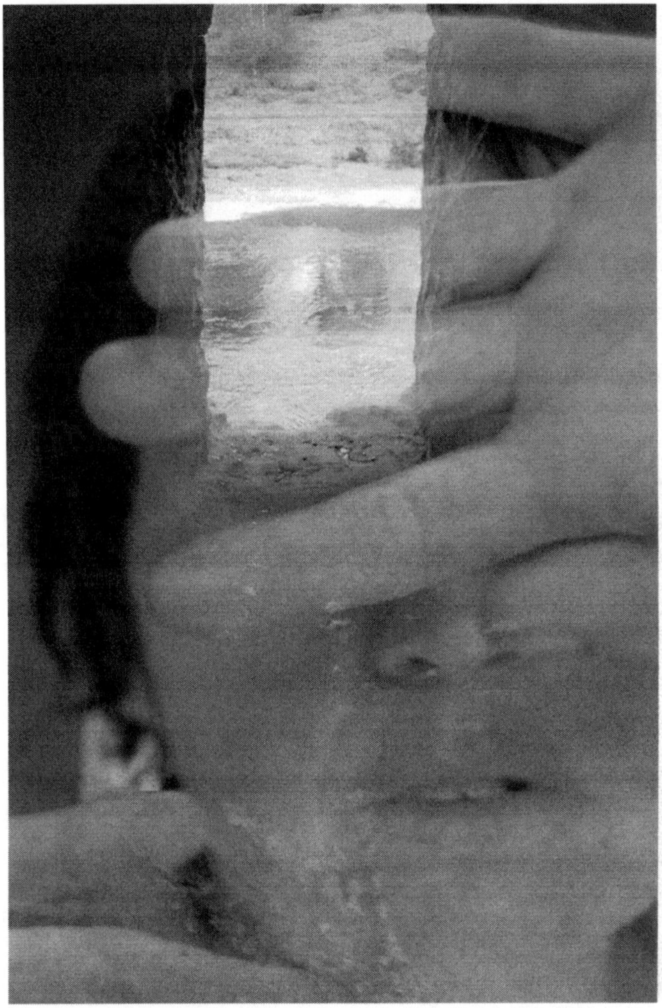

Miranda Tufnell, Study for *Wing*. Photo: Caroline Lee.

Wing is a film about body and land, a collaboration between Miranda Tufnell, musician Sylvia Hallett, and artist Caroline Lee. *The film was composed through a layering of images of landscape and details of the moving body. In this play of scale, we sought to make visible the invisible world of touch and sensation felt beneath the skin.* Miranda Tufnell.

Seen... unseen

The flowers swim like fish made of light upon the dark, green waters. I hold a stalk in my hand. I am the stalk. My roots go down to the depths of the world, through earth dry with brick, and damp earth, through veins of lead and silver. I am all fibre. All tremors shake me, and the weight of the earth is pressed to my ribs. Up here my eyes are green leaves, unseeing.
Virginia Woolf, *The Waves.*

What lies beneath the surface?
Gather materials.... make and explore
to find what is under the skin

Surface and innermost core spring from the same mother tissues and throughout life they function as a single unit, divisible only by dissection or analytical abstraction, every touch initiates a variety of mental responses and nowhere along the line can I draw a sharp distinction between periphery which purely responds as opposed to central nervous system which purely thinks. My tactile experience is just as central to my thought processes as are language or categories of logic.
Deane Juhan, *Job's Body.*

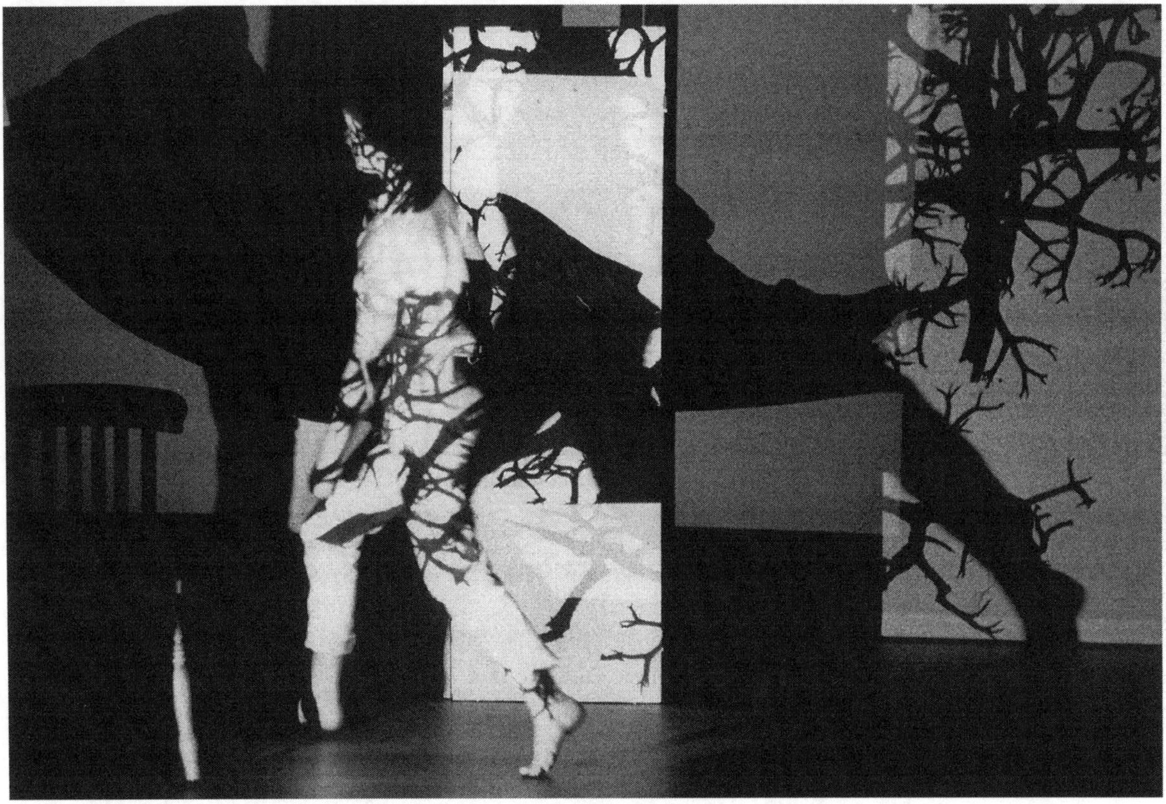

Miranda Tufnell, *Landlight*, 1989
Photo: Dee Conway

Conceal... reveal
Choose something that seems exposed
find how to shelter/ conceal it

Choose something that seems hidden
find ways to give it a voice

***Move** to explore what is there*
Reflect with a partner

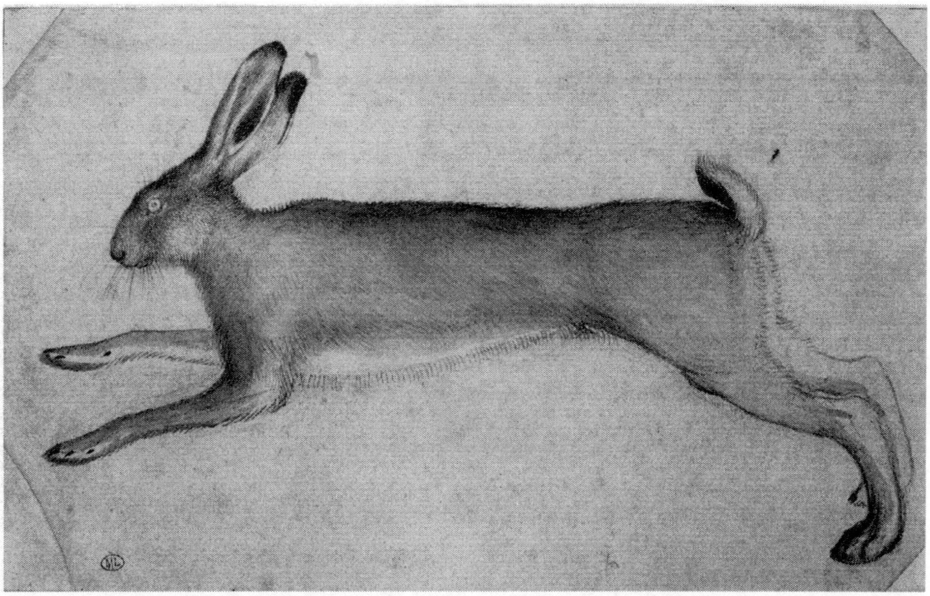

Pisanello, *Running Hare*, c1430-42. Watercolour over black chalk

From outside to inside – the developing skin

In the human fertilised egg, it is the sensitivity and permeability of its outer membrane that allows the constant to and fro of metabolic processes from outside to inside, essential for development and growth. The inner nucleus is the chief carrier of heredity and stability, whilst the surrounding, limiting membrane is the carrier of adaptation and growth.* In the developing embryo, our central nervous system is the folded and in-turned layer of this outer surface, a connection that remains fundamental to our perception, survival and growth. What happens on our skin constantly informs and shapes the responses of our brain and central nervous system.

From the outer layers of the skin over half a million sensory fibres travel inwards to the spinal cord – the periphery of the body creating ever more intricate branchings of neural pathways. The receptors for pain are closer to the surface, while those for heat, cold and pressure are contained within the deeper layers. Skin may be thought of as, "the outer surface of the brain" (Dean Juhan, *Job's Body*), and brain the inturned, hidden lining of our skin.

* Footnote: source – Blechschmidt, *Beginnings of Human Life*

Fay Godwin, *Top Withens*, Near Haworth, Yorkshire.
Black and white photograph.

From all around

Stand or sit still.... outside, in the open air

Close your eyes*.... let your body settle.... let the length of your spine open*
take time to breathe.... letting the outside air.... come in
Sense the life of what is around you
sounds.... movement.... the quality of light, of shadow, of weather, and of air

Let the body be soft as wax.... receiving impressions

Go beneath your skin.... the body has doorways.... windows.... bridges.... passages
Take time... to let impressions in.... sense the movement of response.... in the depths of the body
in the belly.... in the heart.... in the bones.... in the blood

Open your eyes*.... let them rest on whatever you first see*
let your focus soften and spread out.... widening
What is moving at the edges of your vision?

Watch the rise and fall of sensations.... of answering and response.... in the body
let your whole body listen.... speak with.... and be part of what is there

Move*.... to create a small dance or performance for this place*
Write*.... or whisper to yourself, fragments of a story of what is happening here*
Make*.... something to make visible what is invisible*
With a partner.... reflect on all that happened

With listening fingers

Tessa Traeger, *Two Roses*, North Devon,1997.

It is with our hands that we reach out to touch and explore the world. Through touching we discover and feel the other – my hand a bridge between us, connecting, opening a pathway between what is you and what is me. We lay a hand on a frightened child or animal – touching to calm, soften, reassure. The touch of our hands reaches beneath any words and wherever we are touched, a door opens both inwards and outwards and memories may rise and flood us like dreams. As the smallest whisper of sound vibrates on the skin of the ear drum, awakening the tiny bones of the inner ear, so the gentlest of touches resonates and affects us.

What I feel with my hands depends on how I 'use' them. If I let my hand gently spread open and 'give it into' what I touch, I begin to feel an answering movement and form rising to meet my hand. If I loosen and soften my hand as a pathway that opens upwards through my wrist and forearm, my sense of what I am touching deepens, as if I am letting it in to myself. The hand is formed from 27 small and separate bones, which allows its extraordinary delicate and intricate precision of movement. In our everyday use of the hand, we grasp and take hold of what is around us, forgetting the sensitivity with which it can also receive and 'see'. There are more nerve endings within the fingertips and lips, and more of the cortex is devoted to them, than any other part of the body. For blind people, the thousands of nerve endings and sense organs in the fingertips substitute for eyes.

Development of the hand

The upper limb begins to form ahead of the lower (around 26 days), visible first as a tiny ridge or fin developing opposite the ventricles of the heart (the lower limb grows in association with the umbilical cord). As it grows the upper limb curves around the front of the body, the hand and fingers moving over the pulse of the heart. By the eighteenth week, the hand has developed its opposing thumb which generates its extraordinary range of skills and precision of movement.

Figure – *nkisi,* of the Kongo spirit *Mavungu,* into which hundreds of pieces of metal have been hammered by a diviner to activate *Mavungu's* power against the evils of witchcraft. Made before 1892 in the Kongo area of Central Africa (Democratic Republic of Congo/People's Republic of Congo). © Courtesy of the Pitt Rivers Museum, University of Oxford (1900.39.70).

Untouched

Choose something that feels untouched.... untouchable

spend time quietly with it.... imagine its voice.... its stories

Without any plan, or knowing what you are going to do

***make** a place for it*

What begins to emerge?

Look and explore what is there with a partner

***Move** in response*

***Write** to find its story*

Blindfold journey.... a world of proximities

Exploring surroundings through touch and other non-visual senses

Work with a partner, one with eyes closed, one with eyes open

(Although this is a common exercise, it is a very effective way both of awakening the body to sensation and of getting to know a place.)

Person with eyes open

Take your partner on a blindfold journey
bring them to places.... that may interest/ surprise them

guide them gently.... silently
watch that they do not fall/ injure themselves

Sense their impulses to linger.... or to move on
Give them time to take things in.... explore

Person with eyes closed

Take your own time.... explore details .... qualities,
savouring the sensations, rather than trying to identify things
sense...... temperature... contour... texture... sounds... smells...

Some other ways of exploring with eyes closed

Sharing impressions (a variant on the above)

Person with eyes closed speaks their track of attention out loud (a monologue)
partner simply listens

Revisiting a chosen spot (another variant)

Wherever you feel most engaged, ask your partner to plant a flag or marker
Afterwards (with eyes open) return to one of the places marked
Make something there.... in response to your impressions.... then and now....
Then: **write** and **move** in response
(from a workshop in collaboration with Sharon Higginson)

Blindfolded I was carried by my two partners into a building. I heard the creak of hinges on the barbed wire door and felt the flutter of wings on my legs as I was lowered onto a cool, slimy mud and shit floor. Loud cooing and chicken hollers surrounded me as my partners retreated and the door slammed shut"

From an account of a workshop with Min Tanaka intended to heighten sensory awareness. Alissa Cardone, *Losing One Sense to Heighten Others,* Contact Quarterly, Winter/Spring, 2002.

Alone, with eyes closed

Spend time outside on your own with eyes closed
Wander.... what draws you along?
Choose when to open your eyes.... What do you first see?.... What words or images does it call up?
Bring back something from that spot.... connected to what you have seen
Find a place for it inside

Make.... *find what other ingredients are called for*
What appears?
Move or write *to find how this place touches you.... what it speaks of*

Hidden forms – working with clay, eyes closed (about 20 mins)

Let all parts of your hand spread open.... receive.... the mass of the clay
Sense.... what seems to lie within.... as a seed

Give the fingers time.... to follow what they discover
what the hand enjoys.... goes to meet
Touch... see... feel.... with listening fingers

Sense what wants to happen throughout the emerging 'landscape'
drawing out what is immanent.... sleeping within
hollow.... ridge.... animal.... face.... scene

How does the hand itself.... want to move?
Allow both hand and clay.... a voice

Listen.... make.... in conversation with the material
Let images/ stories arise and drift as you work
What is moving up to the surface from within?
What wants to appear?
What comes in from you?

Afterwards; without looking at what you have made
Write.... *from the experience and sensation of making*

A conversation of touch and movement with a partner

person accompanying

Let a hand come to rest on your partner.... as an ear listening
Let the hand soften to receive....
Soften the lengths of your wrist and arms.... open the length of your spine

Wait.... listen as your partner breathes.... watch how they 'arrive' into your hand.... a meeting
as a fish rising to the surface of the water.... a presence under the skin
Let your hand.... your body.... open.... to receive

As in conversation, let your hand give an impulse to your partner
receive... rest on... propel...
Give time.... to let your partner answer.... meet.... your touch

Trust.... your hand in knowing when to let go and where next to settle
Allow the timing and quality of your touch to vary
let your body touch.... support.... give resistance
(resistance often gives the leverage to move)

Let the rhythms of breath guide your working.... expanding.... softening.... pausing
as a wave.... allow each impulse its own time
let your hands and body.... move/ change.... seeing/ responding.... differently in each moment
following.... what is emerging

person moving

Take time to receive.... let in.... the touch.... let it settle inwards
Notice the answering of feeling.... of sensation.... within the body
touch is felt not just on the surface but registers deep within

Take time to.... sense the impulse of response
Allow the touch to call up movement
answer.... call back.... resist.... slide off.... ignore.... go into orbit
Play in the waters of suggestions
How long does a response travel through you?
discovering.... answering.... touch

Gradually.... find a dialogue of touch and movement between you
each changing.... discovering

Eva Karczag on an exploration of moving from touch

Excerpts from a working diary covering a period of sustained exploration of movement combined with Alexander Technique – a collaboration with Irene Koditek, Arnhem, 1999.

We enter the room... you haven't slept all night you tell me – the asthma again – breathing.
Caught in the past history of your body, you want to find the way out.

My hands and intention are drawn first to your belly – to create space, to energise,
to ground you – to help it open, so it can receive the tight ball in your centre chest.
Then, placing one hand on the half moon of your face I am considering detail as I sink
into the orb of your eye.

My hand calls your energy to move –
and I ask myself, am *I* still moving?
Am I feeling the inner space between front of spine and inside of breast-bone,
and the strength that rises through my neck?

Your face opens,
bones shift, muscles soften, and structure becomes more visible. I let
myself drop below the layers of your skin, and into the space
between your jaw and neck,
gliding down into your heart.

I enjoy our talking – making this strange activity connect to real life.
But I am in there with you – with the way the density of your body thins,
so I can feel into your centre, into the movement of your energy.

Connection between pelvic floor opening and widening of underside of jaw
releases energy in your body that talks to the whole of you.
You lighten on a cellular level.

You say – Every little touch, although it also offers something, contains this question –
"are you going with me or not?"
It invites... the result is a very different movement quality.

The more one knows about the body,
the more precise, the more subtle the question can be.

The softness of your torso moves with increasing detail and articulation.
You are the energy of your moving, you are the space. I can see through
your body, and I can see movement through you. You are beyond your
boundaries and barriers, touching an essence that fuels your moving –
vulnerable, present in this moment, fearless and alive.

I can no longer see the shape that is normally you.
Instead I see the detail and subtlety that lies
beyond the physical/emotional borders that you create for yourself.

Getting drawn into a movement duet is a seamless connection - you're with me,
we're speaking body to body, skin to skin, intent to intent, response to
response. Surprises, when movement erupts from both of us, or direction changes,
or touch comes where touch is wanted. This feels good.

Then your role moves into toucher. I stand and wait – information enters my body, and I begin to change.

Unknown forms... drawing from touch

Take some charcoal and a large sheet of paper
With eyes closed.... get someone else to hand you a surprise object

Explore the object through touch
see what your fingers notice –
a lip, a ledge, a broad curving smoothness – an abrupt change of plane or angle, a contrast of texture or temperature

Open your eyes.... but keep the object to one side.... out of sight
Continuing to explore the object through touch
invent your own way of making marks on the paper to register these tactile sensations
Look at your drawing.... but not at the object
(Draw large enough to involve your whole body in the work)

Feeling with the eye... drawing with touch

In a second drawing.... do the reverse of the above –
look at the object.... and draw it without looking down at your drawing

Let your eye travel over the object as your fingers did before
Feel the lines of the object.... in the movement of your hand.... on the paper

The feel of our edges

Boundary surfaces, with their rhythmical processes, are birthplaces of living things. It is as though the creative, formative impulses needed the boundary surfaces in order to be able to act in the material world. Boundary surfaces are everywhere the places where living, formative processes can find hold; be it in cell membranes, surfaces of contact between cells, where the life forces are mysteriously present; in the great boundary surfaces between the current systems of the oceans, where various currents flow past each other in different directions – these are known to be particularly rich in fish;... Theodor Schwenk, *Sensitive Chaos.*

The skin wraps and contains us from head to toe and front to back, enclosing and separating what is me from what is not me, moment by moment protecting the deeper, softer tissues of the body - keeping out what may harm, warning us through pain, and quick to repair itself when damaged or breached. All living things need containment, a boundary between their internal world and the flux of elements within which they exist. Without containment - membrane, shell, skin - what is within any life form is vulnerable, easily dispersed, or scattered. Without the protection and defence of the skin we die. And a sense of what is 'me' and 'not me' is crucial to our sense of identity and our capacity to interact with what is around us. Moment by moment the feel of our skin changes. At times we may feel all edges – prickly, brittle, hard – at other times we may feel we have no skin – exposed, fragile and raw.

The skin has many functions that maintain the over all balance of the body, thin (only 1-2 millimetres in depth), yet strong, it forms a barrier and first line of defence for our fragile insides, protecting against foreign bodies and bacterial invasion. It also plays a crucial part in the regulation of blood pressure, blood flow and body temperature. The skin stores and metabolises fat, salts and water to both cool and warm us. The sebum, from sebaceaous glands, lubricates skin and hair and insulates against rain and cold. Sunlight on our skins synthesises Vitamin D, essential to the body's inner chemistries of digestion and nerve function.

Bill Viola, *Five Angels for the Millennium* (2001) ii. "Birth Angel", Video/sound installation. Five channels of color video projection on walls in large, dark room; stereo sound for each projection. © Bill Viola.

Make a skin

Gather materials.... to make a skin

What skin feels needed?
What does this skin cover.... protect.... keep in.... keep out?
What appearance does it present?
What qualities might it give its wearer?

***Move....** as the skin.... Find what lies beneath its surface*
To whom or what might it belong?
*With a partner **write** and reflect*

Fur and feathers are often worn by shamans because
they carry the animal's power to see what is happening far off.

silky rough raw baggy shiny clear stretched worn transparent scaly thick

Changing skins

Magritte, *The Taste of Sorrow*, 1948
59.5 x 50 in.

I am not I.
I am this one
Walking beside me whom I do not see,
Whom at times I manage to visit,
And at other times I forget.
The one who remains silent when I talk,
The one who forgives, sweet, when I hate,
The one who takes a walk when I am indoors,
The one who will remain standing when I die.

Juan Ramon Jimenez, *I am not I.*

The soles of our boots wear thin, but the soles of our feet grow thick the more we walk upon them....
D'arcy Thompson, *On Growth and Form.*

Our skins are always changing. They record the daily weathering of our lives altering in texture, scent, temperature, and colour, according to our health or emotions. As we age, our skins lose their fullness and moisture, they wrinkle, loosen, harden and thin, yet still give us the familiar appearance by which we are known and recognised. There are many stories of skins lost, stolen, or used as disguises to enter different worlds, or a means to a different point of view. Inside our skins we are rarely all of a piece. We move in and out of different voices that jostle within us like a cast of characters. Throughout our lives we are compelled to shed old skins, old appearances, and to accept new ones. Over a seventy year life time we 'shed' as many as 850 skins.

> *Multiple personality is humanity in its natural condition. In other cultures these multiple personalities have names, locations, energies, functions, voices, angel and animal forms, and even theoretical formulations as different kinds of soul.*
> James Hillman, *Archetypal Psychology.*

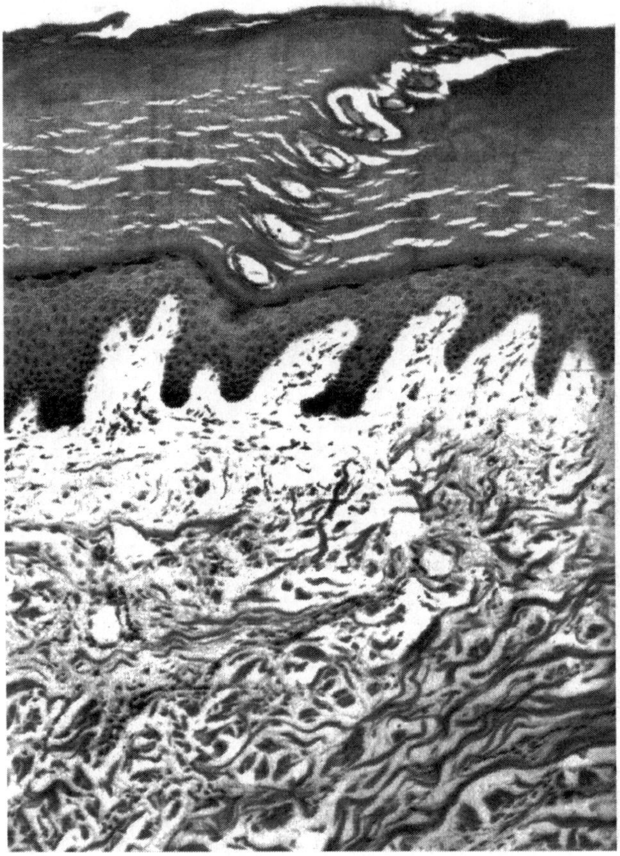

Vertical section through skin, from the sole of the foot

The layers of our skin

The resilience and strength of our skin comes from its progressive layering. The most superficial layer or epidermis is itself formed by four separate layers whose cells are continually being shed and replaced. Our skin is in a constant state of renewal, new cells continuously being formed in the deeper layers of the epidermis which then migrate upwards and are shed at a rate of over a million an hour, a 27 day cycle of renewal. The epidermis functions as a waterproof barrier of protection against bacterial invasion for the inner workings of the body. Its depth varies according to need and use... thicker on the soles of the feet, thinner and more delicate on the lips, eye lids, nostrils and anal canal. There is no blood supply to this outer layer which relies on the underlying dermis for irrigation. The dermis is the thickest layer of the skin and contains the blood and lymph vessels for the epidermis. It also contains hair follicles and sweat glands. It is densely laced with loose connective tissue which gives the skin its resilience and also its anchorage down into the yet deeper layers of subcutaneaous fat and muscle. The connective tissue also produces the fibroblasts responsible for healing injuries to the skin.

Ansuman Biswas and Jem Finer, *Zero Genie,* 2002.
Still from a video made at the Cosmonauts 1 Training Centre, Star City, Moscow.

The video was shot on board an aeroplane following a parabolic flight path. As the aircraft climbed and fell it passed through alternating fields of double gravity and zero gravity. In science fiction mythology Man sheds his earthly skin to ascend to the next stage of evolution amongst the stars. According to conventional wisdom we are dependant upon huge thrusting rockets and the bulky second skin of a spacesuit to fly in space. The Zero Genies are here to show that people of another race have found the thin membrane of a carpet quite sufficient. Ansuman Biswas.

A new skin

This hexagram means in its original sense an animal's pelt, which changes in the course of the year by moulting. I Ching, Hexagram 49, 'Revolution'.

Shedding a skin

Take a large sheet of soft paper (newsprint is good) as large or larger than yourself
Close your eyes.... take time to feel its qualities.... and the response of your body to it
Listen to it.... hear its presence.... imagine it.... as your 'skin'
explore with it

Let a conversation grow.... between you and the paper
find as you move.... the body's need to... wrap... bare... disguise... mask... enclose... cover... shed

When you are ready.... let it fall.... How does the body feel? What does the paper.... become?
Open your eyes.... how do you feel?
***Write**.... and reflect*
(Derived from Miche Fabre Lewin)

Writing in response to 'shedding a skin' (Miche Fabre Lewin)

In the curve of the sea, sheltering, sheltering.... And the call and throw of the next wave
Green blaze.... and I burn skywards.... A cry piercing the still of the throat
Speechless and gaping no sound.... But a cry that echoes through creation
Slowly the slow woods breathe.... A gentling of dark cooling the skin

Come and the ache bleads itself white to the moon.... calling.... calling
Somewhere she came a hand dropping gently through water.... Silently cradling, gently recovering
What was lost.... Mother of bone.... Day bleeds itself bare, sinking
To shadows gathering – feathering the skin's night.... What is remembered dissolved in the whispering corn
Come and come here – Oh my mother skies
I have hung and drawn myself for you.... Pierced and torn open
Myself for you.... Did you hear?.... The pain leaves no room, did you hear?
The robin is singing in the winter trees

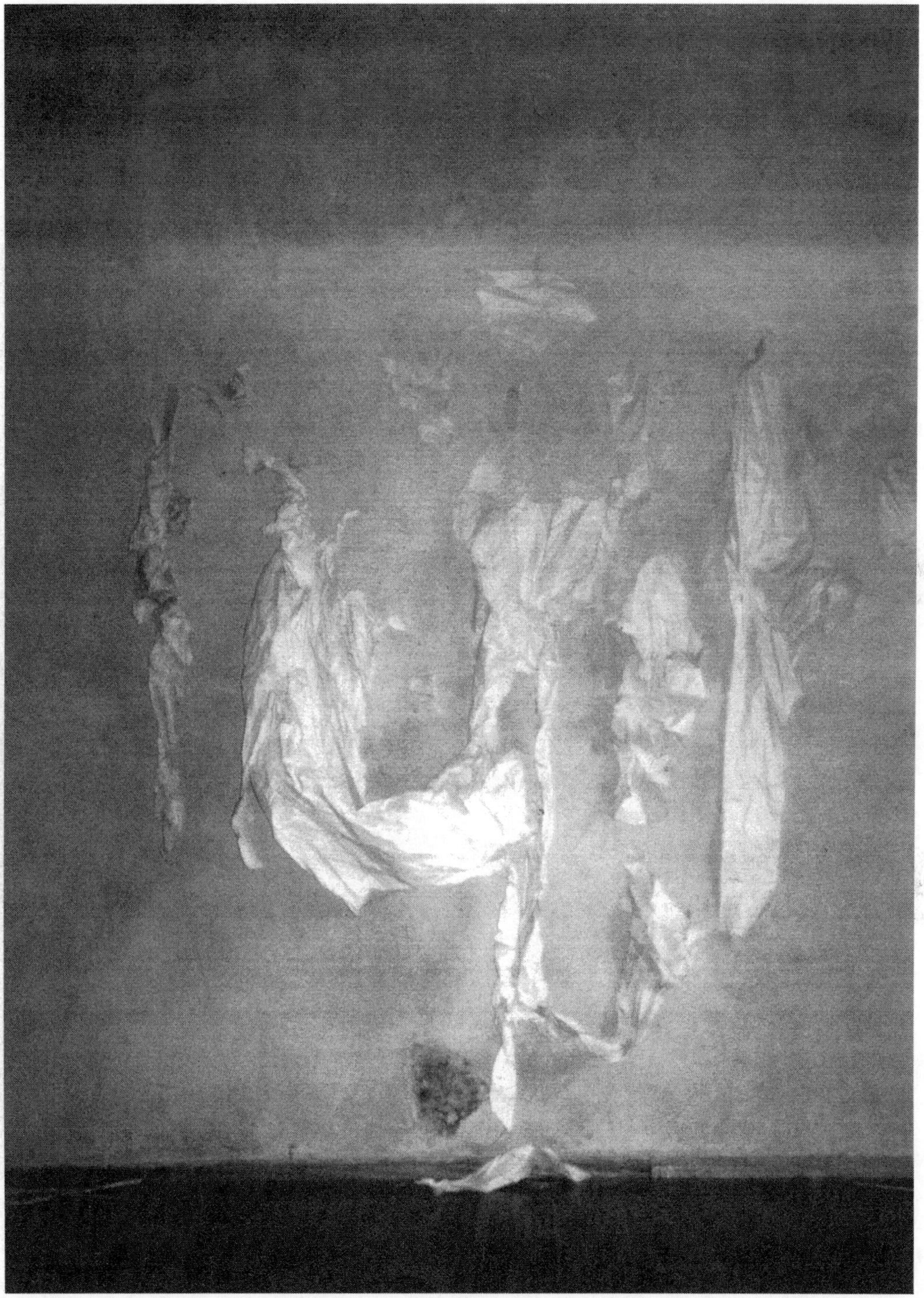

Miche Fabre Lewin, *Mother of Bone*, 1999.
Medium: newsprint role and body movement

Imagine you have no skin

Move.... *find how to 'cover' yourself*

Find.... **something that seems 'wounded'**

Through making on or around it
explore ways to heal the wound.

Make:

a skin.... for another world.... a stolen skin.... skin for a child.... for an old man

Wear them.... speak to them.... listen to them
find places to shed them

***Write**, to find their voices*

Disguise

Make a skin that changes your appearance –
modifies/ disguises.... what you are
*Wear it.... **move** with it*
***Write** from moving*

Camouflage

Become more like your surroundings
***move** to explore – how does your seeing change?*
***Write**, to gather up impressions*

[They] rub their faces until a second or even third skin appears – the new skin visible only to initiates....The old skin must disappear and make room for a new translucent and delicate layer.
Eliade, *Shamanism.*

Border

Make.... *a place at the border*

Your hand opens and closes, opens and closes
If it was always stretched open, or always closed, you would be paralysed
Your deepest presence is in every fine folding and unfolding
The two as perfectly balanced and coordinated as birds' wings.
Rumi

Between places

How we feel and respond is shaped both by our need to be closed and contained, and also to be open, permeable. Paradoxically, it is the sense of containment that frees us to move out. In the living cell only when the surface membrane has become sufficiently enlarged through a drawing in of nutrients from outside, is there room for the core or interior to grow and develop. In our own lives there may be a regular, almost seasonal need to let go of the familiar boundaries and wander out. We may find ourselves heading for unknown places not knowing what we may find there or who we may become, yet somehow following an instinctual and intuitive need for something to change and grow.

Borders are places of connection, of separation, and of transition. I go from one place to another, from one condition to another, often losing or leaving something of myself behind. I cross a threshold from outside to inside the house, or I cross a threshold in my life from one stage to another, and at the moment of crossing I may linger... here I am in what feels like a no-man's land. Who am I now? What am I doing? This is a place without a name – a place where I do not know myself; a place of change where anything might happen.

Turning point
Janus, as in 'January': the god of beginnings,
a god who looks both forward and back.

...it may be difficult to admit that we have ever experienced a void. It is difficult and terrifying even to imagine having been no-one, for most of us have always wanted to be or have been someone and its hard to imagine being nowhere for we have always striven to be or have been somewhere. Bani Shorter, *Border People.*

Emergence

Make something that is just emerging

What shape is taking form?.... What is shed?

Move** to explore its point of view, then **write

Sankai-juku, *Unetsu*, (the Egg Stands out of Curiosity).
Photo: Masafumi Sakamoto

A gentle stream of water, a steady flow of fine sand, an egg swinging from side to side, a pool of water sparkling in the darkness, shaven heads, whitened bodies, red fingertips as the only note of colour... Unetsu... explores the processes of life and death and of man's spiritual quest. Sadlers Wells leaflet.

...the caterpillar which hangs in the aerial and temporary tomb of the cocoon, changes into the inert chrysalis, and then comes out into the light in the perfect shape of the butterfly; the wings are still inept, weak, like crumpled tissue paper, but in a few instants they strengthen, stretch and the newly born lifts in flight. It is a second birth, but at the same time it is a death: what has flown away is a psyche, a soul, and the ripped open cocoon, which is left on the ground is the mortal remains. Primo Levi, *Other People's Trades.*

6. Materials
the substance and surface of things

material, matter *L. materia,* substance.... *L. mater* mother
substance *L. substare,* literally to stand beneath

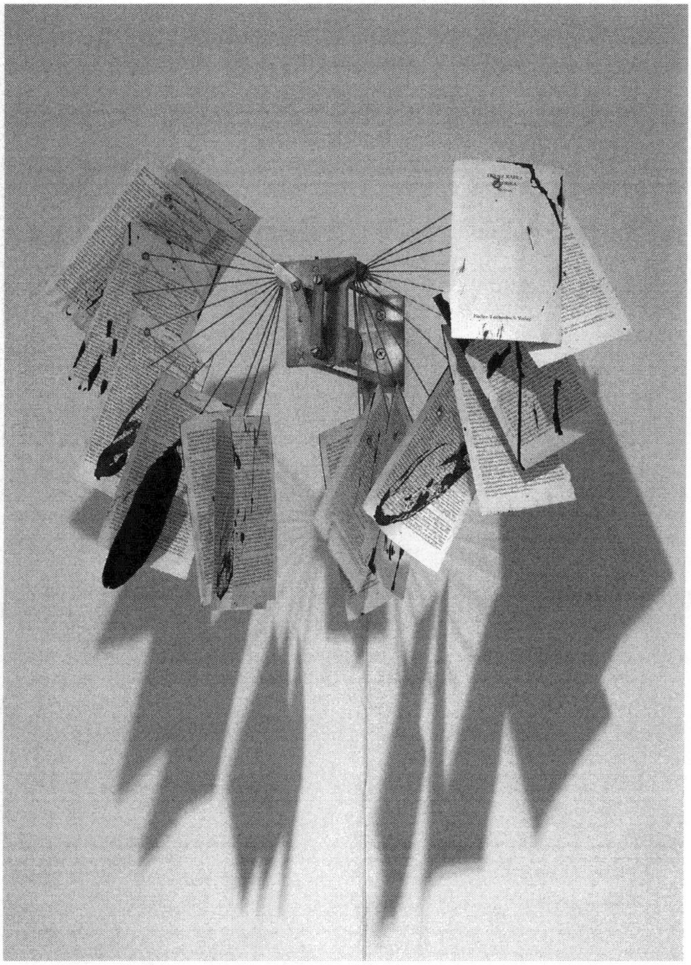

Rebecca Horne, *Kafka Papers,* 1994.
Book pages, colour, feather, metal construction, motor

In our daily lives we continually sense and feel the materials of our surroundings. As we wash, dress, cook, communicate, operate machines.... each moment of our day involves some connection with materials and material things; between finger and thumb or with the finger tips we explore the roughness of an unshaven chin, the smoothness of ironed sheets, the coolness of a leaf, the slipperiness of soap. And throughout life our bodies learn to relate to the materials around us – the material world wraps, supports... sometimes hurts, our bodies. A chair is harder than my body... the sea more fluid... wire bends in my fingers... grain runs through them.

Jean Mohr, photograph.
From: John Berger and Jean Mohr, *Another Way of Telling.*

The feel of things

We all have materials that we specially enjoy and relate to – we like the feel of them... perhaps the touch of hair, or skin, or water, or tips of grass. In our homes we surround ourselves with a particular chosen world of materials. With a few of these we may feel a deeper resonance –we are drawn to them for their sensuous appeal, and perhaps because, without us knowing it, they embody an image or quality we are seeking in our lives.

What quality of materials are you most drawn to?
Collect some that attract you now
Make something with them
See how they come together
View what you have made with a partner

Ada and Ruby spent much of the autumn working with apples. Apples had come in heavy and had to be picked, peeled, sliced, and juiced: pleasant clean work, out among the trees handling the fruit. The sky for much of the time was cloudless blue, the air dry. The light even at midday, brittle and raking, so that by angle alone it told of the year's waning. In the mornings they went carrying ladders when the dew still stood in the orchard grass. They'd climb among the tree limbs to fill sacks with apples, the ladders swaying as the limbs they were propped against gave under their weight. Charles Frazier, *Cold Mountain*

Remember materials in your childhood
Whisper to yourself.... anything you remember about them:
their qualities.... the circumstances surrounding them.... to amplify the memory
Write*.... in response to these memories*
Share and reflect with a partner

Familiar-strange

What are the materials and objects in your daily life?
in your pocket or bag.... in your home.... in your job
Choose some you like the feel of
Spend time exploring their properties – (how they behave, what they'll do)
as you work, let these familiar things become strange to you
form something with them
What emerges?

The feel.... of materials.... of people

Come together in a group
Secretly.... choose another member of the group as your starting point for working
Wander.... to find materials.... which have the feel of this person

Returning.... arrange the materials in a place and in a way
that also has the feel of the person you chose

When all are finished.... go round each piece of work
and, together.... sense and discuss the feel of it
what you notice.... associate.... with it
Who is it?

Miranda Tufnell, *Invisible Forces of Silver*, 1999, performance in collaboration with musician Sylvia Hallet. Performance installation using cane, feathers and copper wire, created by Caroline Lee. Photo: Keith Pattison.

A page of textures and consistencies

wet slippery slushy sloppy slimey
damp

chalky stony gritty raked sandy muddy
loamy leafy

grassy twiggy spiky thorny mossy petal soft

peach smooth

flabby furry wrinkly hairy fluffy downy greasy stubbly feathery dry
shaggy bony combed warm

oily treacly crisp frothy runny viscous sticky
crunchy crumbly brittle

silky velvety tweedy woolly leathery rubbery feathery

crumpled

soapy bristly spongy papery

waxy

friable flaky

bouncy bendy

sharp hard springy

fluid fibrous crystalline

A Place of Sounds

Using sound qualities to explore the surface and substance of the things around you.

Most of the materials that surround us in our daily lives have their own evocative sound - snip of scissors, click of a lock, sizzle of fat, crunch of gravel under foot...

Wherever you are, listen to the sounds that are present
textures of sound.... reflections, resonances, silences.
a thud... a whisper... scratching, scraping, tapping, scuffling... a creak, a squeak...
Using the materials/ surfaces/ objects present, and your own body, intervene in this 'sound space' to create a place of sounds

What are the qualities of this place you create?... what does it evoke?

***Record** some of the sounds that most appeal to you*
*M**ove** with these sounds to explore their qualities further*

Butterflies... make great sounds when they're just flapping their wings...
The sound is like a kite catching in the wind. It really does sound like flight.
Musician Mira Calix, working with the amplified sounds of insects.

Janet Cardiff & George Bures Miller, *The Dark Pool* , 1996
mixed media, dimension variable.

The installation was like an attic or store room, crowded with an assortment of books, furniture and other objects. As one moved around the space into its intimate corners, one unexpectedly encountered odd sounds and whisperings, as if one had stumbled upon some obscure human drama.

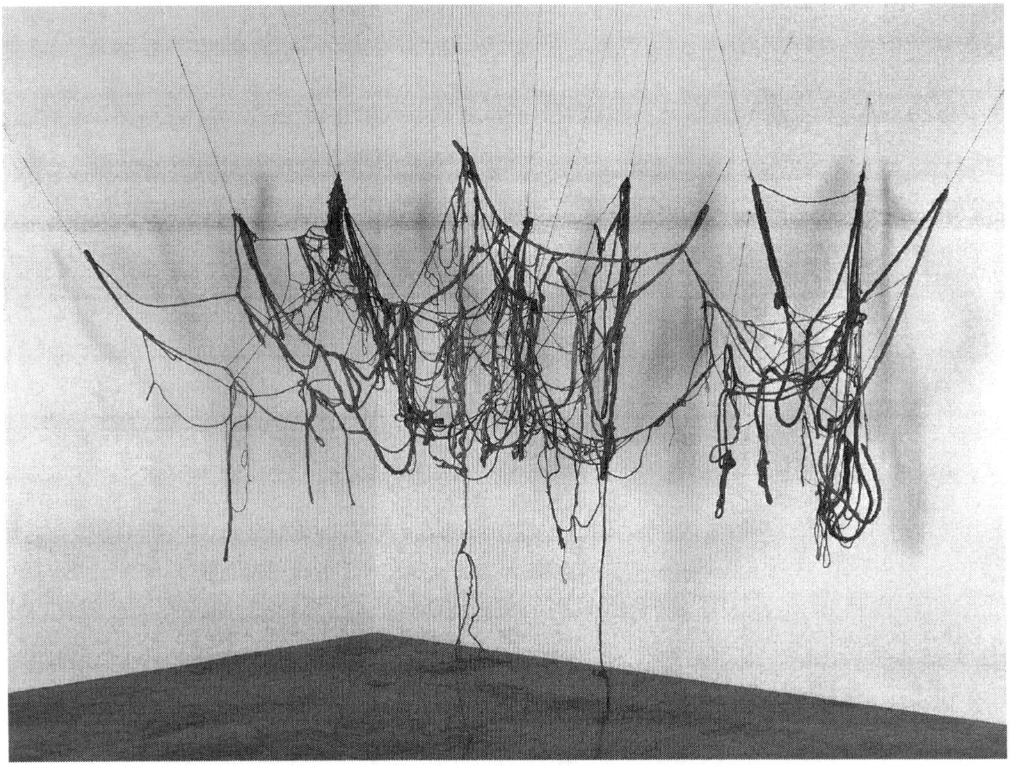

Eva Hesse, *Untitled* ,1970. Latex over rope, string, wire, 3 strands
(A work made shortly before her death at the age of thirty four.)

When it's completed, its structure could be chaos. Chaos can be structured as non-chaos. (Hesse)

The piece has been called "unfinished"; its installation is half the work and must be done by someone extremely familiar with Hesse's ideas (Lippard)

It was first made by Hesse directing David Magasin (a friend who had nothing to do with art): "It was something she'd had in mind [she had made notes and drawings for it as early as November 1969] Life magazine was coming to photograph in a couple of days. I went to my uncle's place and got cable cord of all sizes. I came back and she said 'Do something.' 'What?' 'Whatever you feel like doing... Do you want to make a knot?' 'Yes'. So I made a knot" He dunked it in liquid rubber and strung it up. (Lippard quoting David Magasin)

All the above quoted from: Lucy Lippard, *Eva Hesse.*

Taking apart – bringing together

The material ingredients of any specific setting – a bakery, a swimming pool, a greenhouse –have evolved together through use and not only belong together, but look and feel like they belong. The particular surfaces, colours, fittings, implements, etc., we associate with each of these settings are self consistent and we read them as all-of-a-piece. Yet in working creatively with materials or objects from disparate sources we partially (or wholly) let go of their usual significance and their normal place in the world, in order to discover new connections and meanings arising between them. These new connections are likely to be felt, rather than logically arrived at.

Natural Theatre Company, Brighton Festival 1998
Photo: Roger Bamber

One universe brushing up against another

Range widely to collect.... objects/ images/ materials.... from entirely different contexts (e.g. from indoors, from outdoors – natural/ man made - from contrasting scales: microscopic, miniature, human, giant, cosmic – with contrasting contexts of use... cultural background... historical period... etc.)

In a chosen place.... begin to find how these may come together
to resonate with each other.... unexpectedly
combinations/ arrangements.... you feel drawn to.... find appetising and interesting
Explore with a partner what stories/ associations they evoke

Two objects cannibalised to make a third

Choose two things that are no longer in use -
an old arm chair and a step ladder.... a hoover and a garden fork.... a book and a basket
what they are made of should in some way appeal to you
dismantle.... break them apart.... into their constituent materials
(discard whatever you find unappealing)
With the remaining pieces
slowly.... find how they may recombine as a single object
Share and ponder the result with a partner
What is happening to it? If it could speak, what might it say?

Sheila Clayton, *Fireplace Folly*, 1984.
Various woods, marble, felt, nickle silver, silver leaf, wax, lead, and bronze.

This work celebrates the mythic qualities of male and female children. It consists of a tableaux of objects, which through their colours and forms evoke the feel of a victorian nursery. The fire surround clearly connects to hearth and home. My work generally includes an element of personal narrative. In this case the work related to my own two children, a boy and a girl (It includes a crown for each child). Sheila Clayton, 2003.

Reverse view of the above

Creation - making a world

Cultures throughout history have described the origin of the material universe. Some creation stories involve crafts – the Egyptian God, Ptah, produces the world on his potter's wheel. In Chinese mythology P'an Ku, the creator, sets to work carving out the world with a chisel.

About 4.45 billion years ago, the earth began to develop an atmosphere of methane, ammonia, hydrogen, and carbon dioxide. This highly ionised, violent atmosphere seethed with gigantic lightning storms for about a half billion years, charging and changing the primeval earth and seas. From this one-time (as far as we know), spectacular manifestation of universal winds, the first living cell arose.
Neil Douglas Klotz, *Desert Wisdom*

Cornelia Parker, *Cold Dark Matter: An Exploded View*, 1991.
A garden shed and its contents were blown up and then reassembled, the carefully collected pieces hanging in space with a central light that throws shadows on the walls of the gallery

Out of darkness
Gather materials
go into a dark place
make, to discover
what wants to emerge in the darkness

Elements

element L. *elementum,* a first principle

In the Alchemical system of elements, earth/ air/ fire/ water were considered, not as substances in themselves but as qualities or dynamic tendencies possessed by all things in varying proportions:

earth – the quality of substance, solidity, firmness, shape, outer form
air – the quality of expansiveness and inner movement
fire – the quality of warmth, liveliness, radiance, light, outer movement
water – the quality of fluidity, flow, depth, moistness, inner form

It was these elements that were believed to connect the particularity of individual things to the totality of the universe – human body to the world body, the human soul to the world soul (derived from Robert Sardello, *Love and the Soul*).

blend transmute distil separate

Katherine Stinson (American, 1891-1977) She earned her pilot's licence in 1912.
© Courtesy of Library of Congress, Prints and Photographs Division, 2.5.03

In your element

With which of the four elements – earth, air, fire, water do you feel an affinity? (perhaps two together)
***Move** with this element, or mix of elements, in mind*
Start from resting – let it, or them, move you
without pre-judging what kind of movements would be appropriate.
Remember, each element exists in many forms -
eg. water: as drip, as damp, as dew, as rain, as flood, as torrent, as sea....

***Write** from the moving*
*Then gather materials to **make** a 'world' .... that evokes your elements*
With a partner watching, find a place for yourself in this world
What are you drawn to do in it?

Stories of water

Take any memory of water that comes to you
***Write** an account of it.... as if what happened then.... were happening now*
Read your account to a partner or group
***Move** with the story in mind*
*and again.... **write***

Brighton Beach:
I am playing Chicken with the waves on a jetty.
a massive wave pushes me off and my life is passing from me
as does my coat, torn from my body. But my friend saves me...
Rachie (student project)

River Avon Bristol:
Walking through the woods near my home with my father, mother, brother and sister, we come to a clearing. My parents stop and remark how beautiful it all is. We children are puzzled as we cannot see beyond the long grass... I am picked up and placed on my father's shoulders and now see what they were looking at – a vast lake with birds bobbing around on its glittering surface...
Ron (student project)

In the raw

To imagine or to encounter materials in the raw - in their place of origin - holds a particular fascination in our manufactured and shaped world. Although the extraction and refinement of raw materials is often associated with exploitation and excess, it never-the-less remains a source of wonder and mystery that glass can emerge from sand, cloth from cotton plants, perfumes from oil, paint from coal. Materials in their origin and transformation have the power to shape history, to sustain or wreck lives, to enrich or ruin nations. The simplest artifact can include an astonishing amalgam of raw materials. An ordinary household safety match is a combination of pine wood, ammonium sulphate, paraffin wax, sulphur, sand, clay, phosphorous and formaldehyde (and this is before you get to the box!). And when I strike a match I experience a multitude of tiny sensations set off by this mix of material properties - the touch of the thin square wood between thumb and finger, the scrape of head against box, the small sharp explosion of chemicals, the smell of burning, the heat of flame on the fingers.

stone age, iron age, bronze age

> **bronze:** an alloy of copper with tin, was developed in Mesopotamia (now Iraq) in about 3,000 BC., but it was not known in Europe for another thousand years. Replacing flint implements, bronze tools allowed more rapid clearance of land for growing crops and for pasture, more food and a consequent increase in populations. Bronze weapons and trade in bronze and other metals led to accumulations of wealth and power, which in turn led to the forming of larger settlements, the beginnings of towns and cities.

Wander to find raw materials (or what you can treat as raw materials)
clay ... feathers... discarded corks... water... old clothes
Explore them as they are
gradually.... through working with them, or combining them
let them transform.... take on other qualities
How do they change?.... or perhaps resist change
***Move** to explore this process further*
***Write** from the moving*

When the time came, I took the porcelain boat out of the quartz tube, let it cool off in the vacuum, then dispersed in water the powder, which had turned from greenish to a dirty yellow: a thing which seemed to me a good sign. I picked up the magnet and set to work.
Primo Levi, *The Periodic Table*, describing the extraction of nickel in the laboratory.

Raw into formed

The great mystery of wood is not that it burns, but that it floats Anne Michaels, *Fugitive Pieces*

Each material has not one, but many qualities, depending upon its state, its context and how it has been treated – aluminium as tinfoil or as a ladder. In making things, it is often the impact of tools on materials that we interpret as the quality of the material itself – the ring of stone when struck with a hammer, the clean slicing of card under a sharp blade. Tools and machines change our sense of material properties – the hard body of a car crumples like paper in a car crusher, a road flattens like pastry under a steam roller.

Forming/ transforming:

carve.... explode.... throw.... drop.... mash.... cut out.... draw.... knead.... forge.... grind.... roll out.... twist

roll up.... fold.... bend.... hammer out.... model.... mould.... stretch.... burn.... crumble.... crush

grow.... weave.... bake.... dissolve.... dry.... cure.... scrape.... peel.... slice.... smooth.... gouge out.... tear....

Substance and process
For a week go out everyday, each time to a different place, and choose a material
Explore ways of forming/ transforming it within its setting
Allow something to grow out of this process
Be adventurous - try the unlikely, the impossible!
Use whatever tools/ devices are to hand
***Write** each day in response to what happens*

Joining:

place together.... lean.... prop up.... rest on.... stack.... balance.... heap up.... tip over.... scatter.... sprinkle

fling together.... press together.... bundle up.... weld.... rivet.... staple.... mix.... blend.... stretch over

suspend.... hang over.... hook on.... wrap around.... weave.... knot.... pin.... sew..... knit.... plait.... tie.... zip up

bind.... tangle.... stick in.... cover over.... wedge together.... clip on.... glue.... nail.... screw.... solder.... hinge

Coming Together
From what is immediately to hand
Choose two materials - one to be joined.... another to join with
Let the joining process be a central part of what happens
What emerges?
View with a partner

I enjoy the freedom of just using my hands and "found" tools – a sharp stone, the quill of a feather, thorns. I take the opportunities each day offers: if it is snowing, I work with snow, at leaf-fall it will be with leaves; a blown-over tree becomes a source of twigs and branches. I stop at a place or pick up a material because I feel that there is something to be discovered. Here is where I can learn.

Looking, touching, material, place and form are all inseparable from the resulting work. It is difficult to say where one stops and another begins. The energy and space around a material are as important as the energy and space within. The weather – rain, sun, snow, hail, mist, calm – is that external space made visible. When I touch a rock, I am touching and working the space around it. It is not independent of its surroundings, and the way it sits tells how it came to be there. I want to get under the surface. When I work with a leaf, rock, stick, it is not just that material in itself, it is an opening into the processes of life within and around it. When I leave it, these processes continue.

Movement, change, light, growth and decay are the lifeblood of nature, the energies that I try to tap through my work. I need the shock of touch, the resistance of place, materials and weather, the earth as my source. Nature is in a state of change and that change is the key to understanding. I want my art to be sensitive and alert to changes in material, season and weather. Each work grows, stays, decays. Process and decay are implicit. Transience in my work reflects what I find in nature.

Andy Goldsworthy

Sadie Spikes, detail from *The Sugar House*, 1997, An installation in a dockside cottage, Bristol
materials: baby shoes, flowers, tissue paper, cake boxes, treacle, baking tins, spoons

The materials that I use in my work, which include: ribbon, sugar, treacle, gelatine, thread, porcelain, silver cutlery, satin, net, wax, flowers, bones, shells, feathers, etc., are chosen for their particular resonance, often imbued with a certain nostalgic quality. When combined, the materials and objects create metaphors and narratives. My work with materials often involves baking, sewing, embalming, or boiling, and these processes add another dimension of meaning to the final objects. Sadie Spikes, 2003.

A web of connections – materials and what they mean to us

A web of connection grows out from what we know of the physical qualities and behaviour of any material – a network of stories, instances and applications that enlarge our sense of what that material is or means to us. Materials are also widely reflected in our language, in sayings and everyday expressions, each substance giving rise to its own cluster of associations and metaphors – sand: 'built on sand', 'kick sand in your face', 'sandy haired', 'countless as grains of sand'..... Thus materials are not only physically part of our world, but also exist as 'image' in the way we think and communicate.

Excavating meanings
Go out to find an object
What material(s) is it made of...? – if several choose one of them
Make a list of words and phrases that come to mind
as you ponder and savour this material
***Move** with the feel of one of your words or phrases*

Iron a will of iron... iron fist in a velvet glove... iron out... ironic... rusty

Is it not strange to find this stern and strong metal mingled so delicately in our human life that we cannot even blush without its help.
John Ruskin, *In Praise of Rust,* from: *The Two Paths,* 1859.

Sandro seemed to be made of iron, and he was bound to iron by an ancient kinship: his father's fathers, he told me, had been tinkers (magnin) and blacksmiths in the Canavese valleys: they made nails on the charcoal forges, sheathed wagon wheels with red-hot hoops, pounded iron plates until deafened by the noise; and he himself when he saw the red vein of iron in the rock felt he was meeting a friend. Primo Levi, *The Periodic Table.*

Grass field... a blade of grass... turf.. wild grasslands... out to grass... graze... grass roots

Karen Rann, *Spirality: rim to hub*, 2002, Tufted Hair grasses and PVC. Photo: Simon Fraser

The above was created during an artists residency in Northumberland, 2001-2002. During this residency I was living on very high open moorland. The Spirality series was the result of collecting local grasses and studying algae growing in the bog pools. I used the grasses in combination with PVC to create sculptural forms that suggest or recall cell structure, single celled protozoa, and spiral forms found in nature.

In 1991 a Neolithic hunter's body was discovered
preserved in ice along with clothing and belongings.
His cloak and his conical cap were made of grass.
Joyce Laing in: Art Extraordinary,
The Scottish Collection of Outsider Art.

...At that moment a very small man came in.
I can spin that straw into gold, but what will you
give me in return? he asked.
Grim Brothers, *Rumplestiltskin.*

Glass *viscous (neither solid nor liquid)... window... mirror... glass house... message in a bottle... glassy stare*

It came up the river, its walls like ice emanating light, as fine and elegant as civilisation itself.
Transportation of the glass church in: Peter Carey, *Oscar and Lucinda*

Louise Bourgeois, *Precious Liquids*, view of installation.

Precious liquids *relates to a girl who grows up to discover passion instead of terror. She stops being frightened and experiences passion. Glass becomes a metaphor for muscles. It represents the subtlety of emotions, the organic yet unstable nature of mechanism. When the body's muscles relax and untense, a liquid is produced. Intense emotions become a material liquid, triggering the secretion of a precious liquor. Thus when you allow yourself to weep, the tears mark the end of suffering, and when perspiration occurs on your back due to a state of apprehension, it indicates mastery and resolution of the fear. The secretion of fluids can be intensely pleasurable.* Louise Bourgeois

Feathers flight... feathery... ruffled feathers... in fine feather... to feather an oar... Icarus

Paper
a blank page
wrapped up
paper thin
papering over cracks

Earth
earthy, earthenware, unearth
dig, plough, plant, bury
feet of clay
dust.... mud

Earth built mosque, Dougouba Mali
Photo: James Morris

Stone
rock solid
turned to stone
rock face, boulder, wall
jewels
stepping stones, mile stones, grave stones, mill stone, key stone
weathered
stone circle
stony faced, flint
drop like a stone

igneous rock: formed in fire (fast)
sedimentary rock: formed in water (slowly)

Rough, natural stones were often believed to be the dwelling places of spirits or gods...
Aniela Jaffe, *Symbolism in the Visual Arts*

Salt

Ruth Jones, *Salt of the Earth*, detail of mixed media installation

Electrons, the charged particles that circle an atom's nucleus, are always seeking to attain the lowest possible energy state for the atom; they will share, donate and transfer themselves to achieve this end. Sodium and chlorine are two restless, unstable creatures. Sodium has a lone electron in his outer shell – charged and potent – active. Chlorine has seven electrons requiring an eighth to balance herself. The charged electron of sodium shifts into the outer ring of Chlorine to make both atoms equal, balanced and united. The marriage forms a crystal, which in the consumerist complacency (of the eternal supply and demand of materials) has been named 'common salt'.

Salt is born out of the purest of parents, The Sun and The Sea, said Pythagoras. For Plato it was a substance held dear to the Gods. 'God is warm, moist and salty' sing the Massai women of East Africa. 'Our God is compassionate, our God is free and will have no dealings with exclusion, no dealings with power, no dealings with barriers'. (A Warm, Moist, Salty God, Edwina Gateley)
I work with salt because it is an edible rock which dissolves in water, it corrodes metal and preserves flesh, it is barren and life giving, it has been used to bless and to curse, it slips through all categories because it is two into one, it is neither this nor that – it confounds the duality of my experiences.

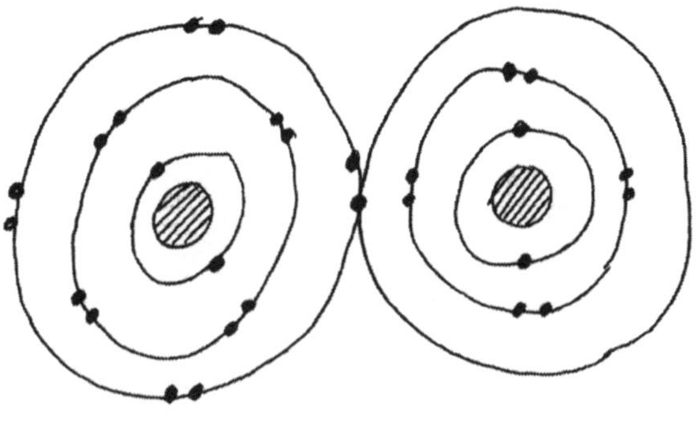

Drawing and text above by Ruth Jones

Exploring a chosen material – what it means to you

Go out to find.... a material (raw, or as part of something made)
See what material you are drawn to today

Spend time with it

Speak to a partner about what it evokes....
qualities..... connotations..... associations....
memories.... feelings.... images

Move in response
lightly holding in mind the aspect, the quality that stays with you most strongly

Gather more of the material, or any others that feel connected

Make from the moving
Where does the making take you?

Write from the making....What further associations and images arise?
Share and reflect with your partner

Lines of need and desire

At certain moments in history, a single material has become in one way or another crucial to survival – as fat is to the Eskimo, salt was for preserving meat before refrigeration, coal and steel were for the industrial revolution, or oil is now for present technologies. What may be regarded as 'essential' is of course not necessarily a matter of survival. For example tulip bulbs became 'essential' and frantically sought after by thousands of people in Holland in the 1630's. Where survival is a factor, it may be more for those who supply the material rather than those who need it. Throughout history, links of supply and demand have created a web of connections across and between continents, and have provided primary reasons for exploration and discovery. During the time of the Old Kingdom, the ancient Egyptians travelled to mines in Syria, Nubia and Punt to obtain gold and silver. In the 5th century B.C., the Phoenicians, needing tin to make bronze, discovered routes from Carthage in the Mediterranean to Southern Britain. From 100 B.C. the Romans imported silk from China via the famous Silk Routes.

> **Silk** is taken from the cocoon of the Mulberry Silk Moth. Over a period of eight days the caterpillar spins its cocoon from a single continuous golden thread. Silk is one of the oldest known textile fibres, recorded in China as early as 2,700 B.C. The Silk Routes established a 4,000 mile trade link between Rome and what is now Xian in China. Wool, gold and silver travelled from Rome in exchange for the silk. The Chinese guarded the secret of silk production until 300 A.D., when the emperor Justinian sent two monks to steal both caterpillar eggs and Mulberry seeds, which they hid in their walking staffs. (source: Encarta digital encyclopaedia)

Basic need

Go out to find a single material that is important to you in your life
Make a place with it.... a 'settlement'
With a partner, explore what might happen there?

Material.... immaterial

In contemplating the world of materials, we also open ourselves to the immaterial – to ideas, feelings, beliefs. Within the rituals of each culture – the mass, baptism, burial – materials such as bread, wine, corn, earth, ash....take on a special spiritual significance – In an equivalent way, we find significance within the material world through what we make. As we work to bring about change in our materials – sorting, sifting, scattering, warming, pouring, mixing – we connect with them both physically and emotionally and become open to change in ourselves.

WU Chun-hsien in *Songs of the Wanderers,*
Performed by Cloud Gate Dance Theatre of Taiwan
Photo: YU Huei- hung
(performance sequence with a floorscape of rice)

Rice is sacred in Asian culture, the staple of life, the sustenance of both man and Buddha, whose shrines are surrounded by rice offerings............ As the performance continues, a figure with a rake appears on stage and starts drawing the mounds of rice into swirling patterns. At the end, long after the dancers have taken their bow and departed, this figure remains alone on stage, intent on gathering all the rice and turning it into a single concentric pattern.
Lyn Gardner, *Grains of Truth.* Review in: *The Guardian,* April 7th, 1999.

7. Stories

We all tell stories. We all recount odd incidents that have happened to us. In so far as we talk at all we are generally telling something of a story. Some of us go further and make stories up at great length, imagine how it would be if this or that happened to us, what would follow, what would happen next and next. In fact you could not live if you were not continually making up little stories. Ted Hughes, *Poetry in the Making.*

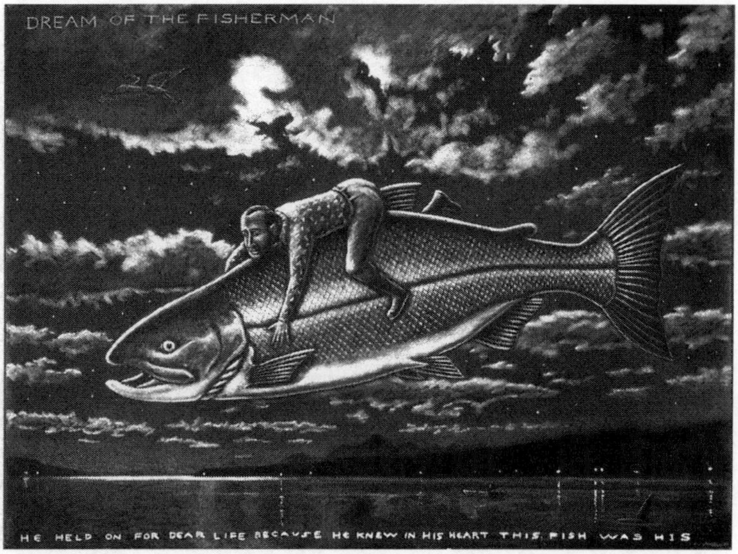

Ray Troll, *Dream of the Fisherman*, 1987. Charcoal on paper.
He held on for dear life because he knew in his heart this fish was his.
© Ray Troll 1987

Whenever we begin to work or to attend to something we have made or collected, a world of images opens up before us. As we move or make, write or speak, we bring into existence the stories of that world. As we work we may feel we are on the edge of some story that we do not know, or moving in and out of different stories whose shapes we cannot quite see. And as we continue to work and to respond to what we have made, these fragments may begin to cohere as clusters of images or loose narratives. These are not necessarily stories in words, nor are they generally the conventional type of story with a narrative line, a beginning and an end. But as we work we begin to get a sense of an emergent world with its own elements, its own way of coming together.

Stories develop through a feeling response to the ordinary details around us. They are not so much stories we invent as stories we listen out for within the fine grain of our sensing, moving and making. What we sense, but mostly cannot quite define, is that these fictional worlds we create have some connection with the ongoing stories of our lives. Yet they are different to the stories we usually tell about who we are, or what our world is like. Thus we discover histories, voices, within whatever we find and touch, and we find aspects of our own story in everything around us. As we begin to weave stories around what we find or make, it is as if we open a door and are drawn deeper into the landscapes of our lives.

As a dream gathers up the ordinary details of the day and throws them together differently, offering us other ways of seeing our worlds, so each of these, often discontinuous and incomplete, image/ stories, is an attempt to give form to what is happening within us. These stories enable us to imagine our lives from a fresh point of view. What is it that I know, see, move towards? In these 'fictions' that emerge in our working, we attempt to piece together a more personal sense of things. And there is never just one story to tell – stories exist in many layers, on many levels, as the 'storeys' of a building.

Our stories are an attempt to find position and direction – in this sense they are like the early maps of the world, or modern maps of the universe... a way of positioning the elements of territory that is just being discovered, beyond the edge of the known. And it is in letting these stories, these mappings of emergent worlds, appear that we begin to trace more fully the undercurrents of our lives.

Penelope, wife of Odysseus, waiting for the return of her husband despite news of his death, sets up a loom in her home and begins weaving a large and delicate piece of work. She promises her many suitors that she will marry one of them when the cloth she is making is finished. But each night, by torchlight, she unpicks what she has done during the day. In her constant making and unmaking she suspends the moment - holds back the completion of a story – knowing in some part of her that Odysseus will return. In her seemingly endless task, she resists the pressure of events, and the insistence of those around her, somehow trusting in the eventual outcome she desires. So too, as we speak of our lives, we weave, unweave, and weave again our story worlds in search of a meaning that brings together what we know.

Living words

Let a word or a phrase lie within you
'step'.... 'greeting'.... 'key'
'the door left open'.... 'feeding the birds'.... 'beneath the mound'

*Savour it.... **move** with it*
***Write** its associations*
*Gather materials and **make** a place for it*
weave a story around it

Tall story

With a partner or in a group
Pick something.... from what you are carrying around with you today
Give an account of where it belongs in your life
how you come to have it.... what it connects with
Then tell a wild, invented story about it
What emerges?
Let the ingredients of these two stories be a starting point
*for **moving**.... or **making***

A story which includes: a bear... a mill wheel... a storm... a shaking house

Remembering

Igor Nitoraj, *Light of the Moon*, 1992. Bronze. photo: Erik Hesmerg

The present is infused with the past. Our memories of places, times, people, events, break the surface of our lives like islands. Memories are always on the move, rising to prominence - at one moment occupying the immediate foreground of our lives, forcing themselves on our attention, at another becoming the merest whisper, sinking away, or frustratingly refusing to come forth when most needed.

Memories lie as shadows beneath our day to day activity, adding their emotional charge to the way we see and feel things. Some incidental quality – the taste of a certain type of biscuit, the smell of dusty streets after rain – will suddenly evoke a distant memory or the feeling of a memory. In this sense, the reservoirs of memory are not confined to our brains, they lie all around us in the world and in every cell of our bodies. To be touched on the arm may unexpectedly trigger a sudden feeling of despair, of laughter, of comfort – reawakening some memory that has been held there suspended. Our past lives may seem to hold us at times within a revolving door, and we may feel destined to endlessly repeat ourselves, seeking out versions of the same people, places and problems again and again. Yet it is through excavating and exploring the layers of our memory through images, through stories, that we begin to perceive and feel the past differently.

memory Gk. *mermeros* anxious, care, thought L. *memor* mindful, remembering

Imagination is the active, creating element
of memory that goes beyond the past.
Robert Sardello, *Love and the Soul.*

Let a story grow... from a fragment of memory

Remember a moment –

a scrap of memory that comes to you:
your earliest memory... a moment before you were born... a moment aged five... last event of your childhood... a time of illness... a dream that recurred... a loss... a remembered person... a celebration... a favourite place... a treasured object... a garment... an unwelcome visitor

Spend some time sinking into the details and textures of this fragment of memory
Let the fragment expand.... grow.... gather round it the sense of an event

What is happening?.... has just happened?.... is about to happen?

Let the memory loosen.... dream around it.... allowing it to fill out in your imagination in all its sensory detail – What can you hear.... smell.... feel in your body?

From the fragment.... let a whole scene emerge
Ask questions.... invent.... elaborate
Where am I?... Who is here?... What season is it?... What size am I?... What can I see from my point of view?

Whisper the elements of the story to yourself

Then: ***write**, in the present tense, as if it were happening now*
As you write, inhabit the memory along with all the sensations and feelings that go with it

Later: *gather materials and **make** or **move***
while holding your story in mind
Work only from the mood or feeling of the story
(not trying to illustrate, simply to respond)

> *Then – as if she'd pushed the hair from my forehead, as if I'd heard her voice – I knew suddenly my mother was inside me. Moving along sinews, under my skin the way she used to move through the house at night, putting things away, putting things in order.*
> Anne Michaels, *Fugitive Pieces.*

Life line

Spend some time picturing the phases and stages of your life
***Make**...."the line of your life"*
Look at it with a partner
What do you notice?

Family history

Take a story that a member of your extended family
tells, or told, about their lives
Collect materials that in some way evoke that story
***Make** a place with them*
let the place become a world
What happens in it?

There was a Young Person of Smyrna
Whose grandmother threatened to burn her;
But she seized on the cat,
And said, "Granny, burn that!
You incongruous old woman of Smyrna!"
Edward Lear, *The Lear Omnibus.*

Let your body tell the story of your life in movement

Spend some time quietly.... pondering the course of your life
Then.... wipe the slate clean of knowing anything
let go the idea of self.... the old familiar story
***Move** in the present moment*
What do you sense.... see.... now?
Who/ what appears?

Give a new context or story to something old and familiar

Choose an old garment, or piece of cloth,
that has belonged to you for a long time
***Make** a place for it that explores its presence*
Discover the story of this place
What happens there?

Mapping a life

Pilgrim's Way, A cartographical rendering of
Bunyan's Pilgrim's Progress, England 19C

Everything we make holds both a story and is also a map of our world. Maps do spatially what our stories do in time or sequence. To call something you make 'a map' is to see it as referring to a wider field than its own immediate presence. A map charts where one thing lies in relation to another – a weaving together of elements. With the help of a map we place ourselves in the world, find out where we are. In all our creating, we work as the early explorers, charting territory previously unknown to us.

Where have I come from?... Who goes with me?... Where am I now?...

Make.... a map

Choose ingredients of any sort
let them form a 'map'
Simply take the idea of a map
don't know what the map is going to be of
let it emerge in the making
Then, view with a partner

Map your life/ world

(Your map could include: people, thoughts, feelings, places, dreams, memories...)

Choose one ingredient - an object.... a material
let this begin a process of mapping
bring in other materials you need as you work

Explore how things want to go in relation to each other
What is happening between them?
What turns out to be: small/ large.... central/ peripheral.... in your map?

Are you part of this map?
What is happening in it?

Afterwards: spend time exploring this map with a partner
its form as well as its content
discovering its stories

on the map
off the map

Dreams and stories

It is working with our hands on invisible connections where we cannot see, deep in the body of the night, penetrating, assembling and differentiating, debriding, stirring, churning, kneading – this constitutes the work on dreams. Always we are doing precision work, but with invisibilities, with ambiguities, and with moving materials.
James Hillman, *The Dream and the Underworld.*

The images of our dreams are akin to the images in our stories. Through their metaphors they seem to offer messages that can reveal what lies hidden from our everyday consciousness. Yet, the images that come to us, whether in our stories or in our dreams, are always in some way a mystery – they seem to speak in riddles, in puns, in allusions – parts we may recognise, feel familiar, yet other parts puzzle us, we cannot grasp their sense. If we take dreams as a starting point for making, moving or writing we can begin to feel our way into their labyrinths. As we play with them, create around them, we enter the dream landscape and as we continue to work, the images find connections and develop a kind of sense for us. Then we no longer feel, as it were, outsiders, trying to look into the dream; instead we enter the dream image and begin to sense how it belongs and moves within us.

Entering a dream image

First, tell the dream to a partner, or draw or write it
Then: ***move****....* *or* ***make****....* *to explore the dream*
State this as an intention.... let go of it as you begin to work
Start just with a detail of the dream.... allow the other parts to find their own way in

Write*, from the moving or making*
Reflect with a partner on what has emerged

Nightmare

Remember a nightmare
Write or draw it, including even the most incidental details
Move *from it, whispering to yourself the story*
Write*.... in the wake of moving*
Make *and then view with a partner*

An account of working with a partner in response to a dream

Sharing the dream... exploring it in movement... writing after moving... and a partner's responses in moving and writing

In my dream: it is late evening and the season is closing in, I am digging in the garden at the back of a house. There are some large fish swimming below me in a stream. Though the water is depleted, like some forgotten backwater, the fish have grown large. A clod of earth falls into the stream from where I am digging; as it does so, it crosses my mind that this could harm the fish. Then, the place where I am standing turns into a spacious conservatory; I am arranging plants and colourful sculptures. A young man, who in real life once lived next door (a person who is inclined to speak and behave with unusual formality), appears carrying a whitish papery female figure. This figure reminds me of an Egyptian mummy – but underneath the surface appearance, she resembles the woman who now (in real life) lives next door to me. Her eyes are almost closed, just slits, yet I can just make out a tremor of life within. I say to the young man, "she needs to be taken home".

A friend to whom I tell the dream: remarks that it contains some things that suffer from neglect or are endangered (the depleted stream, the fish at risk from a falling clod of earth, the woman who needs to be taken home), and some things that are being conserved (the conservatory with its plants and sculptures, the fact that the man is carrying the woman and that she seems to be wrapped like a mummy).

In starting to move from my dream: I think of the fish, grown large despite the unpromising water, and now endangered (from the clod of earth) and the woman who needs to be taken care of. I find myself moving wildly at first, I rush to and fro in the space, brushing my hands against the walls. As I end, I stand stock still for some time, frozen to the spot, tensed, my head bowed, one hand locked, clenched.

> **Phrases from my writing include:**
> *a sword stabbing the heart, blood flowing, unabated... haemorrhages.*
> *Wide eyed... on the edge of the cliff, looking down... crash!... cast a line to rescue.*
> *Corralled... all the horses stampeded to one end of the compound, their necks steaming, their eyes bulging, kicking up the dust*

As my partner moves in response: she puts her arms each side of a glazed door, as if they were looking through the glass at each other. She goes outside, tears up some blades of grass and brings them in, placing them on the bare floor. Then, again outside, I see her framed in the doorway, walking slowly backwards... moving her arms repeatedly in winding motions as if drawing in threads with her hands... She tilts her head to the sky as if listening. She tells me later that for some reason she wanted to say to me, " turn your head".

> **Phrases from her writing include:**
> *a closed book... he listened... hit the walls, break... break up... break down.*
> *let in the deep murmuring for which his heart yearned... he waited on the top of the hill... for miles around the land seemed empty of people, events... he wished... prayed... the fish would swim by him, touch him ever so gently... carry him with them in their mysterious river voyages*

Looking back: this was for me an unusually clear and detailed dream. Even now, a year or two later, it is still vivid, and somehow rings true to an aspect of my life. I think it would have just slipped away, like most dreams do, and been lost, had I not shared it and created something around it.

Graciela Iturbide, *Yucatan*, Mexico. Photograph.

I came to the bend and said, "Buenas noches." The person answered me with an eerie, gruff, inhuman howl. The hair on my body literally stood on end. For a second I was paralyzed. Then I began to walk fast. I took a quick glance. I saw that the dark silhouette had stood up halfway; it was a woman. She was stooped over, leaning forward; she walked in that position for a few yards and then she hopped. I began to run, while the woman hopped like a bird at my side, keeping up with my speed. By the time I arrived at Blas's house she was cutting in front of me and we had almost touched. I leapt across a small dry ditch in front of the house and crashed through the flimsy door. Carlos Castaneda, *Journey to Ixtlan.*

Letting in the unexpected

What is knocking?
What is knocking at the door in the night?
It is somebody wants to do us harm.

No, no, it is the three strange angels.
Admit them, admit them.

from: D.H. Lawrence, *Song of a Man Who Has Come Through.*

Visitors

Often as we work, figures, presences, surprisingly appear in our imagery, as when strangers come unexpectedly to the door. They come into our written stories; we sense or discover their presence when moving; or they emerge among the materials as we make something. These 'visitors' come from outside our immediate world, and yet we feel that they have in some way been sent. Sometimes, they may come as helpers, advisers, with something to offer or tell us if we are prepared to listen, just as animals or dwarfs impart crucial information in fairy tales. At other times, they may seem to be destructive or persecuting figures, that can make our lives difficult. Whoever they are, such figures offer a different point of view, a different quality, even though they may puzzle us by what they suggest.

I will give you an iron wand and two little loaves of bread; strike the iron door of the castle three times with the wand and it will open...
Dwarf gives the young prince some help in:
The Brothers Grimm, *The Waters of Life.*

An arrival

Make.... *a place*
Who or what arrives there?
What begins to happen?
Write *or tell the story*

From a childhood story

Remember.... a character from a story in childhood
Who comes to mind?
With a partner.... describe this character
Gather materials and ***make...*** *a place*
that evokes your sense of them
Briefly, explore it with your partner
Then, be still.... listen.... locate yourself somewhere near what you have made
Let your body ***move*** *to discover more*
then ***write****.... and share again with your partner*

Koffi Koko, performance, Benin, 2003

His physicality is... fuelled by embodying different deities and peoples, but also working with imagery of nature, animals, elements and plants which is a vital source for the dance of Benin.

The necessity for dancers to be able to let go... in a process of 'emptying oneself out', so that something else can enter the body whether it is a god, an animal, or a new dance technique. This 'emptying out', brought about by repetition of particular movements or rhythms, happens in other performative rituals... Josephine Leask, *The Multiculturalism of Koffi Koto,* Dance Theatre Journal

In my understanding the basis of Koffi's dance is ritual. Koffi said 'dance is a prayer'. When you dance you are in touch with the energy of the world. Everybody that watches the dance is part of this energy. The power of all the people present gives strength to the group. The piece starts with a kind of ritual and then Koffi develops his dance. If you see him dance you feel that everything that happens on stage is growing from inside the dancer. The difference between 'embodiment' and imitation is that you feel what happens on stage is more than what you see. Kerstin Feuerstein

Animal Visitors

animal L. *animal* a living creature Gk... *anima* breath, life

Slowly I begin the final metamorphosis. I must drive out my old self and let the universe in. The creatures will come creeping back – not as gods transmogrified, but as themselves. Beaked, furred, fanged, tusked, clawed, hooved, snouted, they will settle in us, re-entering their old lives deep in our consciousness. David Malouf, *An Imaginary Life.*

Meeting an animal

Warm up.... awaken the senses
scent the air.... listen to the ground.... see beyond the walls
Then.... ***move****.... go on a journey to meet an animal*
not knowing what it may be
What do you find?
Make *something as a message for it*
Move *from the making to find out what happens next*

Animals remind us of a world in which we are not the only players. They awaken us to what we have forgotten in ourselves, to a more instinctual part of us. Animals sense things that we do not see: vibrations, scents, presences, sounds beyond the range of our hearing, colours beyond our own visible spectrum. In the wild, they often surprise us with when they appear.

Sightings

The Museum of Scotland houses the enormous skeleton of a blue whale, washed up on the coast in the 1920s.

The man went up to the bedroom where his wife was still asleep and woke her. 'There's a unicorn in the garden,' he said. 'Eating roses.' She opened one unfriendly eye and looked at him. 'The unicorn is a mythical beast,' she said, and turned her back on him. James Thurber, *The Unicorn in the Garden*, in: The Thurber Carnival.

Animals hold us to what is present: to who we are at the time, not to who we've been or how our bank accounts describe us.
Gretel Ehrlich, *The Solace of Open Spaces.*

Pep Ramis (Mal Pelo), *Thousands of months,* 2001. Dancer: Constanza Brnčić. Photo: Jordi Bover.

The piece was about silence, about holding tension and stretching time, about embodying present time. It was about us as humans, about our animal selves and our sophistication. The dog was performing without any control, any order – four dancers and a dog, a kind of anthropological research in watching them all together. Pep Ramis

Animal story
In a group
each tells their own animal story
Then: each ***moves*** *to find a vivid detail*
Write *a story from the moving*

owl... horse... mouse... deer... bee... tortoise... lark... swan... hare... cat... nightingale

Coming to life
Choose something that is inanimate
Imagine it alive
***Make** its world*

Getting to know a dream animal
An animal has appeared in your dreams
or in something you have made/ written
Without trying literally to represent it
***Make**, to explore its presence*
***Move**, to tell its story*

Half man, half beast
Imagine.... what combination of human and animal you might be
***Move**.... to explore*

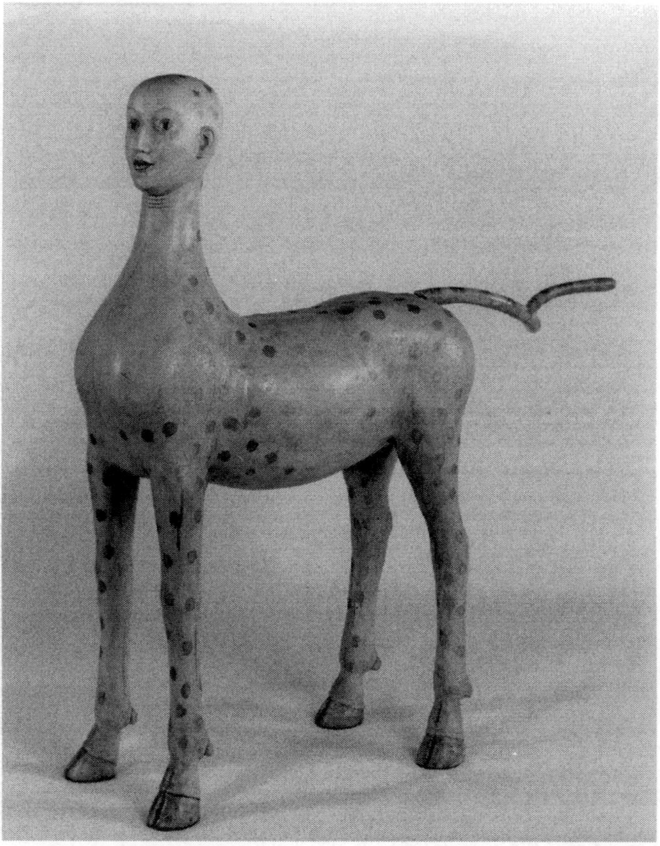

Dhruva Mistry,
Creature, 1983. Plaster

Journeys.... looking forwards.... looking back

Journey M.E. *journee* a days travel, F. *journey* a day, a journal, a daily record.

J. Kaiserer, *Suggestion for a dirigible balloon,* Vienna,1801.

> *The landscape you see when looking back is startlingly different from the one you believed you saw when the journey lay ahead. As such the story continues.*
> Alida Gersie, *Reflections on Therapeutic Story Making.*

Every day of our lives is a kind of setting out. What will happen to us? Where will we be by the evening? And every time we work we set out on a journey to find something we need or have lost, as characters in folk tales who must leave home to seek their fortune. To travel in any sense opens out our ways of seeing and knowing. We go out from ourselves and something else is able to come in. In our continuing work with images we gradually trace out the directions of our lives.

leaning into the wind... blown along
holding a course

Setting out

Within the place where you are
Move.... to go on a 'journey'
Sense where your body leads you
What do you move towards?.... Whom do you meet on the way?

What you take, what you leave, what you find

Tell a partner.... about a journey –
remembered.... imagined.... dreamed of...
***Make** four things:*
Something to carry with you
Something collected on the way
Something to greet you on arrival
Something to leave behind
Find how to place them
***Move** or **write** to explore their collective story*

Alfred Wallis, *Three-master on a Stormy Sea.* Oil on card

How do you cross huge distances with no obvious physical guides? Oceans are a complex interaction of tides, currents and wind-driven wave patterns that are replicated in cycles over time. The steepness of waves, their pattern of refraction, or the amount of cresting can all indicate location. Star configurations and their movement are markers that can be used with equal reliability. Species of birds that nest on land fly at a variety of distances from the shore......Sea colors, sounds, water temperature, and phosphorescence change with depth, as do the type and variety of sea creatures that can be observed. Floating debris and smells travel in predictable patterns."
from: *Eye Memory: The Inspiration of Aboriginal Mapping,* in: Doug Aberley, ed., *Boundaries of Home: Mapping for Local Empoerment.*

Travellers' tales

Ancient travellers, setting out into the unknown, took to the sea, navigating along the edges of land or ice, following routes determined by wind and current, or walked across whole continents, risking marauding bandits, deserts, mountains, and returned with fabulous tales. The Greek explorer Scylax, who in 510 BC. undertook the first Greek exploration of the Arabian Sea and Red Sea, returned with tales of men with one eye, of people who slept in the shelter of their own enormous ears, and of the 'Shadowfeet People' who used their feet to ward off the sun. Marco Polo, in his book, *A Description of The World,* published around 1300AD, gave accounts of birds that eat elephants, hairy fish sixty metres long, cloth that fire cannot destroy, a celestial city with 12,000 bridges. Mythical tales of epic journeys such as the Odyssey and the Illiad, often incorporated versions of actual histories, or customs and rituals of the period transformed into heroic stories. Conversely, actual journeys were informed and coloured by myths - Alexander the Great, setting out in 334 BC on his 11 year journey to explore and conquer the Eastern world, carried with him a copy of Homer's *Illiad.* His fragmentary picture of where he was going assumed that the earth consisted of lands surrounded by a vast ring of water.

Imagined journey

In conversation with a partner
use questions and answers to invent a traveller's tale –
One asks questions, the other answers – both working spontaneously, without knowing what is coming:
Where are you?... Who/ what are you?... Why are you setting out?... Do you know where you are going?
What is lying in your path, right now?... What do you take it as a sign of?... What do you do with it?
Is there someone else around?... What have you got in your bag?... What did you forget to bring?
What accident befalls you?
Invent questions, let the answers develop into a story

Leave a message

Imagine you only have ten words
Find ways .... to leave a message with them
for someone who will arrive.... after you have left

A discovered destination

Gather materials
Imagine a journey
***Make** the place you arrive at*
Tell the story of this place

Shrine, Puri beach, Orissa, India, 1986. Photo: Bobbie Cox

The above is a temporary shrine to the three 'Jagannath' made on the beach as the focus for a personal dawn ritual involving chanting and immersion in the sea. The Jagannath religion, for which Puri is the centre, worships the god, Lord Jagannath, together with his brother and sister. In shrines to what are known as 'The Jagannath Trio', Lord Jagannath is placed to the right and has a black face. On the left is placed his brother Balabhadra who is identified with white. In the centre is Subhandra their sister for whom the colour is saffron. (The flags in this shrine are coloured black, saffron and white accordingly). These three characters are normally represented with painted wooden posts – in this case sticks. Three balls of sand just visible at the base (sprinkled with red colouring) may also correspond to The Trio. In an annual festival, 50ft high chariots are used to carry these deities through the town. It is said that in past times many devotees would blindly throw themselves under the wheels of these vehicles, only to be crushed to death. From this tradition of the Jagannath religion, we get our word 'Juggernaut'. (from a spoken account by Bobbie Cox – information originally drawn from the writings of Stella Kramrich and Mildred Archer)

8. Bone

The 'Star of Shetland' returning from the Alaskan fishing grounds around 1920.
Photo: Wayne Barnet
© collection: San Francisco Maritime National Historical Park

The human body is vapour materialised by sunshine and mixed with the life of stars. Paracelsus

...a scapular of sea
between islands: smooth, shining
as thin bone

feather, mouse-skull, broken
chambered shell
the clean death
by water and salt wind...

from: Frances Horowitz, Orkney.

Bone is the hard edge within the soft verges of our bodies. The constellation of bones that form our skeleton creates a living, changing framework of support within us. As a tree that grows and branches inside us, the presence of bone opens out the interior of the body, creating space throughout. The intricate fibres of bone create a curving, shifting architecture – of bridges, stairwells, chambers, corridors – through which the tissues of the body are defined and held, as within the most delicate and sensitive fingers. The bones endlessly adjust and reshape themselves to support the living, moving weight of our bodies. Born out of connective tissue which binds us together, the hard crystalline forms of bone spread out our length, depth and width, which in turn allows all else in the body to function and to move. Hidden beneath the skin, the presence of bone defines our shape – I am this tall, this broad, the landscape of my face rounded, angular according to the bones that form it. To trace the pathways of bone within us, feel out their directions, curves, edges, angles – is to discover an open and dynamic structure of support within the body. Without the leverage of the many bones spreading out and supporting our bodies, movement would have none of its precision and delicacy; through bone we are able to climb, run, dance, and manipulate the most intricate of tools. To forget bone, to feel 'boneless', is to lose a sense of space, shape, resistance, articulation and movement in the body.

Fine boned, bony, hard nosed, thick skulled, back bone, skin and bone, marrow of the bone, wish bone, bone of contention, cut to the bone, bone to pick, rag and bone, bag of bones, bone headed

Imagine you have no bones

One by one.... let your bones soften.... and disappear
let go the small bones of hands and feet
let the ribs melt between front and back.... let the length of the spine.... dissolve
and the long bones of the arms and legs.... slowly vanish
Sense how the body's weight.... softens.... falls
Sense your weight.... as liquid.... spilling.... spreading out

Let in the drift and tides of breath.... into the fluid depths of the body
Sense gravity.... the slow mass of the earth beneath you.... supporting.... turning

Take time.... moving.... with no bones
roll... ooze... spill

Slowly.... one by one.... replace the bones
24 small bones into the pathway of spine.... 5 deep bones fusing into sacrum
tiny curling bones of tail.... coccyx
Sense length of the spine spreading out through your back
Replace.... long bones into the centre of arms and legs.... open the length of the limbs
Replace the curved bones.... of ribs.... of pelvis.... of head

Sense roundness.... depth....volume
Let the breath fill into the marrow of the bones
sense the geology.... of their form
Let bone be as land within the liquid flow of your body
Let the hardness of ground.... meet the hard edges of bone

Move.... to explore the voice.... and quality of bone in the body

Give me a place to stand and I will move the world. Archimedes

The forming of bone

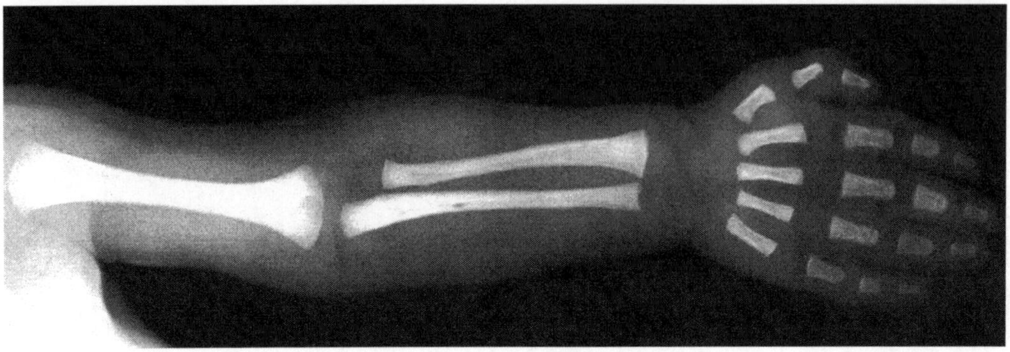

Radiograph of neonatal arm

> *...at birth every joint in the body is composed of membrane or cartilage, not bone. There is softness everywhere, the body like liquid gold. There is less of a sense of division than at any other time.* Hugh Milne, *The Heart of Listening.*

The formation of bone begins early in the liquid world of the womb. At 16 days the beginning of the embryonic spine is already visible, and by the sixth week, when the foetus is no bigger than a small finger nail, the embryonic 'seeds' of every structure of the body are present. The bones of the skull, jaw and collarbone are formed by the activity of the periosteum, the tough outer sheath that surrounds the surface of bone and through which, later, bone is repaired. Most of our bones begin as cartilage. From within the flow of connective tissue, chondroblast cells begin to appear which secrete cartilage. This cartilage creates a mould for the particular shapes of what will later become our bones. These chondroblast cells then expand in size and change their function, becoming osteoblasts (bone producers) secreting a chemical which precipitates into crystals of mineral salts absorbed from the blood. These interlocking crystals are deposited along collagen fibres within the cartilage and layered onto the surface of the cartilage base, creating a weave of fibre and crystal. The cartilage base is gradually dissolved leaving a hollowed interior, traversed by filaments of bone (trabeculae) that create an intricate honeycomb structure of support within the bone. It is this trabecular architecture of bone that both lightens its weight and gives bone a unique strength, elasticity, and tensility in response to mechanical stress. The spaces thus created are also sites for bone marrow and blood production. In some of the facial and cranial bones these spaces are filled with air, as in the wing bones of birds, to lighten them.

In the infant, cartilage and bone lie like stepping stones, condensations within the liquid flow of the infant's tissues. The sutures of the infant's skull are open at birth, and the edges of the cranial bones smooth to allow them to glide over each other in their passage through the birth canal. These same joints of the skull allow the brain to grow, breathe and move – the cradling strength of the cranial bones and their subtle movement protects the brain against impact and trauma. The skeleton of a new born is full of spaces between one part and another, an openness that allows for growth and movement. As we develop, cartilage hardens into bone, providing anchorage for the muscles that move us, and the body becomes denser and heavier. In the forming of bone we may find a parallel to our own processes of making – a journey from liquid to solid, from amorphous to shaped; a delicate feeling out of what something may become; a gradual emergence of form in the play of different elements and needs.

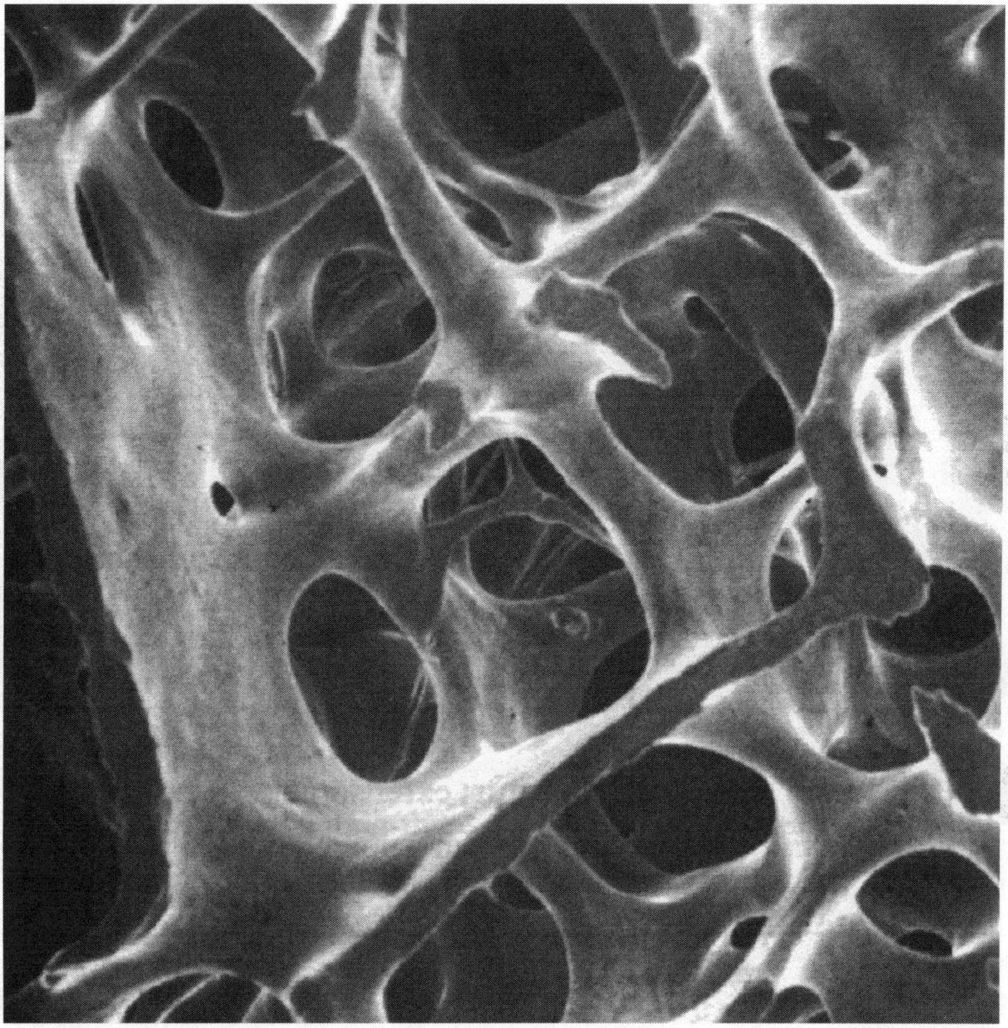

Electron micrographs showing trabecular structure of bone (from the human femur)
© Whitehouse and Dyson, 1974

...the whole skeleton and every part thereof, down to the minute intrinsic structure of the bones themselves, is related in form and in position to the lines of force, to the resistances it has to encounter; for by one of the mysteries of biology, resistance begets resistance, and where pressure falls there growth springs up in strength to meet it.
D'Arcy Thompson, *On Growth and Form.*

Snowflakes are born in chaos. The delicate balance between order and disorder: in a growing ice crystal, diffusion pushes toward instability, breaking up the boundary; the contrary force of surface tension tries to smooth it again, make an even skin like a soap bubble's. A competition emerges, one force trying to sharpen the crystal, another trying to flatten it. Like living organisms, the snowflake at once seeks and abhors equilibrium. James Gleick, *Nature's Chaos.*

Choose:
something shapeless.... find ways.... to give it form
something fragile.... strengthen it
something hard.... soften it

Gathering... growing

Bone is formed out of connective tissue through a process of sedimentation of mineral salts from the blood. The hard crystalline shapes of bone forming around the softer tissues of blood vessel and nerve that nourish its growth, as a village grows around the essential waters of stream, river or well. Skeleton from the Greek *Skeletos,* meaning a dried body, implies dry brittle bones, but living bone is plastic, resilient and saturated with blood and fat cells. Bone crystals create a labyrinth of mineralised tissue – branching, curving spiralling – that encloses nerve and blood vessels. It is constantly reabsorbed and deposited according to the body's need for support. As 'inside shells', the bones grow and change, thickening where the stresses are greatest as in the bodies of the spinal vertebrae or pelvis; membraneous and translucent as a bird's egg where the pressures are least. The hard tissue of bone is constantly altered by the soft tissues that depend on it. In the forms of the skull it is possible to see how delicately bone grows and responds to the movement and growth of the brain it contains and supports.

Something... growing
Choose something very small.... a scrap or fragment
Gradually.... begin to make around it
How does it grow?
What does it become?

Living bone

Beneath the skin, bone is flexible, changing, listening and responding to events in our lives. Bone holds our deepest and oldest memories, it reacts to joy or shock, breathes and fails to breathe. Our skeletons may be somewhat pliant and malleable, or rigid and brittle, according to what happens in our lives. Diet, trauma, work, and sensory stimulation, all profoundly affect the growth and quality of our bones.

Bone carries the imprint of all that we do, and of where we have been. Throughout our lives our bones subtlely change and record the directions we have taken. As we ourselves are shaped by how we live, so the geology of our bones – their density and mass – alters within hours in response to changes of use or to shifts in the gravitational field of the earth. In response our bones become fragile, porous, brittle, dense, plastic, or heavy, (the weightlessness experienced by astronauts in outer space causes immediate and significant bone loss). The structure of bone constantly reorientates itself according to the forces acting upon it – a cycle of depositing, dissolving and redepositing to meet demands in balancing this cycle of change. Lack of compressive stimulus on the bone is as crucial as overloading it – a case of 'use it or lose it'.

Anil had worked with teachers who could take a seven-hundred-year-old skeleton and discover through evidence of physical stress or trauma in those bones what the person's profession had been. Lawrence Angel, her mentor at the Smithsonian, could, from just the curvature of a spine to the right, recognise a stonemason from Pisa, and from thumb fractures among dead Texans tell that they had spent long evenings gripping the saddle on mechanical barroom bulls.
Michael Ondaatje, *Anil's Ghost.*

Arriving form

Take a lump of clay.... let it rest within your hands
Sense what moves it from within.... and from without
Sense the undertows, currents.... of what is pushing it.... pulling it

Allow.... something to emerge in the clay from these forces
nudge... press... twist... shove... squash... lift
***Move and write** to explore its voice*

The hidden presence of bone

IOU Theatre Company, *The Patience of Fossils,* 1983. Photo: Mike Laye.

IOU uses painting, sculpture, dance, mechanical devices, specially composed music, prose and poetry, working on the senses to evoke strong atmospheres and emotions through a dream-like unfolding of episodes. Richard Sobey

Everything that gives light is dependent on something to which it clings, in order that it may continue to shine. Thus, sun and moon cling to heaven, and grain, grass, and trees cling to the earth.

I Ching, Hexagram 30, The Clinging (Richard Wilhelm trans.)

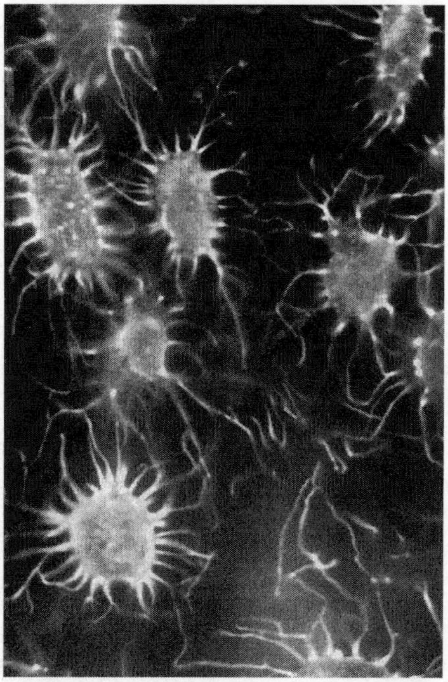

Osteocytes in rat parietal bone

All parts and systems of the body depend on the hidden presence of bone. Its hardness forms a protection and support to the softer tissues of the body and creates the essential space for brain, heart and lungs to function. Respiration, circulation, defence and immunity, nervous and digestive systems, all depend on bone. From the marrow of our bones comes the streaming of blood that sustains life within us. There are around 25 billion red blood cells in the body (carriers of oxygen and nutrients to every cell). Each has a life span of about 120 days. Each second millions of red blood cells are launched into the body from the marrow of the bones. White cells (central to the body's defence) exist in smaller numbers. They vary in types and lifespan (many less than five days) and their production rate varies hugely – high in states of acute infection. Bone forms a storehouse of calcium, phosphorus and other minerals essential to the body's chemistries of digestion and to the nervous system. 99% of the body's calcium is in the bone, and calcium in the blood and tissue fluids constantly exchanges with calcium in the bone. The dense branching of capillary and blood supply within bone provides both metabolic support for its own nourishment and renewal, and also avenues of entry and exit for rapid calcium exchange between bone and the tissues and fluids of the rest of the body. As the waxing and waning of the moon draws the earth's tides and affects the life and growth of all living things, so the body depends on the changing chemistries of bone – every system of the body affected by its hidden, anchoring presence.

Sink inwards to the marrow of the bones.... *to the movement of blood*
Open out through the branches of bone
Let the bones spread and illuminate the interior of the body
see.... you are a galaxy of stars

the *osteocyst* cells from which bone grows are *stellate* (star shaped) - L.*stella,* a star

Boundaries and hard edges

Bone defines our shape, sets our edges, defines our weakness and strength. And in our lives, our sense of limits gives definition to what we do. Without limits our energies dissipate. To come up against hard edges focuses and concentrates our efforts.

> Unlimited possibilities are not suited to man;
> if they existed, his life would only dissolve in the boundless.
> I Ching, Hexagram 60, *Limitation* (Richard Wilhelm trans.)

Exploring resistance

With a partner

One moves.... the other tries to prevent all movement

Block.... intercept.... obstruct.... all their attempts to move
sit on... hold back... hold down....... every impulse of your partner

***Mover**: don't give up..... use your wit.... escape.... change shape.... deceive.... keep going at all costs!*

***After moving:** gather materials and use the energy generated to*
***make**.... something.... be bold!*
What appears?

It is surprising what comes to form, what is liberated, when our blood is up.
Contact Improvisation began with dancers hurling themselves at each other and exploring impact.

An office worker confronts a line of tanks, Tiananman Square, 1989. Photo: Stuart Franklin

What do you say "No" to?

Explore in movement.... separately or with another

Yes.... No.... Maybe

Work against... work with... accept... question... balance

***Make** and **write** from what emerges*

...by saying no to the sad charm of disenchantment, we are saying yes to hope.
Eduardo Galeano, *We Say No.*

The many bones of our selves

Alexander Calder, *Sumac V,* Mobile,1953. wire and metal, painted red

The shape and form of each bone in the body is unique and particular to its function within the overall structure. Most of our bones are preformed in hyaline cartilage which is gradually replaced by the crystalline hardness of bone (except for specialised layers which remain as protection at joint surfaces, or as soft walls for larynx, bronchi, trachea and external parts of nose and ears). Most of our bones are formed through a precise and exquisite coalescence of separate elements that join together to form a complex whole. The temporal bones (that house our hearing and balance), ossify from ten different centres beginning in the seventh week after conception and are still in three parts at birth (Milne, *The Heart of Listening*). The sacrum is formed from five fused vertebrae, each having seven centres of ossification, the occiput (the bone that supports the base of the brain) is formed from four separate parts. It is the demands of movement and support that stimulate the fusion of all these parts. In the womb there are as many as 600 tiny 'bones'; at birth we have 350 separate bones; in the adult skeleton these have fused to 206. Head, hands, feet and spine each have almost the same number of bones (26/27), reflecting the needs of these structures for a subtle and responsive flexibility to whatever they support or come to meet. The last bones to ossify (to change from cartilage to bone) are usually the sacrum and the breast-bone at around 25 years (Sometimes the breast-bone remains as cartilage even longer).

Imagine you are made of.... a single bone
How does the body feel?
Imagine you are made of four bones.... how do you move?
Continuing in movement
gradually.... let in other bones
Sense how the body changes
***Write**, to give it a voice*

Find the bones

With a partner:

Use your hands.... to feel and trace out.... the pathways of bone in any part of the body
Let your fingers take a walk
around whatever bone draws your attention

Be curious.... dare to dig in with the fingers!
Look.... see.... touch.... discover - not trying to change what you find
simply let your fingers notice
Explore the density, fragility, edges, curves.... the shape and quality of each bone
mapping
delicate.... as a bird.... in the eye socket
curved.... as the prow of a boat.... in the pelvis

Feel out.... hoop of the jaw.... of chin.... dome of the head.... wings of the shoulder....
pebbles of hands and feet
Let your fingers wander.... exploring.... mapping.... surveying
Sense how each bone has a particular place and voice
within the constellation of the whole body

Gently begin to move your partner
Sense the direction of each bone within the body.... Which way does it seem to go?
Sense the openings of the joints
How does each limb like to move.... dream?

Listen and support the direction of your partner's moving bones
Sense their momentum
Gradually.... let them move alone

***Move**.... to hear the voice of bone in the body*
Write

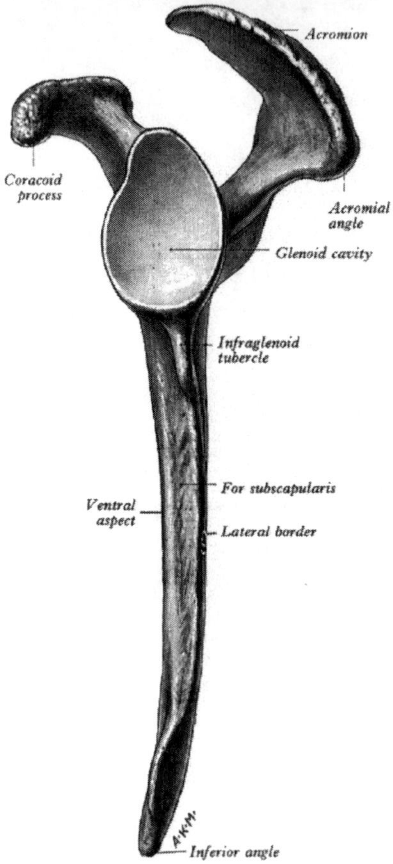

Left scapula, side view

Bone story

Choose a single bone.... look at it in detail.... its forms and qualities

Imagine the 'world' it comes from....What is its voice.... character?

Move as this bone

Gather elements to make.... its world

***Write**.... to give voice to its story*

***clavicle** or little key (opening shoulder out from the body)*

***coccyx** or cuckoo's bill*

***fibula** or brooch bone*

***atlas** supporting the world of head*

***axis** turning the head*

***sacrum** or holy bone*

Egyptian model boat. Painted wooden boat representing a magical re-enactment of the journey to Abydos, sacred city of Orisis. Middle Kingdom, c. 1900 BC. Length 77.5 cm.
© The British Museum

Beginning again

To 'feel something in the bones' describes a sensation of something fundamental and deeply known – something on which our whole understanding rests. When the rest of us has dissolved, the bones remain. From fragments of bone we can reconstruct the lives of those who lived thousands of years ago. The skeleton has become an image of death and fear – the bare bones to which we will be reduced – but to tribal peoples, bone is the symbol of life, wisdom, strength and renewal, a link to the divine and eternal. Bones of the dead are consulted in times of need to guide and inform the living – skulls of ancestors preserved and treasured. For hunting peoples, bone is the source of life from which the animals on which they depend will return and be reborn. In the Judeo-Christian world, Adam is formed from the earth, but Eve is born from Adam's rib.

Essence

Take something you have made.... or found
strip.... reduce.... discover its bare essentials
What is left?.... listen to it
What does it call for?
Take time to let it form.... a new world for itself

Spine – creating length and space

Gaby Agis, *Duet,* London, 1991 – a collaboration with Shelley Lasica. Photo: Hugo Glendinning

At this time, my work was especially concerned with responding both to an internal sense of the body and to the external space in which I was moving (This piece was performed in an art gallery). In this particular movement I was conscious of sending my body on an upward diagonal – an image of elevation while retaining a sense of connection to the floor.

The resilience and hardness of bone allows us to stand and to withstand the compressive forces of gravity. Our upright posture frees the hand and arm with which we shape our worlds. The many small clustering bones of our feet form a living arch through which we rise and walk. The long bones of our legs allow the swing of a walk, enabling us to move in all directions. They pass our weight downward to the ground and support us upwards into the bridges and arches of the pelvis. The moving curves of the pelvis in turn support the length of the spine, lifting the head high.

The spine forms the central axis of support throughout the body, around which the rest of the body spreads out and grows. It creates a moving pathway between head and pelvis that maintains an essential length and width and depth of the body, and allows the vital functioning of heart, lungs and digestion. The length of the spine spaces head from thorax and pelvis and connects all other parts of the body; legs and arms take their rooting from the spine. The many bones of the spine protect the nervous system (spinal cord), as it elongates and flows downward from the brain, branching outwards through the body. If the spine shortens and the spinal nerves are even fractionally compressed or irritated, numbness and pain will occur.

Find the spine.... a pathway within

Feel the length of the spine.... flowing upwards and downwards through the back
Sense the weight and roundness of the head.... sense the tip of the spine rising behind the eyes
Let the senses.... awaken
let what you see.... hear.... smell.... resonate throughout the length of your spine

let the weight of each vertebra descend.... slowly.... falling through curves of:
neck.... thorax.... lumbar spine
let the spine spread out as a river.... into the valleys and slopes.... of pelvis and sacrum
Let the tip of the coccyx gently uncurl.... as the tip of a fern.... downwards
Let the many bones of the spine be as stepping stones.... between head and pelvis
let them open.... separate

Let the pelvis listen to the head through the spine.... let the head hear the pelvis
In your mind's eye.... travel the pathway of the spine

Let the legs and arms.... open as branches.... from its length
Open the soles of the feet.... sense the ground
Open the crown of the head.... let in air.... light

Let the whole body open and move from the length of the spine

***Write** and **make** to give the spine a voice*

Standing up

The spine is formed from 24 separate vertebrae, 5 fused sacral and 3-5 coccygeal vertebrae – our vestigial tail. Between each vertebra lie fluid-filled discs that allow movement and act as shock absorbers, cushioning and spacing the vertebrae from each other. We are taller in the morning, losing up to an inch of height (sometimes even more) throughout the day as the discs compress. The discs have no blood supply and maintain their fluid tone through a balance of movement and rest, without which they become fibrous, and may bulge or rupture.

....

In the developing embryo it is the agitation of the embryonic spinal chord (notachord) that stimulates the layers of the embryo to grow. By the 2nd week of embryonic life, three layers are formed: one from which the skin and nervous system will grow; a second from which the gut and respiratory system develop; the third and last to grow is that of muscle, bone, blood and connective tissue. Its function is to support, protect and to move our nervous system. This embryonic spine, develops from a dense and lively group of cells which burrow upwards towards what becomes the 'mouth' thereby creating a length that is organised towards the mouth and head end. This movement of the developing 'spine' is a highly charged impulse upwards – from tail to head. Conversely the bones of the cranium and spine develop downwards – from head to sacrum.

....

In the body there are no straight building blocks of bone, no tongue and groove joints or symmetrical hinges. No bone is straight and no joint is stable, each is curved, irregular and rounded, within the weave of muscle and connective tissue that forms our body. Our length and depth is maintained through a constant shifting of balance between the different parts – it is the subtleties of movement allowed throughout the body in the interaction between the tissues that prevents our bones from stiffening or being worn away. We do not have to 'hold' ourselves up – the length of our bodies is suspended in a living and dynamic weave of tissues.

Balancing

Gather several elements.... consider different weights, qualities
Find ways to balance them.... delicately
Explore.... balance.... off balance
even if they fall.... persist
What comes to form?
Discover its story?

High place

Go up high.... find a vantage point
cliff edge, tower, hilltop...
what part of it are you drawn to?
Gather materials
***Make** a place there.... at any scale.... large or tiny*
What do you imagine happens in and around it?
With a partner.... find the story of this place

Between above and below – near and far

Stand still.... sense the ground.... go down beneath your feet
Sense the sky high above
Sense what is under your nose.... the horizon far beyond
Let your attention travel between these dimensions
Moving in close.... moving far out and away
What images begin to appear?

***Move** to explore their presence*
Share with a partner

Flag

***Make** a flag for yourself*
Raise it high

Tower

***Make** the tallest tower you can with anything to hand*
boxes... bicycles... chairs and tables... sticks... suitcases... kettles
Let this tower speak...what does it see?
What happens to it?

From a different point of view

Imagine your body as tiny.... moving under.... and in and out.... of things
Imagine your body as enormous.... looking down.... stepping over
***Move** to explore changing your sense of scale*
***Write** from the moving*

among the roots... under a stone... bottom of a pond... in a gutter
from a bridge... from a crane... with the eye of a bird... at the top of a tree

Deborah Jones, *Intimate Landscapes*, 2002. Site-specific photo work
(A residency commissioned by the Creative Arts Department, University of Bath)

As Artist in Residence on the campus of the University of Bath, memories of my childhood on a very similar campus at York were my starting point. There had been this fantastic landscape on my doorstep - vast grounds with a lake, expanses of grass, an amphitheater – all interlaced with futuristic (sixties) buildings and walkways. It was a world where I could roam and run and daydream, playing for days on end with friends or alone. Returning to that sense of occupying such a vast place in my imaginary play-world, I recalled a sense of countless tiny worlds existing within the vast, visible one which the grown-ups around me had seemed to pass through like strangers. As I explored the Bath campus, I positioned small toys around the site, photographing them as I went. New halls of residence were under construction. I invited staff to write messages of good luck to future students, transferred these onto the small construction workers and vehicles (featured in the photographs), and then buried them in the walls of thew new buildings. Deborah Jones

Behind the eyes

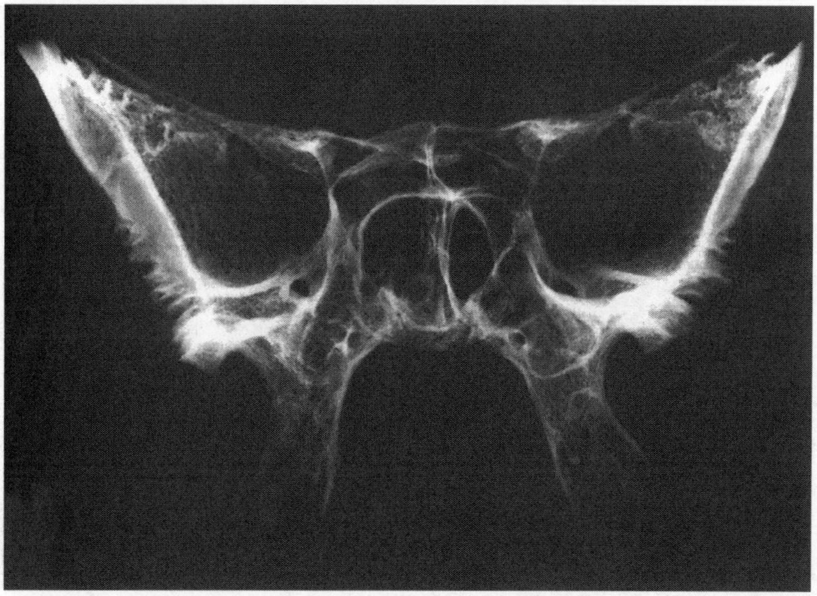

Micro radiograph of the sphenoid bone

The head is formed as a small galaxy of 29 separate and particular bones. These many bones delicately woven together collaborate to support and protect the fragile moving world of the brain and senses through which we perceive the world around us. Fourteen separate bones form the face – eight cradling bones support the dome and weight of the brain. Behind the eyes lies a bone, the *sphenoid,* shaped like a dragonfly – that spreads its four wings through the centre of the the head. Its 'body' provides anchorage for the muscles of the eyes. The optic nerve runs through it on its journey to the optic lobes at the back of the brain. The frontal lobes (where we plan and make decisions) rest on its lesser wings, the temporal lobes (memory) lie on its greater wings. From its drifting feet are suspended the muscles of the throat. Its fissures and corridors are threaded with nerves and air sinuses which help cool the brain, its back forms a saddle into which the light-sensitive pituitary gland sits (which sets the clock of our circadian and biological rhythms). The movement of the sphenoid dipping and rising within the head, milks the pituitary gland of excess venous blood and transmits the movement of the brain to the rest of the body. Every other bone of the cranium touches and is affected by the spread wings and gentle flight of the sphenoid within the centre of the head.

> *For the Chukchee the human soul usually takes the form of a fly or bee. They believe that a shaman can replace a person's soul by opening the skull and introducing a fly. Alternatively, the soul can be inserted through the fingers, the mouth or the big toe. As other Siberian peoples, they believe there are several souls. At death, one flies up into the sky in the smoke of the funeral pyre, another descends into the underworld, where ordinary life continues as on earth.* (derived from Mircea Eliade, *Shamanism.*)

Temporal bone

Listening balance

Our sense of hearing and of balance are housed within the two temporal bones that form part of the cranial base. Each temporal bone is shaped as a small boat which rocks and 'sails' in the sides of the head. The balance of our whole body shifts according to information received through these two bones. Sound tells us about what inhabits the space around us. To be deaf, shuts us off from the world – as we open our ears and listen, our whole body is enlivened. Sound tells us what is there and what is arriving. The sensitivity of our hearing and balance inform and protect the head. Noticing what we are hearing frees the balance of the head on the neck, thereby opening the pathway of the brain as it flows downwards into the body.

Many mammals have large movable ears to "catch" sound. Our ears are small and less mobile; instead we use our neck to turn the head. Bats fly in complete darkness and depend on sound to 'see', calling and hunting their prey by echo location. Locusts have ear drums on their legs – nocturnal moths on the sides of their bodies. The skin of our own bodies is sensitive to the vibration of sound.

After I went blind, I could never make a motion without starting an avalanche of noise. If I went into my room at night, the room where I used to hear nothing, the small plaster statue on the mantelpiece made a fraction of a turn. I heard its friction in the air, as light a sound as the sound of a waving hand. Whenever I took a step, the floor cried or sang – I could hear it making both these sounds – and its song was passed along from one board to the next, all the way to the window, to give me the measure of the room. If I spoke out suddenly, the window-panes, which seemed so solid in their putty frames, began to shake, very lightly of course but distinctly. This noise was on a higher pitch than the others, cooler, as if it were already in contact with the outside air. Lusseyran, *And There Was Light.*

Ray Chung, *Solo improvisation.* Photo: Theodora Litsios

Moving from listening

Open each ear.... listen
Hear the sounds.... of what is around you.... each sound as a note of music
feel.... their resonance in the body.... touching.... left.... and right ear
sense.... space.... silence

let sound enter.... and move the body
touching.... sounding.... each bone

Listen.... to the sounds close to.... within the body.... heart.... breath
sounds of the room.... distant sounds

Let the length of the neck soften
Sense how the head turns in response to sound
Let the whole body open.... as an ear

Let the sounds you hear move the body

***Draw** the qualities of sound*
talk with a partner about your drawing
***Move**.... as a sound*

Pierre Boucher, Photograph

Make *something.... that listens*

The structure of each ear is like a shell gently spiralling inwards to the membrane of the ear drum. The vibrations of sound are transmitted through the air-filled cavity of the middle ear via three tiny bones – hammer, anvil and stirrup – the last of which touches the oval window that connects into the fluid-filled labyrinths of the cochlea. Here sound vibration is translated to nerve impulse. Movement of sound waves vibrates the fluid, and jostles the hairs of thousands of audio receptor cells. Similarly, as the head moves, tiny hairs register movement of minute calcium crystals floating within the liquid of the semicircular canals – our organs of balance and equilibrium. These register the smallest shifts in our movement. Nerve fibres of both balance and hearing join to form the vestibular cochlear nerve. Vestibular pathways in the brain itself connect both to the limbs and to the eyes. Hence both hearing and balance guide our seeing and moving.

The first embryonic cells are sound sensitive.
By 4 1/2 months in the womb, the baby's auditory system is complete.

Sacrum.... sacred bone

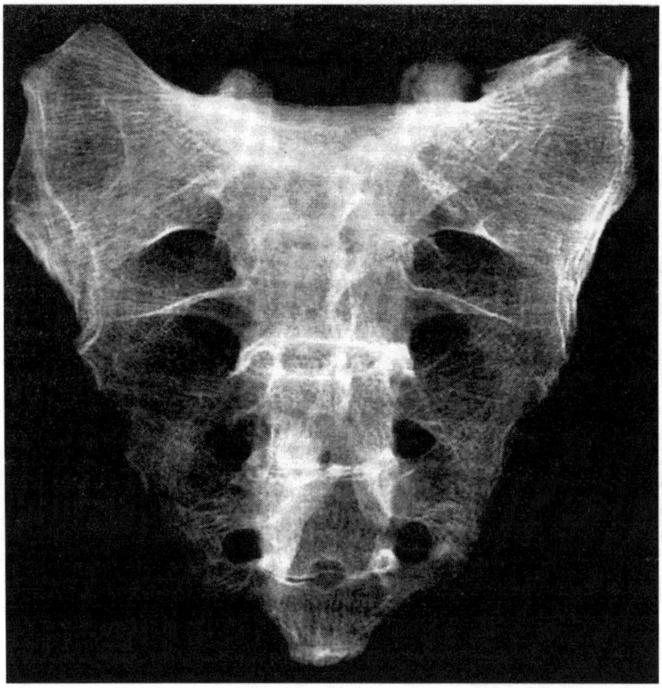

Sacrum, from: *Cunningham's Textbook of Anatomy*

All things return to their root Lao Tse

'Sacrum' means sacred or holy bone and was once believed to be the bone from which the body would be resurrected. The sacrum is the 'root bone', that spreads our weight downwards to the earth, and also, as the keel of a boat, supporting the rise of the head and spine. The diaphragm, or muscle of breathing, is a major influence on the movement of the sacrum. The sacrum carries within it our need both for movement and also for anchorage, stability. Formed from five bones that fuse slowly over the first twenty years of life, it creates a stable base for the ascending column of spine and head. It is this fusion of several bones in the sacrum that gives it flexibility and makes it one of the strongest bones of the body. The sacrum, more than any other bone, is shaped by the movement and weight that passes through it. To feel the presence of the sacrum is to find a sense of grounding and moving support. The *meninges* or membranes, which support and protect the brain and spinal cord, are woven into the cranial bones, and then hang loose around the length of the spinal cord, attaching within the sacrum. Hence the movement of the head profoundly affects the movement of the sacrum – and movement, or lack of movement, in the sacrum restricts the head. Similarly, if the lower back is tight, the sacrum stiffens and the whole spine tightens, causing restrictions in the thorax and shoulders. We cannot find our length, spread out and go up, if we cannot also find our way down to the roots, to what we depend on. To find the essential length of the spine, sacrum and head must be able to move away from each other.

In the roots

In your imagination.... travel down.... the curves and length.... of your spine
falling.... giving way
Sense the base of the spine
feel the depth.... density.... of its form
Let the breath reach downwards.... to the marrow of the sacrum
feel the support of the ground under you
Take time.... to imagine your roots.... uncurling downwards

Slowly.... return upwards.... outwards
to the throat.... to the heart and hands

***Make** something.... that is coming up.... from below.... from underneath*

Keystone
In a chosen place
gather materials to
***make** something that gives support*

Winifrid Nicholson, *Winter Hyacinth,* 1950s.
Oil on canvas 61x 62.2 cm

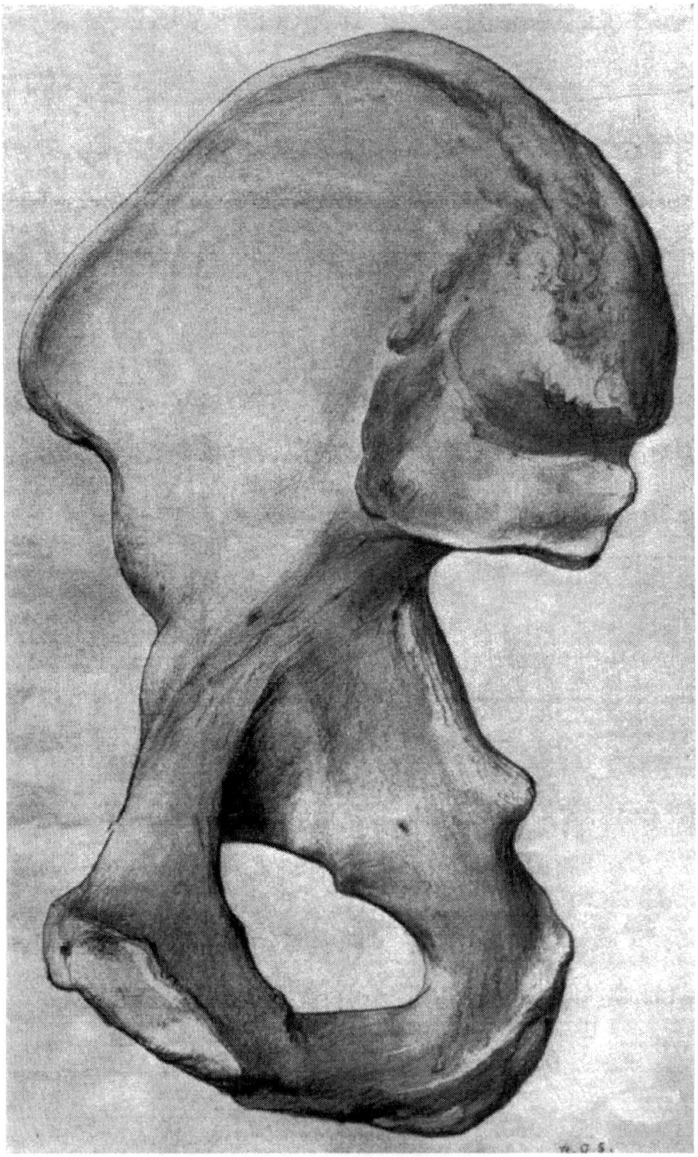

Right hip bone seen from the medial (inner) side showing Illium at the top and Ischium at the bottom

Steve Paxton: notes on the pelvis and the spine

After 40 years of dancing, my body sometimes feels overly familiar. As an improviser, I suppose I should do something to retain the adventure of unknowing. This is basic housekeeping for the mature improviser. Life goes on, as they say, in ruts. Occasionally the road takes an unexpected turning and to stay the course we have to call on unknown reserves within. As far as the improviser's work is concerned, there should be no ruts. Unexpected turns are supposed to be normal. A certain brinkmanship is required. But my body, having found the brink of whatever ruts were forming, settles in comfortably there. It is a creature of habit. As its consciousness, it is my job to watch with dismay as it continues its routines.

In 1985 I began teaching technically, no longer investigating improvisational forms, focussing instead on the spine. It was a helpful focus during improvisational performance. I could let my mind review the spinal material I'd felt, and my movement potential would change, with its roots in an inner riff of thoughts – flick; much like a slide show, a vision of an evolving spinal deportment in space. When that became routine, needing a change, I began an examination of the shoulders and pelvis. Currently the bones of the pelvis are my 'slides'.

The pelvis is like a butterfly, like the twin hulls of a catamaran, the ballast of a balloon. The sacrum and coccyx are similar to the body of a butterfly, the ilia and ischia are similar to the upper and lower lobes of its wings. The pelvis seems designed for lightness, despite the considerable weight bearing it does. The ilia are essentially receptacles for the knobs of the femur and an anchor for numerous muscles. Yet this is accomplished with remarkable economy of materials.

The ischia, the sitzbones, are the twin hulls of the catamaran; they are easily known when we are sitting, but also operate when we stand or move in that they point the weight of the torso downwards to the earth where it is anyway drawn. The three elements of the pelvis, the two hips and the sacrum comprise a sort of container. The volume contained in this 'basin' is the centre of mass of the body, achieved with the weightiest part of our digestive process. The mass serves as a basis for movement of the spine, arms and legs. Movement may originate in its centre, a principle which the Eastern martial arts have employed.

This vision of structure + mass is rather like a catamaran which lets me view the soft tissue – the muscles, tendons and ligaments – as rigging. The spine becomes a mast, the shoulders and arms are articulated booms. The head would be the lookout, the crows nest, I suppose, although it is obviously a mass-centre as well, articulated at the top of the spine with two types of rotation (which we use for 'yes' and 'no'). This message may apply to other weight masses of the spine; the pelvis and the shoulders/ ribs – their connections, how they rotate; their interconnections, how the rotations relate.

The final analogy, the hot-air balloon, ignores the skeletal structuring of the catamaran. It is a reflection of the mass below and the lungs above. It speaks of a relationship between earth and air. The mediating tissue, the diaphragm, is moving the lungs and simultaneously massaging all the organs at the bottom of the basin.

We see the workings of a basic principle in operation at the core of the body; stability achieved via opposing forces, the directions pulling the torso being: inflation and rising, vs gravity and falling. For me there are several teachings in this image. In order to move, to reach, to utilise our sphere of activity, we rely on gravity, and falling. There is a direct and constant dialogue between our own mass and the mass of the earth. If often limiting our movement, it also gives us stability. We may not fly but we can rise.

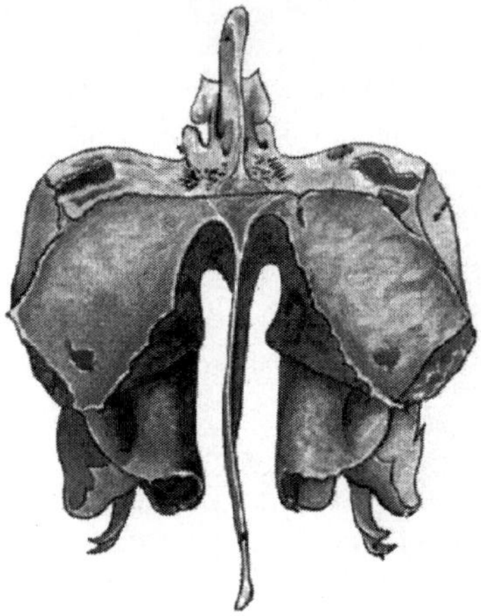

Ethmoid bone, seen from behind

Direction - following your nose

Within the sinuses of the Ethmoid bone of all vertebrates lie magnetic deposits which are like a compass or navigational system for the body (vital for some migratory birds and mammals), informing the body of shifts in the earth's magnetic field. These crystals lie close to the pineal and pituitary glands, and rotate slightly. Disturbance of the earth's magnetic field affect the growth and stability of every cell in the body.

> *One thousand feet down in the depths of the Pacific Ocean a just-hatched eel measuring three millimetres sets out on a 2,000 mile voyage to the rivers of Eastern Australia. Riding the currents over the next 12 months, she dodges predators and reaches the estuary where she must climb a 35ft dam and waterfalls as high as two - story houses. A lake near the river is her home for the next quarter century, but she will then tackle the return journey to the Pacific to lay her eggs and die. How she accomplishes this is barely grasped. Why is utterly unknown.*
>
> Francesca Turner, *Watching Brief*, The Guardian, Jan 16th. 1997

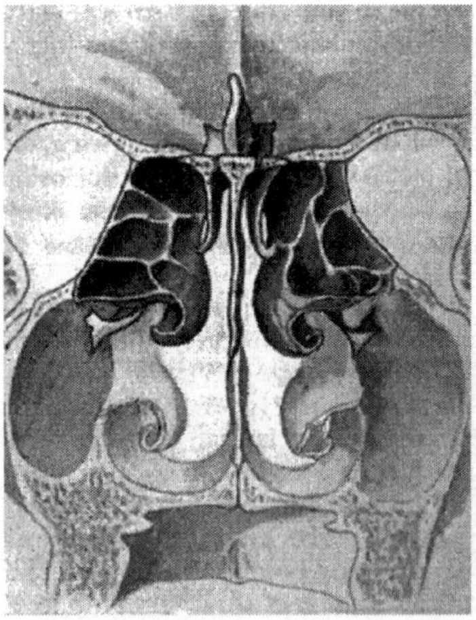

Ethmoid bone, shown in frontal cross section of the skull

Listen to the voice of the wind and the ceaseless
message that forms itself out of silence. Rilke

Moving beyond

Sense the flow and direction of your bones.... spreading out through the body
Where are they pointing ?.... move and follow
pass through and beyond your edges

9. Places

Karen Rann, *Deep Water 2,* Dunaujvaros Spring festival, Hungary, 1994.

The performance site was the side of a ten story housing block in a new town originally called Stalin Town. This 'vertical dance' was about giving wings to disused and unloved buildings. A sister piece was an installation on the side of a disused hotel in Budapest. The netting symbolises that a building is about to be transformed, to be 'made better'. Karen Rann

Place for me is the locus of desire. Places have influenced my life as much as, perhaps more than, people. I fall for (or into) places faster and less conditionally than I do for people. I can drive through a landscape and vividly picture myself in that disintegrating mining cabin, that saltwater farm, that little porched house in the barrio. Lucy Lippard, *The Lure of the Local.*

Places and what they mean to us

The story of our lives includes many places – places lived in, visited, remembered, heard of, dreamed about. Some of these hold a special significance – the place we were born, the place we regard as home, places we love to go, places we avoid. Every place is many places – for you and for me each place will be different.

It is difficult to capture the sense of a place we feel within us. Each place has its own qualities of space, of texture, its own smells and sounds, its particular light and colour, its own feel and associations. In returning to a familiar place we recover a particular sense of ourselves. I go to a spot on the coast that I often visit, a bay like a huge dish with its long curving shingle beach, its changing character with the weather and time of day, its salty air and crunch of gravel underfoot, or I come back to the room where I work, with its intense clutter of books and strewn papers, its interior silence only broken by the whirring of a computer, its framed view through net curtains of my small front garden, cars parked outside and occasional passers by. In each of these places I feel different, their different mood and feel are somehow a part of me.

What a place means to each of us depends upon what happens or has happened there, an ongoing story that is both personal and collective. There I walked home everyday from the tube station; here I visited friends; there, behind closed curtains, lived a woman who was invariably drunk; here was once a greyhound racing stadium; here is a city place with a country name (Green Lanes). Every place is resonant with stories – as I enter a place, I re-enter the stories that belong there. In traditional cultures, a person's identity is closely connected to the land, the territory they live in, and the collective story worlds of their tribe or culture that inform that place. For us, the link between ourselves and places is more ambiguous and transient, yet places and their stories still play an essential part in our lives.

Places exist on many different scales – London, Siberia, and under-the-bed are all places. The moment I call something I am making, 'a place', however small it may be, it starts to become somewhere, it belongs with other places... things could happen there.

Christian Boltanski, *Ombres* (Shadows), 1984, Installation view.
Tiny figures made from pieces of cork, paper, cardboard, copper and tin, whose shadows are cast on the surrounding walls by means of three light sources. The whole cast of characters is gently set in motion by a small fan.

Making a place

In an empty space.... choose a spot

Collect ingredients

three chairs.... four bones.... a newspaper

a reel of cotton.... twigs.... feathers.... red paint

Make a 'place' with the elements you have collected

Move.... write.... view with a partner

to explore the stories of the place you have made

Getting to know a place

(What you notice in a place when you are not trying to notice anything in particular)

Sit quietly in a chosen place, with paper and pen to hand
Throw open your attention.... see what comes
as you sit.... (without looking down at what you are writing)
Make a list of sensory impressions.... sounds.... sensations in your body.... colours...
whatever calls attention to itself

As you persist and relax into doing this, not just the naming of each impression (dog barks, car passes...), but the qualities of it, become more apparent - what kind of bark? yapping... yelping... wolf like... growling?... how does the car pass? slips by... roars... struggles... trundles...? The more you sink into the present moment of your sensations, the more distinctive and qualitative your list will be.

After a while, read back your list to a partner or group... discover what each person noticed.
From your own list see whether some impressions were stronger than others.
These, or what triggered them, could become starting points for working.

'Look at the spider's web on the corner of the balcony,' said Bernard. 'It has beads of water on it, drops of white light.'

'The leaves are gathered round the window like pointed ears,' said Susan.

'A shadow falls on the path,' said Louis, 'like an elbow bent.'

'Islands of light are swimming on the grass,' said Rhoda. 'They have fallen through the trees.'.....

'Stones are cold to my feet,' said Neville. 'I feel each one, round or pointed, separately.'

'The back of my hand burns,' said Jinny, 'but the palm is clammy and damp with dew.'

Excerpts from Virginia Woolf, *The Waves.*

Norman Hallendy, *Spirit figure in the likeness of a raven,* Baffin Island. Photograph.
(© from: *Inuksuit Silent Messengers of the Artic,* published by The British Museum)

These are stone messages, some as much as a thousand years old, left by Inuit hunters to help others passing that way. They signal safe routes, hidden springs, natural shelters, fishing places, etc, and were often venerated.

Responding to a place.... by making something there

Choose somewhere to go
Spend time there.... wander
allow yourself to be drawn to a particular spot
be still.... receiving
see what impressions come

Is there something here – some quality, or element - that feels like an opening?
as if what you are going to make had already begun

Wander.... to gather more ingredients
find things that feel as if they belong to the spot you have chosen
bring them to this place.... without knowing what you will do with them

What does this place seem to call for?
Explore.... how the elements you have gathered want to go
See them in relation to each other and to the place itself.... how it changes as they are introduced
Gradually.... let something emerge
Then: view with a partner

From what comes up as you view the work
***move**, then **write**.... then read and reflect again with your partner*

Francesca Woodman,
House No. 3, Providence, 1975-76
Black and white photograph, 10 x 8 in

Woodman created many images of herself as a figure within an interior space. In the above, as in many others, she appears to merge somewhat with her surroundings. At the same time, through her delicate presence, she brings to life what would otherwise seem to be a forgotten place.

Neglected

Wherever you are.... find.... a forgotten place
a spot that feels neglected, dulled, empty
Make something there, or move within it, to enliven
to re-enchant it

We started in dust-covered rooms cluttered with discarded objects: items of furniture, boxes, bottles, bits of electric cable, etc. Over several days we arranged and re-arranged these ingrediants, retaining some, discarding others, in order to gain a sense of these places and to re-energise them. Sometimes the sun shone through the windows, creating patches of bright light. At other times the spaces became darkened, shadowy. As we continued to physically change the rooms and corridors we also photographed and filmed each other moving in response to them. At the end of two weeks we had transformed four rooms and a corridoor into a set of linked installations – both a response to the setting and an evocation of the body in movement. Video and slides made during this time became projected images, moving figures brought back into the spaces they came from, but located differently, at oblique angles to the walls, floors, ceilings.

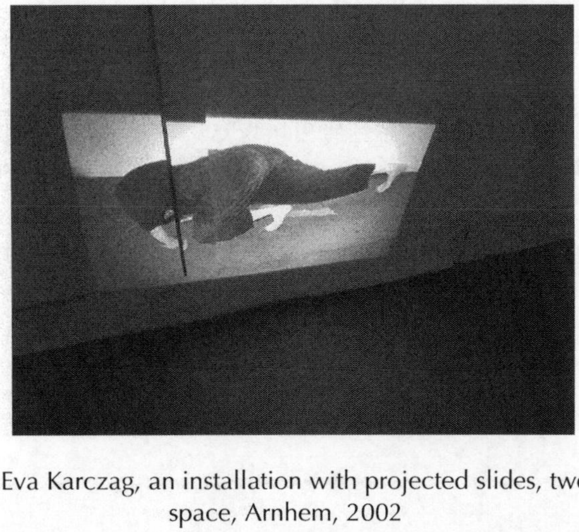

Chris Crickmay and Eva Karczag, an installation with projected slides, two views of the same space, Arnhem, 2002

Home..... a place of belonging

belong M.E. *belongen* , from *be-* prefix and A.S. *langian* to long after

Ken Kiff, *The Journey.* (Sequence No 105), 1979,
acrylic on paper, 55 x 77cm (21 1/2 x 30 1/4 in.)

a local.... a stranger

To belong is one of our most fundamental needs, an endorsement of our existence, a relief from isolation. The very word 'be-long' carries a sense of longing within it. Yet, for much of the time, this need to belong remains a wish rather than a reality. Instead, we are often to some extent in transition from worlds that no longer seem to fit, to others that we seek. The sense of belonging, of having a 'place', is countered by the contrary feeling of being lost, out of place, alien... We move in and out of both these states. A sense of belonging includes having a role, a part to play, and being accepted, but is also to do with a more intangible feeling of compatibility with one's circumstances and surroundings. The sense of home, or feeling 'at home' is therefore a potent one in our lives - an inextricable part of our imaginative landscape. 'Home' is a place we search for, the cause of our wandering. And our actual home may or may not correspond to our need for 'at homeness'.

placed
displaced

Coming home (the ideal)

Home is a dwelling place, the place we set out from and return to – the place of daily rituals. Home is where we expect to feel warmed and welcomed and may choose whether or not to welcome others. To cross the threshold into our own home is to enter a private, protected space over which we have a degree of control. Home is our shell, a roof over our heads, a refuge, a place where we can lock the door, close the curtains. And beyond its sheltering presence, home is also a place we invest with particular meaning, an extension and expression of ourselves and of what we value. At times, home may feel like our only preserve of meaning and coherence in an otherwise disjointed world. Home is a place for intimacy, where we are likely to be caught up in our most intense relationships; home is where we can restore ourselves – dry off, warm up, have a bath, change our clothes. When we go out from home, then home is the place to which we return – to eat, to relax, to sleep. We stay at home to recover from illness.

Elisabeth Vellacott, *Girl in an Arm Chair*, 1955.
Pencil on paper, 18 x 14 3/4 ins

Within a home there may be a part that we count as especially ours – a particular chair, kitchen, bedroom, den. This is the place where we feel most 'at home', our inner sanctum, the place where we keep our most personal possessions, a place that we can retreat into and come out from.

sheltered.... exposed

Make... a place to belong in

Wherever you are, choose a particular part of it as 'your spot'
Gather ingredients that evoke home for you
introduce them gradually into your chosen spot
to make a place in which you feel at home
a place to rest in.... to look out from.... to come and go from

What does this place need? add.... rearrange.... take out
What else should happen to make it feel right?
***Move** to feel what the body needs*

With a partner, spend time getting to know the place you have made
Speak from within it

home/ hearth/ heart

Hermes in antiquity was paired in the city with Hestia, she of the hearth, she who sat still, focused. ('Focus' is Latin for fireplace, hearth.) James Hillman in:
Hillman and Ventura, *We've had a Hundred Years of Psychotherapy and the World is Getting Worse.*

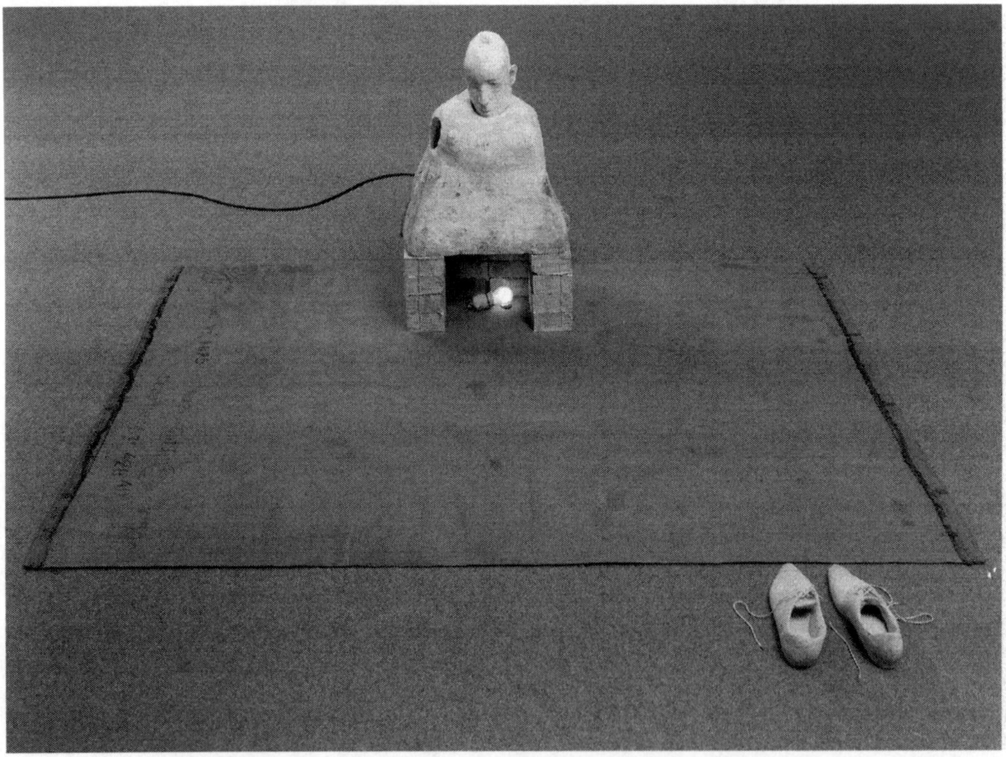

Miroslaw Balka, *Fire Place,*1986. Wood, plaster, bricks, blanket and electric light. © Tate, London 2003

Our belongings

A home that has been lived in for long becomes like an imprint of the lives of its occupants, each corner layered with personal significance. We shape a home, as a bird its nest, gathering things around us that we identify with, that hold our memories, that give us particular pleasure. Knowing where things are kept is a part of being at home – where are the plasters?... the scissors?... the salt and pepper...?

At home

What are the things you choose to give you the feeling of being 'at home'?
favourite: cup... plant... book... ornament... music... photograph...?
Take a favourite thing and **make** *a place for it*
View with a partner

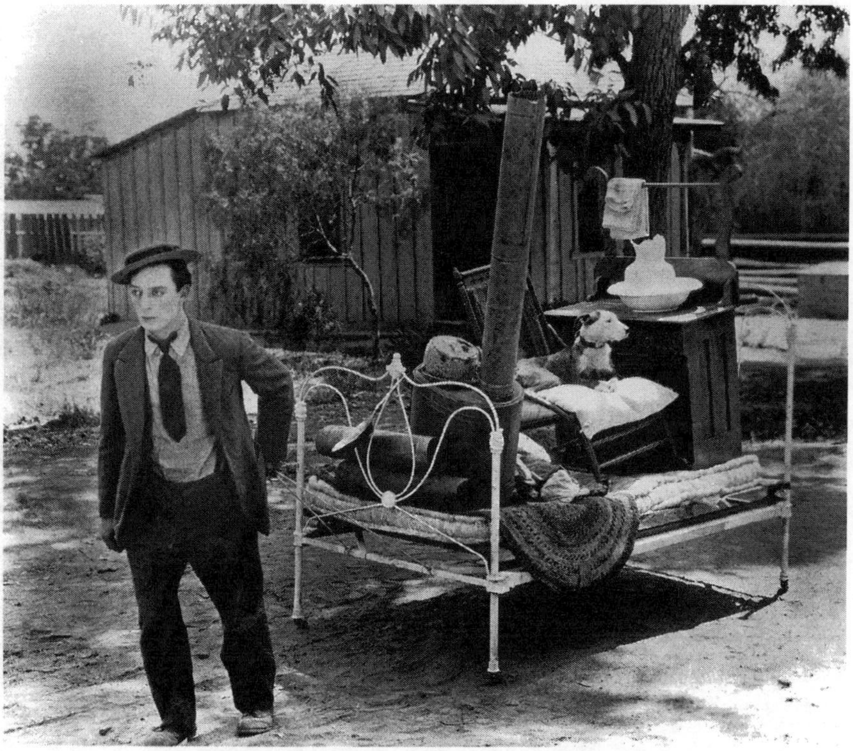

Buster Keaton, *Go West,* 1925. Film still.

"... Cause living plants are so rare in the city and I like taking care of them and they purify the air: it's a real subtle give and take with the plants. I like their shapes and shadows and things like that. Without them my house wouldn't feel so alive to me and I also feel that my plants are real centered kinds of beings. Like if I ever really get angry or something I can go and start working with the plants, repotting them, taking care of them. And it makes me feel better, so I would really feel a loss, they are so sensitive and subtle."

Person living in Chicago imagines life without her plants
(quoted in: Mihaly Csikszentmihalyi and Eugene Rochberg-Halton, *The Meaning of Things*)

Shut out

The very ideal of home we carry in our minds, makes us feel all the more bereft if our actual home feels unwelcoming to us – a place where instead of being warmed, we are chilled, oppressed by those closest to us, worn down by routine, isolated. Or we may have been expelled, pushed out of our homes, in exile, stripped of any sense of belonging.

stuck at home.... not feeling at home... homeless

Sandra Orgel, *Sheet Closet*, Womanhouse Project, 1972.
Photo: Lloyd Hamrol

Outsider

Choose some ingredients that you are drawn to, feel welcoming
Choose others that feel alien.... with which you feel uncomfortable
*What seems to happen as you bring them together.... to **make** a place?*
***Move** to explore this place*
***Write** to hear its story*

Unsafe/ safe

In two groups, or with one other person
*one **makes**.... a 'safe' space .... the other a 'threatening' space*
take a look together at what has emerged
Which actually threatens?.... Which feels safe?
What other qualities do they have for you?

Makeshift

***Make** a shelter with the barest of ingredients*
newspaper.... plastic cup.... piece of string
Give it a voice

IOU Theatre Company, *A Second Soaking,* 1986. Photo: Mike Laye.

IOU strives to create a world that the audience is invited to explore. It is vital that this world has its own logic and, while it may contain fantastical elements, the logic must hold for it to be believable. Richard Sobey.

New home
In your imagination, go underground
come up in a place that is to be your new home
Gather wild ingredients
Make

Garden

Romano Gabriel, *Wooden garden,* Eureka California. Photo: Jan Wampler

Built over a period of 30 years using the ends and sides of wooden orange crates. His sources of inspiration have been memories of people and places he has seen and the National Geographic magazine which he receives each month. Jan Wampler, *All their Own*

Dreaming a garden

With colours, pencils, or clay
make*.... a dream garden*
Start simply with shapes or forms... without naming things
let it grow without knowing what it is going to be like
a dream garden may have any ingredients, however unorthodox they may seem

When it is finished, explore with a partner or group

Later*.... wander outdoors*
find a place that feels connected to your dream garden
Gather materials and make something there
Write *its story*

Make.... a secret place

Sara Levart, something made in a garden
From a workshop session initiated by Chris Crickmay and Alan Boldon.
International arts camp for young people, Luxembourg, 2001.

She found an inconspicuous corner by some steps – a way into the garden from the street. Here she made something that suggested a very small shelter with two people made from clay who seemed to be enjoying some kind of celebration. She said, this place provided protection from a storm that was raging outside.

Alan Boldon, something made in a garden (workshop session as previous page)

He noticed the delicate movements of ants and a snail as they negotiated their way across the rough bark of a tree and drew lines on paper to evoke this quality. Later that day he went back to make something in the same place. Remembering the movement of the ants, he planted little avenues of dried grass stalks in the ground. *The placing of the grass stalks individually allowed me to traverse the compost heap and earth under the walnut tree at the pace of an ant. I followed the contours of the mound and explored the crevices and underside of overhangs, experiencing a different sense of scale and interest in the composition of surface in an ant-like journey.* Alan Boldon

Something hidden

Wherever you are.... look about
Find something that seems shadowy.... hidden
Make something in the vicinity of what you found
or ***move*** *to explore its presence*
What happens?

Miranda Tufnell, *A place for something to happen*, Cumbria, 2000

She took a reel of white cotton and tied a single grass head and drew it towards a step, wrapped the thread around a stone and then went upwards around a branch – a spider's journey, a washing line, on which she later hung roots and feathers... the whole space was guarded by tall goose quills. She called it, 'By the Skin of your Teeth'.

In a landscape

Bill Viola, *I Do Not Know What It Is I Am Like* (1986)
Videotape, colour, stereo sound; 89.00 minutes. Photo: Kira Perov

We realise that we have seen this image before and are constantly seeing it as the diverse forms of nature continue to reveal their deeper common origins. We see the tree against the grey November sky; we see the river and its tributaries from the airplane window; we see the array of blood vessels in the body or the web of the brain's interconnecting nerve cells in a medical film; we sense a thought as it grows and branches out in our minds and lives. Bill Viola, *Reasons for Knocking at an Empty House, Writings 1973-1994.*

landscape G. *Landschaft,* a shaped land

Shaping forces

In the shape of the land we can sense the sculptural processes of its formation – thrown up by fire; shunted into folds by internal pressures; carved, ground and shovelled by ice; shattered by frost and sun; worn smooth by wind; washed away and redeposited by rain and rivers; swept up and dropped by seas... Such formings and deformings happen not once and not singly, but over and over and in combination, each present configuration being simply a moment in a never ending pattern of turbulence. In the aeons of geological time our familiar surroundings may well become many times their opposite... dry hills becoming deep seas, temperate grasslands becoming ice flows. And within the relatively short span of human history, any long standing settlement owes its origin and character to this shaping of the underlying geology and to the disposition of land masses which result. These govern its access to the sea, its proximity to drinking water, its defensibility, its nearness to ways through or across a landscape.

All my early memories are of forms and shapes and textures. Moving through and over the West Riding landscape with my father in his car, the hills were sculptures; the roads defined the form. Barbara Hepworth

The land connects us to a sense of time and space beyond the scale of our own lives. As we look to the horizon, go out into the weather, sense the slow rhythms of growth and decay around us, we feel ourselves entering a larger realm of action. And this is true whether we are surrounded by fields and trees or whether the land for us is partly or wholly urban – as city, suburb, industrial landscape, waste... where growth and decay are more obviously the result of social and economic rather than natural forces.

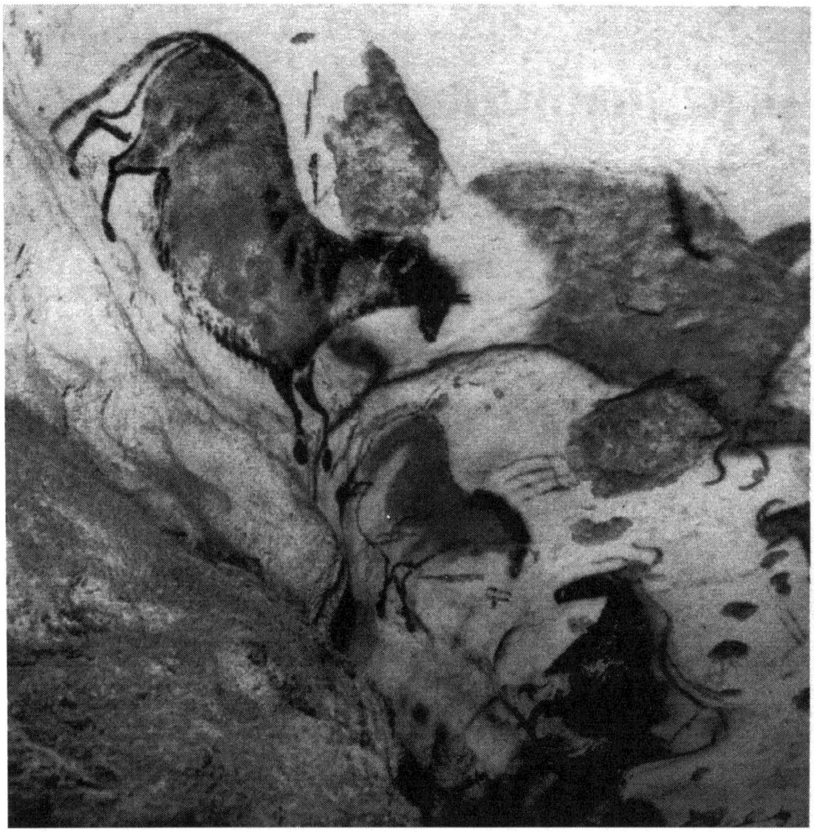

Lascaux cave painting. Photo: Ray Delvert

The Lascaux cave paintings were made around 17,000 years ago using conventions of representation that had already been developing for 13,000 years since the first known cave art. These images (mainly of animals) were created deep inside limestone caves formed over millennia by the tunnelling action of underground rivers. The images were made by the light of lamps made from clay or slivers of stone, burning on a wick of moss or fur, and fuelled with animal fat. One can imagine that as these early men and women moved about in the darkness, the animal images on the uneven surfaces of the cave, weakly illuminated by flickering lamps, would have seemed (as real animals) to appear and then to disappear, or suddenly to move. Colours used were derived from the surrounding rocks and soils: iron oxides for reds and browns, goethite or clay for yellows, manganese dioxide or charcoal for blacks and greys, calcite for white. Pigments were mixed with clay, sand and water to make usable colours. (Sources: B. & D. Delluc, *Discovering Lascaux* and Edward Wachtel, *The First Picture Show*).

I return in my mind's eye to the northern slope of Bald Mountain on which I live. I look around, and pronto. Something happens. I see snow. I jump and curl in the air. Simone Forti

Jake Harvey, *Nocturnal Landscape*, 1980. Forged and welded steel and wood.

This sculpture is one in a series that references 'remembered conscious/ sub-conscious landscape images', rather than referring to 'actual place'. The work echoes a period of working from a studio in the village of Roxburgh in the Scottish Borders. The sculpture embodies an interest at the time in making objects that operated within an elemental landscape language. By combining concept, material and form and sense of movement (here I mean the static, rootedness of earth/ trees, in relation to the ephemeral nature of clouds, rain, murder of crows, etc.) I was trying to make sculptures that possessed (like landscape) qualities of timelessness and amalgams of meaning that stimulated the senses, basic instincts and emotions of the viewer. At this time the Scottish landscape, archaeology, artefacts and symbolism were relevant touchstones and I worked predominantly with earth materials such as stone, clay and forged metal. In a formal sense I used space/negative form as a constructive element in the sculpture. The juxtaposition of solid and negative shapes creating rhythms and different senses of weight and movement over the panorama. Agricultural field patterns, drumlin hill forms, clouds, wee woods, tree forms, river etched landscape, weather, time of year etc. – all fused into the piece. The title 'Nocturnal Landscape' relates to the experience of landscape at night when forms become quite flattened and simplified – like silhouettes. When I was a boy I had the fortunate experience of growing up in the village of Yetholm in the Borders, and often went out poaching salmon and pheasants on moonlit nights. This conscious/sub-conscious episode of my life also had some impact on the work's development.
Jake Harvey

In a landscape

Sense what is around you.... in every direction.... behind.... above.... below

What is close to?....What is far away?

What is the furthest you can see/ sense?

Breathe.... listen.... to close.... and distant.... sounds

Sense the movements.... of weather.... land.... sky.... light

What calls to you.... in this landscape?

Feel your connection with it

***Move** to explore its qualities*

***Make** something in response*

Helen Poynor in collaboration with Annie Pfingst, *Salt and Ash*, Sydney, 1994

My approach is based on forming a relationship with the land and the sites in which I am working, endeavouring to find, through movement, stillness and voice, physical responses to the challenges presented by different terrains and conditions; moving on the hills and in valleys, on cliffs, moors and mountains and in ancient sites; responding to rock, earth and ocean in wind, rain and sun; looking, listening, sitting, walking, lying, crawling, running, waiting, singing, creating; seeking to meet the physical reality of the land with the physicality of my body, in a mutual exchange. Each element of the land elicits different qualities of movement; each location has its own atmosphere, which may change in different weathers or at different times of day. I seek out ways of entering, places of stillness, pathways of movement, exploring the relationship between the form, scale and direction of the place and of my body in movement. Helen Poynor

Traces... what has gone?... what is left behind?

In ancient field patterns and derelict farms, in a track now going nowhere, in long abandoned workings of old mines, the interaction of human presence and natural events is recorded in the landscape. Some of these traces are from small localised events – a tree is blown down in a storm and sawn up, a stream floods and blocks a path, a piece of land is sold to a new owner. Other marks in the landscape record major shifts of fortune – a region is bankrupted by a change in the market, a river runs dry because of a new dam many miles away upstream. In a long deserted spot, we sense the presences of people and past events that still linger there.

At the end of the wide way, to one side of it, in tall grass, were flat shallow boxes, painted grey, set down in two rows. I was told later that they were or had been beehives. I was never told who it was who had kept the bees...... Abandoned now, unexplained, the grey boxes that were worth no one's while to take away were a little mysterious in the unfenced openness. V.S. Naipaul, *The Enigma of Arrival.*

Making visible

Go to a place which has fallen into disuse
old quarry.... empty building.... abandoned railway

Spend time there
discovering what traces remain

Choose one that attracts your interest
Find ways of strengthening its presence
using materials that are to hand

Add to.... change.... remove from.... what is there
to make this trace more visible

Cristina Garcia Rodero, *El Enharinao*, Laza, photograph,1985.

River's edge

Wherever you are

Make.... 'a place by the river'

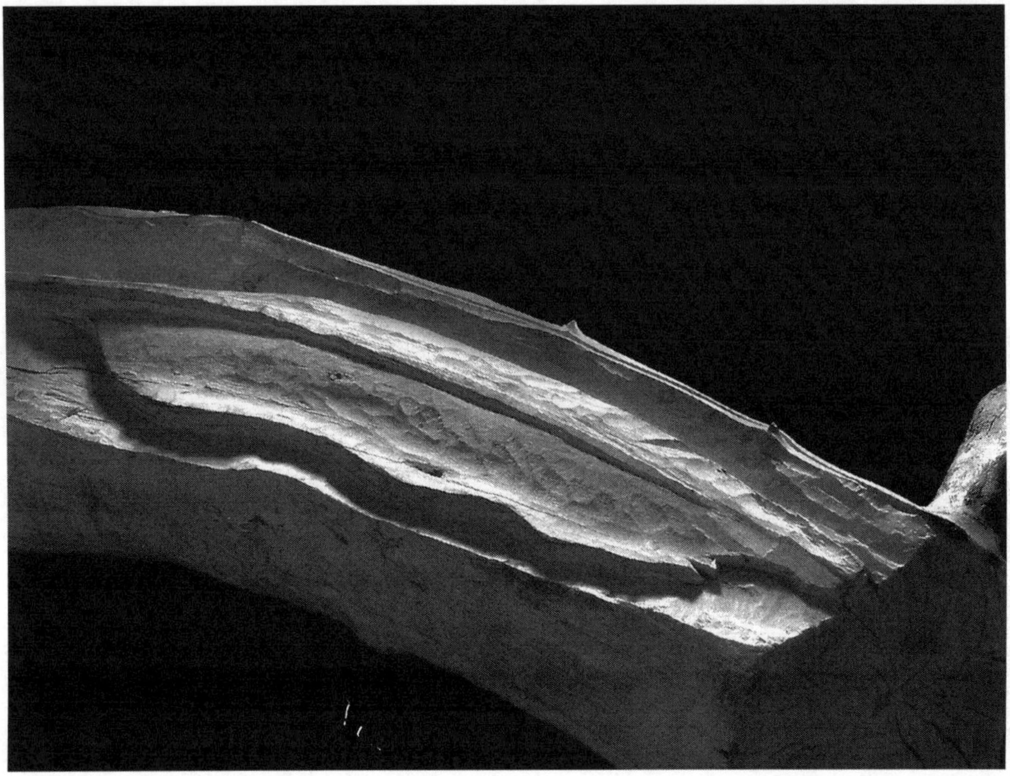

Chris Crickmay, *Seagull's feather in a log,* 1992. Wood carving painted white. Photo: Dan Rack

The river Dart connects Dartmoor to the sea and runs through the town where I live. I decided to visit the mouth and the sources of the Dart (there are two), and to make things based on what I found in each of these places. At the mouth I came across a seagull's feather; at one source a fighter plane flew over at low level; at the other I found rounded hollows formed by bubbling springs.

Sound Mapping the Danube from the Schwartzwald to the Black Sea, for a sound installation blending water sounds and the voices of people living on and from the river, in many dialects - to be completed in 2005. Notes from a work journal. **Annea Lockwood**, 1/12/2002

Germany: April – May 2002
4/29 Brigachquelle (a source) 8:20 am: nice discovery, can record simultaneously at the surface and underwater with hydrophone half in, half out, sometimes

5/1 Fridingen 2:35 pm: air mic – sheep all over the place right down by the river – a whole mob being shorn and protesting to heaven – whole town watching – will make nice break in water continuity.

5/8 Dillingen: dreamed that I dropped my little Denon (DAT recorder) and it vanished forever into the Danube; so insistent that the dream woke me up – very careful all day and need to continue to be - no cut-off date for premonitions.

5/15 Regensburg 6.30 am: underwater - hydrophone drifting in the main current, caught in little vortices – clearly hearing the flow, pause, change in direction and pressure of the water's flowing. A low bumping sound like wind on an air mic, when a gust of water hit the hydrophone; hard to tell through headphones whether this will give good low tones, or need to be filtered out.

Austria-Slovakia-Hungary: October 2002
10/10 Grein, Austria: Michael Froschl, furniture maker/boater: "When the floods came in August and flooded all the roads so no cars could come through, no trains, no ships, then you could hear the river itself" (normally masked) "everywhere, only that."

10/13 Durnstein, Austria 5:45 pm: air mic – road traffic inaudible for once; plenty of river traffic, 'Hron' (a barge), a rowing crew, nice standing waves at shore, very fast current, some wind. Next morning – no wind so returned but it's all changed, no standing waves, and the site's underwater though no rain here overnight. So many interacting variables. Seize the moment. Retakes aren't possible with this river – I like that.

10/26 Domos, Hungary 10:05 am: – camping site strewn with boulders from flooding – fierce waves where fast stream empties into Danube (Duna) and I could get right up to them. Pure river! Recorded three sites descending the stream, then these waves.

10/27 Szentendre, Hungary 6:52 am. Under a bridge on feeder stream, the Bukos patak – early am. Good resonance, joyous dog, dry leaves. Furthest downstream this year. 1650 kilometers to go. Thinking like a river – possible?

Photo: Ruth Anderson – near Stopfenreuth, Austria

Going to town

One man's city is another man's wilderness (bewilderment). Lucy Lippard

Cristina Garcia Rodero, *El Enharinao,* Laza, photograph1985.

Becoming... someone... else

We are drawn to cities as places of adventure, of opportunity, not knowing who or what we may meet – anything seems possible. In the city we can come out of ourselves, break our routines, be anonymous, get lost. And as we look at faces, hear voices, we find ourselves surrounded by extremes of otherness – people quite unlike ourselves, with unfamiliar features, dress habits, languages, ways of being. These extremes of difference shake up our own sense of how things are.

Make:

a place that draws a crowd

a meeting of strangers

something that evokes the sounds of a city

a place of accidents.... of coincidences

something that is lost

a place after dark.... a night spot

***Make** something that calls other things to it, into its orbit.... a magnet*

Holding together... breaking apart

No one can fly low over a city, coming into its airport, without being astonished at the sheer breadth and multiplicity of it – all that effort and ingenuity!... the vast mass of it, growing piece by small piece; the huge amount of organisation it takes (only evident in times of disaster) to provide enough: bread... water... fresh vegetables... and to constantly move its inhabitants and workers in... and then... out again. Even in normal times there is often a sense that a city exists right on the edge of chaos and destruction, that all these arrangements might suddenly collapse – perhaps this is what gives it its life and energy.

On the brink

Make something.... that is almost out of control.... only just holding together

As a city empties and fills... shifts gear between day and night... sweats and shivers in different seasons... our perceptions of it are also transformed. Its changing lights, scents, sounds, impinge variously upon us – we savour or recoil from them. We see its elements mutate and move under our gaze, one thing evoking another: a wet pavement blooms in brilliant reflected colour, orange and red like a cactus flower; a train beats its way down the track, an earth tremor beneath our feet, a hammering in our brains...

George Wyllie, *The Paper Boat*, Tower Bridge, London, 1989.

In Scotland the heady days of big ship building are gone. Clyde shipbuilders now wield scissors, wear trainers, and have cut out smoking at work. They are building 'paper boats'. George Wyllie.

Distanced/ close up

As we enter the city we encounter a mix of official and unofficial worlds. On the one hand there is the postcard world, of monuments and historic sights, the city's calender of festivals and public occasions – all that you might find in a guide book or directory. This official city also includes the city's running narrative of events and opinions, as reported in the media. These are views, as it were, from a distance. At another level are you and I. This is the view from close at hand – the city of conversations, chance meetings, of pedestrian journeys, of glances, of frightening moments, of passionate encounters.

In Venice, because of the lack of motorised traffic,
what one hears is the buzz of conversation

THIS STORY IS TOLD

A new and expensive Mercedes is parked outside a theatre where the rich owner is enjoying a play. A poor street kid walks up to the car and with close concentration begins to drag a coin along its side making a long, deep scar in the paintwork. At this point the owner leaves the theatre.

'You little son-of-a-whore', he shouts, 'what the fuck do you think you're doing!?'

The kid pulls himself up, looks the man in the face and replies: 'What I do with my own money, senor, is my own business.'

Peter D. Osborne, *Milton Friedman's Smile: Travel Culture and the Poetics of a City.*

Gift to a city

Choose.... an outdoor space where you can work
Make something there....to give that place.... something it seems.... to lack

Folake Shoga, *Altar for Elegba* , at Lawrence Hill roundabout, Bristol, 1999
Part of an art work that marked significant points in the Bristol landscape according to Yoruba cosmological ideas.

In Central Park, Manhatten, a group of artists negotiated to paint
all gardeners' implements gold, in celebration of their work for the city

Places beyond... between

Magritte, *Carte Blanche,* Le blanc-seing,1965.
Oil, 81 x 65 cms

I did not go in, but stood there on the margin between the two worlds,
my familiar flat and these rooms which had been quietly waiting there all this time....
Doris Lessing, *The Memoirs of a Survivor.*

Make:

a place at the end of the world
a place without a name
a place of unknown elements
a place where paths cross
a place that is just below the surface

a place that is about to appear

10. Heart

heart Hebrew *leba* centre of courage, intelligence, feeling –
the breast, the mind, pith, marrow, centre, or best part of anything.

Vivian Russel, *Fountain of the Organ,* Villa D'Este, Rome. photograph.

...........Throw that emptiness
out of your arms and into the air that we breathe:
does it widen the sky for the birds - add zest to their flight?
Yes, *you* were needed. Every springtime needed you.
Even stars relied on your witnessing presence
when a gathering wave surged from the past - or when
some violin utterly offered itself
as you passed by a half-opened window. All this was your mission.

Rilke, *The First Elegy.*

The amazing heart

The perpetual motion of the blood in a circle is brought about by the beat of the heart. Harvey, 1616.

The heart is as the sun within the body. As every living thing on the earth depends on the light and heat of the sun, so every cell of our bodies depends on the immense living energy of the heart. The heart forms a pulsating centre to the vast river systems of our lifeblood, its four chambers a meeting place through which two spiralling streams of blood continually move. The flying dynamic of the heart propels the blood through 60,000 miles of blood vessel and capillary – a vascular network that laid end to end could encircle the earth twice over. The electro-magnetic field of the heart is 5,000 times greater than that of the brain – a field that can be measured anywhere within the body and registered at least 2 feet away from it. The heart transports 100 gallons of blood per hour, beating 100,000 times a day or 40 million times a year. It is the beat of the heart that synchronises and orchestrates the vibrational impulses of the 75 billion cells that form our bodies. Despite its great power, the heart is small – you could hold it within your hand.

Within the word 'heart':
hear tear earth eat ear art
(drawn from: Hugh Milne)

Heart of the matter

We depend on the untiring muscle of the heart, its beat, like the beat of a drum, sustains every moment of our lives. Death is registered in the silence and stilling of the heart. As we feel its pulse we can sense the vitality of life within us and become aware of the deep currents of our emotion and feeling. The heart is the centre of our circulatory system constantly receiving and sending out our life blood to the cells of the body. It is not simply a mechanical pump, its tissues register and respond to all that is taking place within our circulatory system. Everything that happens to us, all that we feel, affects its rhythm and pace; our hearts 'leap', 'fall', 'miss a beat','swell', 'soften' or 'harden', and sometimes even 'break'. The impulse and vitality of the heart expands us into the world, calling us towards what really matters for us. In the heart we feel the world entering and changing us. We cannot reason our way towards happiness, or a sense of meaning or value; rather we may sense it in the instinctual and intuitive response of the heart. The heart is our compass, showing us the ways in which our lives may be nourished and renewed.

The Skeleton Woman

While lying beside him, she reached inside the sleeping man and took out his heart, the mighty drum. She sat up and banged on both sides of it: Bom, Bomm!.... Bom, Bomm!.... As she drummed, she began to sing out "Flesh, flesh, flesh! Flesh, flesh, flesh!" And the more she sang, the more her body filled out with flesh. Clarissa Pinkola Estes, *Women Who Run With the Wolves.*

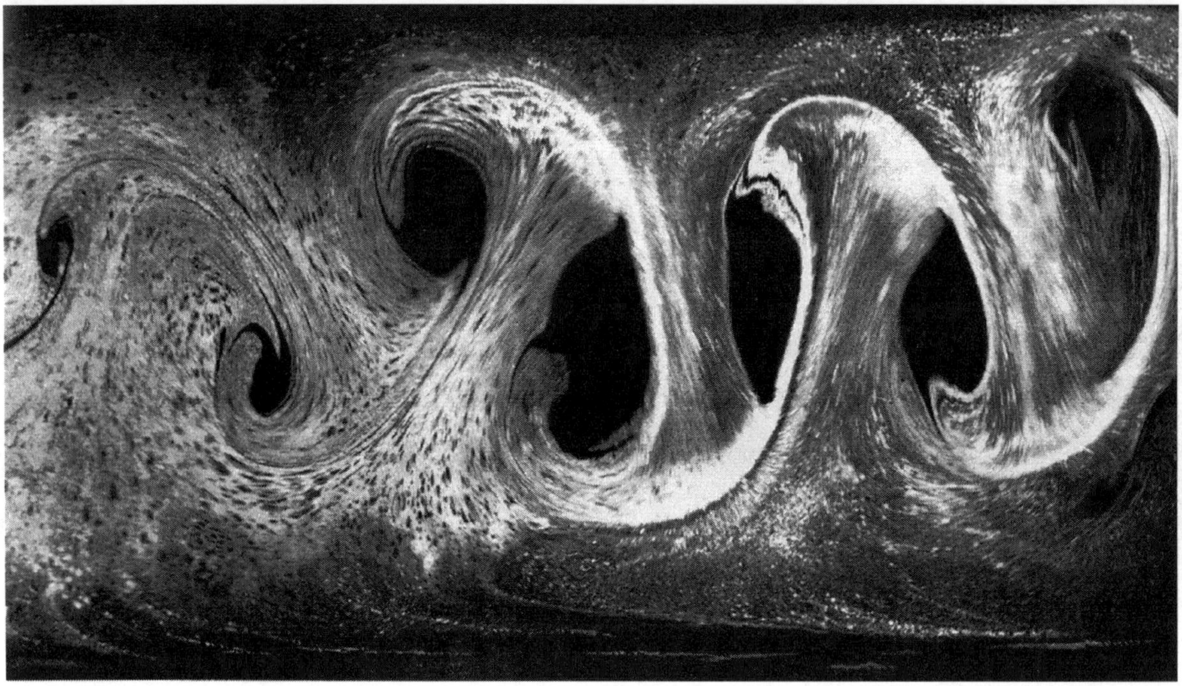

Vortices and their structure

Love set you going like a great fat clock. Sylvia Plath, *Ariel.*

From the core to the periphery... between heart, lungs and the rest of the body

The heart forms the dynamic centre to our circulatory system, constantly controlling and adapting the pressure and volume of blood moving through us. Leonardo da Vinci first noted the fluid dynamics of blood, "whirling around in diverse patterns". The spiralling fibres of the heart itself seem to form through a consolidation of two streams of blood whose swirling vortices open and close the valves or gates of the heart's four chambers. Blood passes through the heart twice. The returning blood enters the right atrium (hallway), from which it is passed into the right ventricle which in turn sends blood to the lungs. Here it picks up oxygen and returns to the left atrium. The left atrium passes blood to the powerful left ventricle which sends it throughout the whole body. Our entire blood supply (8 pints) washes through the heart and lungs each minute – the circulatory system hums from the pressure of this surging blood.

Untiring heart

The heart must not tire – blood supply to the heart itself (via the coronary arteries) is immense, because of its constant need for oxygen and glucose and to flush away wastes that might cause fatigue or cramps. The impulse of the left and most powerful ventricle of the heart could pump the blood 6 ft. into the air. The impulse of the right ventricle (which sends blood into the lungs for re- oxygenation), pumps blood the equivalent of 1 ft. in the air. "The pump work done by the heart is equivalent to lifting a 1kg weight to about twice the height of Mount Everest each day" (Blakemore & Jennett, *Oxford Companion to the Body*)

Find the heart

Warm up.... to get your blood moving.... expand the heart beat.

Then – find a place to lie down comfortably.

Ask a partner to lay their head on your chest and put their ear to your heart.

Check that both of you can sense its beat.

Feel the pulse and rhythm of the heart... movement and surge of blood throughout the body.

When you feel ready.... ask your partner to move away.

Then – **on your own:**

Breathe into.... the heart.... listen
Breathe out.... from the heart.... expand
Listen as sensations or images.... rise.... and fall away through the body
calling of whales... beating of hooves... surging of waves... of wind... cry of a child

Let your face soften
let the weight of.... brain/ of skin/ organ/ bone.... spread out and rest.... on the beat and tides of the heart
Listen.... feel how the whole body receives.... reflects.... the heart's pulse

Sense the delicate 'small circulation'.... between heart and lungs
Sense the colour.... vitality.... generosity.... of the blood's 'great circulation'
streaming out from the heart.... to the furthest edges of the body
nourishing.... sustaining.... carrying away.... what is not needed

And the slow returning movement back to the heart.... gently receiving inwards

Sense the changes.... between systole and diastole.... expansion.... contraction
Sense.... cadences... tones... rhythms...... of the heart's voice
Sense the interchange.... between stillness and movement

Let the beat of the heart fill through the body
Let the body listen.... and turn towards the heart.... as the earth turns towards the sun

Sense.... the impulse arising from deep within, as a seed growing in the darkness
spreading out.... through the body from the heart
Follow.... as sensations rise into gestures.... movements

Let the movement of the heart.... move the body

Where do you go?.... what happens?.... who do you meet?.... what do you become?

Afterwards: ***write****.... and share with your partner*

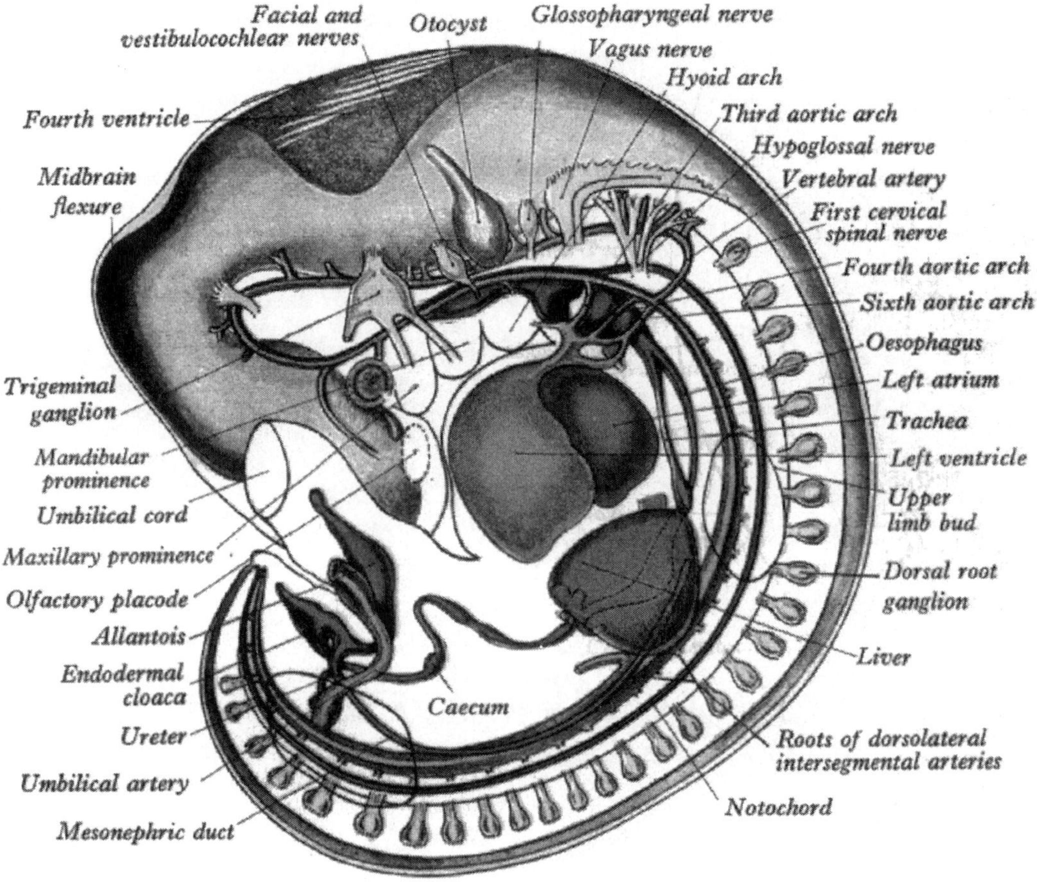

A human embryo of 7mm greatest length, in the fifth week

A Growing Heart

In the developing embryo, the heart is the first major organ to mature and function.
The heart begins to form directly beneath the fastest growing area of the embryo – the head/ brain.
A tube shaped primordial heart is formed at the beginning of the third week and by the end of that week blood is circulating through the early heart which is already pulsating.

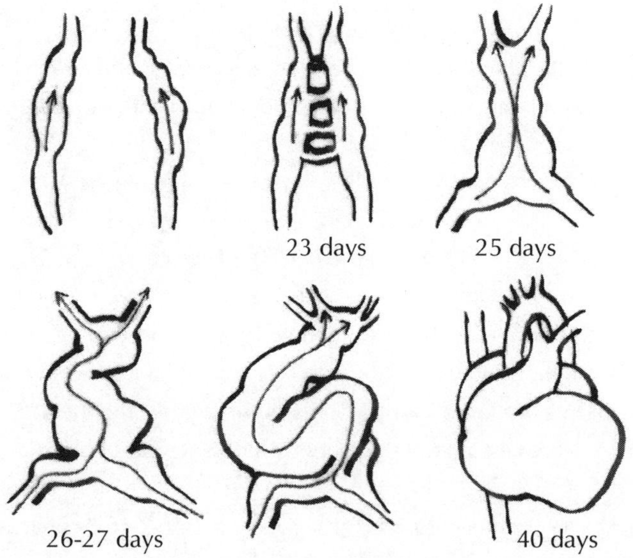

Development of the heart (drawings derived from H.R.Muinos)

The heart begins to form from two minute primitive blood vessels growing alongside each other.
These develop links which draw the two vessels together, fusing to form a single chamber surrounded by a sheath of muscle, which later becomes the unique, untiring muscle of the heart.
The spiralling movement of blood travelling through causes this single chamber to bulge and twist... gradually creating a second chamber.
For the first five weeks the 'heart' is the centre of the embryo's 'body' and is huge in proportion to the rest of it – participating in a flow of blood and nutrients to the embryo which in these early days is doubling its weight every four hours.

the meeting of paths

A constant flow

At first the primitive heart simply accommodates the flow of blood, but within 28 days it begins to propel it.
30 days after fertilisation there is a blood transporting system in the baby-to-be, carrying oxygen and nutrients to the growing embryo.
By the 6th-7th week (42 days) the valves or 'gates' of the heart mature.
These prevent a back flow of blood from ventricle to atrium.
Despite their membraneous transparency, they are strong, parachute-like structures, opening and closing between 4 – 5 thousand times per hour (this is the beat of the heart).

gateways opening.... closing

By 55 days, the heart of the one inch foetus has four chambers,
working as twin side-by-side pumps and creating a one-way flow of blood.
Because the lungs do not function until birth, the foetus's blood is oxygenated by the placenta
and travels from there to the right atrium.
Some blood travels to the lungs to bring them oxygen and nutrients for their growth.
The rest is shunted around the foetus's rapidly developing body.

This one-way flow of blood is essential in ensuring the delivery of oxygenated blood
to all parts of the foetus.
If the valves separating the chambers fail to develop, oxygenated and de-oxygenated blood mix,
thereby starving the developing body of nutrients and oxygen.

moment by moment the need for nourishment

The face and the heart

As the primitive head grows and expands, it curves more deeply around the beating heart.
The folds of the embryo, as it curves inwards around the heart,
become the structures of the face – jaw, hyoid and cricoid bone.
Thus our face is formed pressed up against the heart,
the face an 'interface' between heart and brain.

Muscle cells cannot contract until their internal architecture has been fully stretched and organised.
As the embryo grows, it curves around the heart, thereby stretching the muscle cells of the
back wall of its body, which in contracting, then lift the head upwards and away from the heart.
This in turn stimulates growth and stretch in the muscle cells
of the front wall of the body, which contract.
These movements of growth, towards and away from the heart, are part of a larger rhythm
of opening and closing in the developing embryo – a rhythm echoed by the systole/ diastole of
the heart itself. As the head begins to lift away from the heart, the embryo is now called a foetus.

growing towards and away from the heart

At the first breath, as the lungs begin to function, the foramen ovale
(the opening between left and right upper chambers of the heart), closes - the cord is cut
and the infant now begins to live as a separate and independent being.

My birthday began with the water –
Birds and the birds of the winged trees flying my name.
Dylan Thomas, *Poem in October.*

Beginnings

Imagine yourself as small.... round.... a single cell
Rest within that roundness.... containment
Sense the beat of your heart
Gradually.... notice what touches you.... from outside
drawing you out.... into movement

Your heart... your face

Be still.... listen to the beat of the heart
Let.... face/ throat/ jaw.... soften
Sense the expression of the face.... and what is behind the face
Let the face feel/ remember.... the beat and impulse of the heart
Let face and heart.... listen to each other
Imagine a conversation

***move** to explore.... a duet between face and heart*
***make** and **write** in the wake of moving*
Reflect on what has emerged

Heartland

Go for a walk.... look about you
sense.... notice the qualities of 'heart'.... in whatever you see
Not knowing what you will make.... gather materials
and let them form.... a heart

What connections does it gather around itself?
What flows out from this 'heart'?.... What flows inwards to it.... received?
Where do you choose to place it?
Listen to it.... what does it need?.... what does it speak of?

Share with a partner

Form a face

Remember.... the face of someone you love (or loved).... remember details
Gather materials.... and gradually let them form.... a face
Imagine its voice.... listen to it

***Write**.... then share with a partner*

The brain is literally tethered to the heart through the arteries and veins that nourish and cleanse its tissues, a vital connection that remains throughout life. The mature brain needs 25% of the body's oxygen to sustain its functioning. And after first nourishing itself, through the coronary artery, the heart sends blood to the brain. The pericardium of the heart blends with the diaphragm. Brain, heart, and diaphragm are thus linked in a rhythm of expansion and contraction, each moves and is moved by the other. The transition from dilation to contraction is rhythmical.

The heart receives and expands, before it contracts. The beat of the heart is regulated by the heart's own pacemaker, which synchronises the contraction of the heart muscle. Each contraction (systole), is followed by an expansion or resting phase (diastole). In resting the smaller upper chambers of the heart fill with returning blood. A beat starts as the atria contract, forcing blood downwards to the ventricles. The contraction continues in the ventricles, sending blood to the lungs for oxygenation and out through the body.

Circulation... nourishing life

circulation L. circare, to go around, to explore **circus**, a ring

The whole function and form of the heart is a reflection of the streaming processes of water, where in its movements of expansion and contraction it is as though separate spaces were continually being formed .... The fibres of the heart are a physical echo of the creative movements by which it was begotten. In spiralling paths they swing down to its apex and then rise again to its base. They make the same movements and emphasise the revolving vertical streaming of the fluids within the heart. Theodor Schwenk, *Sensitive Chaos.*

Rosemary Lee, *The Banquet Dances.* Photo: Pau Ros

The Banquet Dances were part of Take Me to the River, a performance event that took the audience by boat down the Thames, stopping to see three performances on the way. The Banquet Dances were made for the Painted Hall, in the Royal Naval College Greenwich. Its grandiose and rather vacuous atmosphere had me longing to fill it with throngs of people, to bring it to life on an immediate and human scale. 50 performers of varied ages, children and young adults, mature and senior performers took part in the event, some never having performed before and others with more experience. Rosemary Lee. (Incorporated into the performance was a lecture on the themes of: river, flow, circulation, transition, and nurturing, given by Dr Tony Burch)

***Make** a procession.... a celebration*
With a partner, explore what is happening there

The need for movement and exchange

Expect poison from standing water. William Blake, *Proverbs from Hell*

All living things depend on the exchange and movement of nutrients and waste throughout their system. Small, single-celled organisms do not need a circulatory system – they breathe and absorb food directly through the cell wall. But larger creatures depend on a circulatory system to transport nutrients throughout their bodies. The vital functioning of lungs, liver and kidneys, the exchange of nutrients and waste in the blood and tissue fluid, all critically depend on the energy and pressure within the circulatory system. Muscle tone, and secretion of glands, are also affected by the rhythms and vitality of the heart.

The electric signal of the heart begins in the heart's own pace maker which co-ordinates the cellular orchestra of the heart. The heart contracts from its pointed base upwards – a wave of excitation that passes from cell to cell, spreads through the muscle of the heart, and impels a varying flow of around 2 gallons of blood per minute (120 gallons an hour) throughout the body. As the heart propels the blood through the body tissues, nutrients and oxygen move from the blood into the interstitial fluid and then into the cells. At the same time the blood takes up wastes, carbon dioxide and heat. Blood needs to move - if blood flow to some part of the body stops, even for a few minutes, that region suffers serious damage. Blood absorbs oxygen from the lungs and nutrients from the intestines and carries hormones from the many endocrine glands of the body. These stimulate, accelerate and regulate the chemical processes of the body – our blood is thus a carrier of signals and messages. Without this movement, and the flow and exchange of nutrients and waste, our tissues become either water logged, or starved of essential nutrients. Backing up of any of these fluids creates both pressure and stagnation.

Map the circulation

Choose colours.... and a large sheet of paper
'Map' the movement and landscape of the heart

Find ways to evoke its rhythm.... flow.... expansions.... contractions
Imagine the different colours of its chambers.... of its changing rhythm
crimson... violet... ochre... amber... scarlet... indigo... gold... silver

Sense...... shadows... whirlpools... blockages... darkness
Follow.... whatever colours draw you
What comes to form?

Explore this map with a partner
***Move** to find the qualities of this heart*
As the partner.... move in response
***Write** then reflect together on what emerged*

Pomegranates sprang from the blood of the murdered Dionysus,
anemones from the blood of Adonis, and violets from the blood of Attis.

Blood vessels in the Liver
from: Janos Vajda, *Atlas Anatomiae,* vol. 2

Changing states

Blood, lymph, cerebrospinal, synovial, cellular and intercellular fluids, are all essentially one fluid, that changes properties and characteristics as it passes through membranes, flows through different channels and interacts with different substances. The movement of these fluids within the body are all affected by the strength or weakness of the heart.

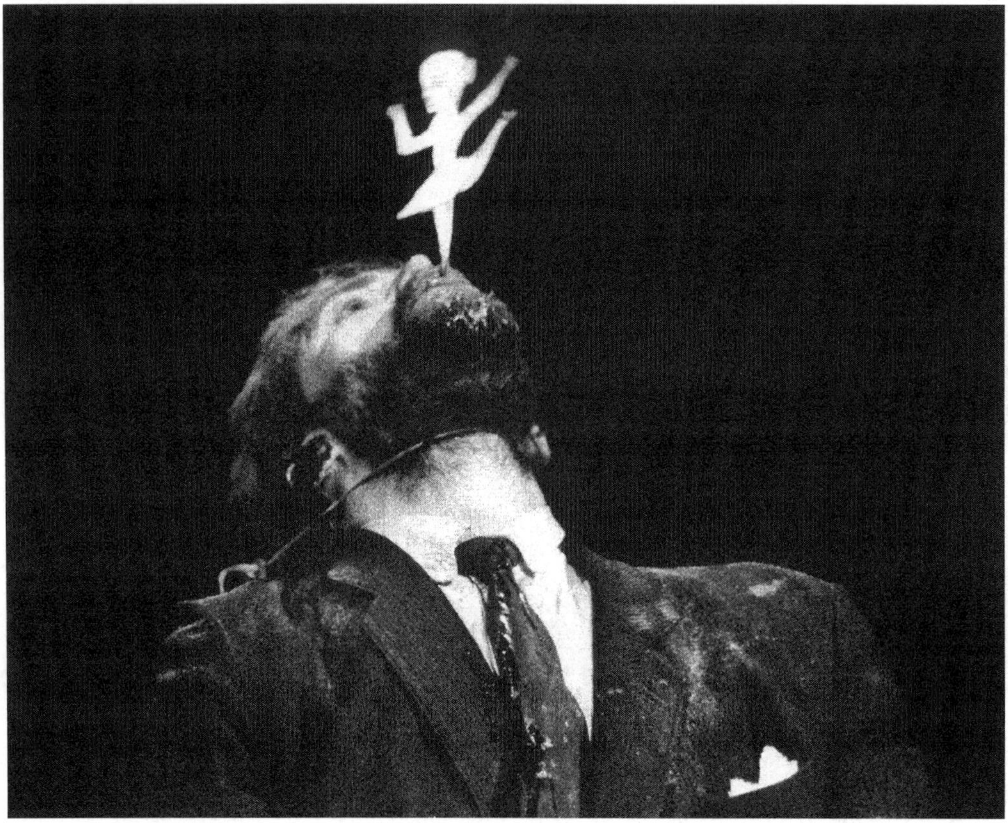

AKHE Theatre. *Pookh i Prakh* (Fluff and Feathers), created by Maxim Isaev, Pavel Semchenko and Jana Toumina, AKHE Theatre, St Petersburg. Performed Edinburgh, 2001. Photo: © Ken Reynolds

Our work is hard and cynical and we do have trouble taking anything seriously. But it is cynicism of the mind only. The Heart stays pure. Otherwise we wouldn't be making theatre. Jana Tumina

communicate OF. *communier,* to talk with,
mutable L. *mutabilis,* changeable

A meeting place

The chambers of the heart form a meeting place for all that comes from the world. What exists outside us – the multiplicity of things, people, and events - is gathered inwards and felt within our hearts. As the circulation of the blood unites every part of our bodies and communicates with every cell, so what we feel for expands our circulation outwards to our surroundings. As the heart itself belongs within the vast branching network of artery, vein and capillary of the body, so, who we are is not separate from all that we love and that sustains life in us.

Message

In making or moving....
send a message from the heart

Heart as endocrine organ

Recent findings in neurocardiology suggest the heart plays a crucial role in many aspects of our overall consciousness and is constantly in touch with the brain in order to organise the energy of the body. Heart cells are full of neurohormones that communicate back and forth with the brain, immune system, and every major organ of the body. As the right atria contracts, the heart produces its own hormone or peptide (ANF) which communicates directly with parts of the brain. (Drawn from Paul Pearsall, *The Heart's Code.*)

A 'family tree' (blood-line)

Remember the presence of important people in your life
parents.... ancestors.... children.... friends and companions
remember moments.... details of their lives

Whisper to yourself words or phrases they evoke
invite them into you.... around you
Listen and move from what you feel

Go out and wander to collect elements that in some way connect to these people and events
allow surprises in what you gather
accept disparate.... unlikely.... even hostile.... ingredients

Take time to explore.... how they come together
to make a 'map' of relationships, a 'family tree'

View with a partner

The purpose of poetry is to remind us
how difficult it is to remain just one person,
for our house is open, there are no keys in the doors,
and invisible guests come in and out at will.
Milosz, *Ars Poetica.*

Horse and Bamboo Theatre, *Company of Angels, The Story of Charlotte Salomon*, 2002.

Charlotte Salomon was a German Jewish woman, a painter, born in Berlin in 1917. 26 years later she was put to death in Auschwitz/ Birkenau concentration camp. In the last year of her life, while in exile in the South of France, she produced an amazing series of gouache paintings – a personal account of her life, yet reflecting the gruesome political background of the time. Drawing upon this colourful visual material, and using various theatrical devices –masks, puppets, animated furniture, mime, movement, projection, and music – the company recreated the story of Charlotte and her imaginative world. Images in the piece appeared at many different scales. In the picture, masked human actors, puppets, a landscape in a suitcase and a miniature hot air balloon, coexist in the same space.

Rhythm

For the fact is, that this seeming chaos which is in us is a rich, rolling, swelling, dying, lilting, singing, laughing, shouting, crying, sleeping order. If we we will only let this order guide our acts of building, the buildings that we make, the towns we help to make, will be the forests, the meadows of the human heart.
Christopher Alexander, *The Timeless Way of Building.*

A changing tune – heart rhythm... world rhythms

The beat of the heart creates rhythm within the body – a cyclical rhythm of expansion and contraction, of streaming outwards from the core, and returning inwards from the periphery – a rhythm or beat which links us to the flow and movement of all life. The rhythmic cycles of the earth - of night and day, of seasons, of growth and decay, of birth and death – echo in the systolic/diastolic beat of the heart.

Natural rhythms are never entirely regular; the rhythms that arise in the heart are as the rhythms and fluctuations of seasons, or as a piece of music that shifts in key, pace and tone. The cells of the heart constantly listen, respond, and beat out through the blood, a rhythm and tone that changes swiftly in response to the body's need. Our health (wholeness), depends on an energetic and responsive flow between all the parts of ourselves. If we lose a sense of the natural and fluctuating rhythms of circulation, of life, we create conditions for illness (disconnection), within us. And if the heart's energy is seriously disturbed, its cells lose their vital connection to each other and are caught in a quivering, lethal fibrillation – a heart attack.

heart as conductor

The atoms and molecules that form us are shaped, held together, by flows of energy.
The molecules within each cell vibrate every thousandth of a second, each molecule resonating with its own unique pitch within the overall chemistries of the body.
It is the energy and beat of the heart that co-ordinates this vast cellular chorus.
(Drawn from: Paul Pearsall, *The Heart's Code*)

cell L. *cella* small room

Heart attack

Heart attack relates to a world of panic, a world that has lost rhythm, pace and tone – a world of anxiety. The acute pain of angina is named from the Latin, *angere,* to choke or distress. In Greek, the word for anxiety is *mermeros,* meaning the division of an entity into smaller and smaller parts, a fragmentation of the whole. Heart attack expresses a dismembered world where the rhythm of the heart is disturbed and the connections between one thing and another is broken, shattered. When we have too much to pay attention to and feel driven by disconnected demands, we lose our capacity to adapt. Thus we lose a sense of the rhythm and connection by which we are able to absorb and move through the events of our lives. "Half of acute admissions to hospital for heart failure were precipitated by gross emotional upset"(Nixon and King)

pulse relates to **impulse, pulsate** L. *pulsare* to throb, beat
L. *pellere* (pp. *pulsus*) to drive
L. *impellare* to urge on
compel... expel... dispel... pelt
appeal L. *appelare* to call upon, incline towards
peal a chime of bells

Finding connections... the responsiveness of the heart

The unique quality of heart cells is their capacity to beat spontaneously and to improvise and beat out new rhythms in response to events and the body's need. (Even when isolated from the body, heart cells beat 35-40 times a minute). Heart cells are also unique in their tendency to synchronise rhythm with the heart cells of another – our hearts literally beat together with those with whom we feel in sympathy.

dawn chorus
a gathering of friends

A shared pulse... moving together and apart

Sense.... or imagine the beat of your heart.... feel it through your whole body
let it take you on a walk.... feel its pulse as you move
Join up with a partner.... walk or run together.... fall into step
find a shared rhythm.... unison

sense as the rhythm between you needs to change
counter.... syncopate.... decorate
Allow surprises.... separations.... re-connections
discovering.... a looser.... more complex rhythm and connection with each other

Afterwards: Find ways to ***make****.... a 'score'.... an image of your shared path*

Between work and rest

All muscles of the body alternately contract and relax. In a twenty four hour cycle, on average, the heart muscle works for an equivalent of 9 hours and rests for 15, a rhythm of work and rest that enables it to keep going throughout a lifetime. As with other muscles of the body, if the heart muscle cannot relax, its chronic constriction will cause permanent damage to the tissues of the heart. (Stretching, breathing, and relaxation help the arteries to open to their full extent).

What is your passion?

Ernest Bloch, *Lady with Mushrooms*, 1912. Photograph.

What heartens you?

Spend time with a partner

Speak of what brings joy to your life.... delights.... heartens

lightens.... your heart

(derived from Patch Adams)

Treasure

Choose something you treasure
talk about it with a partner
What does it.... call up/ speak of?

Slowly.... gather materials.... and make something for it
a gift.... a 'friend'.... an event

***Move** to discover more of how it speaks to you*
***Write**, then share with a partner*

Taken to heart

The Greek word for perception *aesthesis* means a taking in, a taking to heart, from which our word *aesthetic* is drawn. What we feel as beautiful, thus comes from a 'seeing' with heart. Conversely, *anaesthetic* means dulled, numbed and without feeling.

The word 'passion' belongs with the heart. What we love and feel for expands the flow of life through us. From the heart comes our capacity to open and live more generously with all that is around us. This is the energy of the heart, an energy that brings the world to life for us – the means by which we imagine and empathise with what is other than ourselves. Our 'com-passion' enables us to feel-with and for another. It is the vitality and imagination of the heart that meets the world with love, wonder and curiosity – our lives are landscapes formed by friendships, loves and losses. A favourite piece of music, favourite places, people, events, objects... what we enjoy doing – all these are our lifeblood, they 'hearten' us, and our lives grow and change as we allow them in. The smile of a friend or stranger, something shared, lights up our entire day, whereas the unresponsiveness of a 'cold' heart chills, repels, extinguishes us. *'Shitan',* the Hebrew the word for devil means 'no response'... he who cannot respond, cannot empathise, cannot love.

Henri Douanier Rousseau, *The Sleeping Gypsy*, 1897

What is passive, immobile, asleep in the heart creates a desert...... [In mythology] *there is a longstanding association of desert and lion...... the lion's cubs are still-born. They must be awakened into life by a roar....* [So also in our lives] *the heart,* [what we love], *must be provoked, called forth...... Beauty must be raged or outraged into life.* Drawn from: James Hillman, *The Thought of the Heart.*

Back to life
Take something that seems 'dead'
make a heart for it
Find.... what brings it to life
Move.... write*.... reflect*

Valentine L. *valente* from the verb *valere* to be strong

Wild heart

Gallup.... race.... shout.... roar
shake up.... loosen.... all that lies around the heart...... ribs... shoulders... jaw... throat
expand.... the circulation.... warm the blood

Sense the pulse of the heart.... let its beat.... fire.... light up.... the body
shine out through the face.... the eyes
open the heart into the body.... open the body into the heart

Jump.... spring.... find a bounce in the feet.... as an india rubber ball
let the impulse expand through the whole body.... spring.... leap.... bound
expel.... heaviness/ inertia

Brighten...... head... hands... knees... pelvis
open the windows.... open the doors
let the wind/ weather.... blow through

warming... blazing... tumbling... sparkling... cascading
Travel everywhere
welcome whatever you meet, or see

Move...... as lightning... as laughter... as colour... as rushing water
find companions.... surprises.... delights
let an animal.... move with your heart

Follow impulse... take risks... be enormous... change shape
seize the fun
Let the wild heart sing.... dance

Afterwards: gather whatever materials sing out to you, and make something
What appears?
Share with a partner

Lightening up

Tom Brazier, *Morris dancing cockerel,* Peterborough
Photo: John Robertson. 1992.

Creativity, it would appear, should be approached in the spirit of play, of foreplay, of dalliance, doodling, messing around – and then, bit by bit, you somehow get deeper into the matter. But if you go in there with a businessman's solemnity or the fanaticism of some artistic types you are likely to be rewarded with a stiff response, a joyless dribble, strained originality, ideas that come out all strapped up and strangled by too much effort. Ben Okri, *A Way of Being Free.*

The mediaeval carnival was an annual 'time of misrule' when all order was reversed – a seasonal upsetting of everyday values and boundaries – masters waited on servants, rules of behaviour were flouted, etc. – in A Mid Summer Nights Dream a queen falls in love with a donkey. Laughter decreases the flow of blood to the prefrontal and temperoparietal lobes of the brain, thus putting the controlling, thinking brain temporarily at rest. Laughter brings us together – the tears both of laughter and of grief open us towards others, our tears altering the chemistries of stress within the body, dissolving and breaking up what may otherwise break us down.

"Daft as a brush"

change character.... do a crazy dance
walk with disobedient arms.... one mad leg.... rebellious mouth
don't fit in.... be extreme.... wear six hats.... fill up the room.... then empty it

Mishaps

Begin moving.... in your movement tell a story
of having a series of 'accidents'

Anarchy

Gather a crazy bunch of materials
soup.... a telephone.... a tree
Imagine them as noisy.... let them create.... a 'revolution'

The arrival of a good clown exercises more beneficial influence in a town than of twenty asses laden with drugs. 17 century physician quoted in: Patch Adams, *Gesundeit*

Surprise
Begin moving.... in each moment
do the opposite of what you intend
create 1000 surprises for yourself

Unlikely
Move...
to tell a tall story

Bright
Choose something dull
find how to brighten it

Colour
Wherever you are
fill it with 'colour'

Lighten
Choose something heavy
find how to make it lighter

Extravagant
Dress up.... be conspicuous.... enormous.... impossible
(**extravagant** L. *extravagans* wandering beyond)

Party
Wherever you are make.... 'a party '
make or dance.... an invitation.... a welcome

Joke
Make.... a 'joke' object
based on a 'serious' object
Imagine its role in the world
Move to give it a story
let it gather companions to it
Do what it tells you

'The gross and net result of it is that people who spent most of their natural lives riding iron bicycles over the rocky roadsteads of this parish get their personalities mixed up with the personalities of their bicycle as a result of the interchanging of the atoms of each of them and you would be surprised at the number of people in these parts who nearly are half people and half bicycles.' Flann O'Brien, *The Third Policeman.*

Darkening... loss of heart

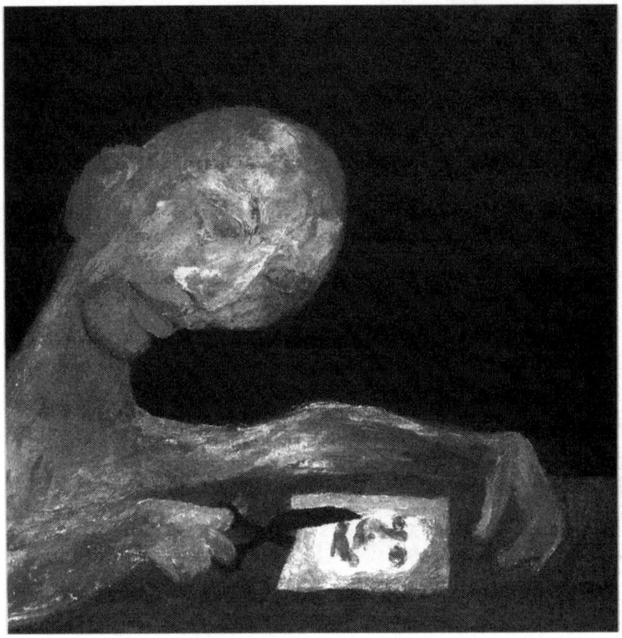

Ken Kiff, *Person Cutting an Image,* 1965 -71
Tempera on board, 61 x 61 cm (24 x 24 in.)

There are lone cemeteries,
tombs filled with soundless bones,
the heart passing through a tunnel
dark, dark, dark;
like a shipwreck we die inward,
like smothering in our hearts,
like slowly falling from our skin down to our soul.

Pablo Neruda, *Only Death,* from: *Residence on Earth.*

There are recurring and inevitable times in our lives, when the heart feels deadened – all sense of life and movement seems to have died away, deserted us, leaving us stranded on what seems a barren shore. Our sense of who we are and what we are doing feels empty, 'without heart'. We feel crushed by confusion, depression or grief; we lose a sense of our own body and feel disconnected from what is around us; to create or engage with anything feels near impossible. Recovering a physical sense of body, in whatever way we feel we can, is a way of bringing some relief. If we take time simply to let the body breathe and allow the touch of immediate sensory detail gently to engage us, some sensation or image may emerge to guide us. In such times a companion is also of great value. Working alone may trap us in what we fear to face, fearing what may surface, overwhelmed by sadness or pain. The presence of another helps us to accept whatever mood or feeling we are in and this subtle loosening of our resistance begins to allow change. To make, move, or write in these times of darkness is a way of anchoring our attention and opening us into a wider field of awareness.

Loss of heart – recovering connection

Let your head fall
Let your face rest against the ground
feel the beat of the heart
rest
Sense the shadow under you
slowly settling.... giving way

Let your feelings.... simply lie quiet.... within you

Breathe
do not expect anything
allow silence.... not knowing.... if anything will come

Allow the breath to come in.... from outside
let it wash through the body
allow each part of the body to give way.... and drift apart

Let the field of your attention gently spread out.... around you
widening.... settling.... as you breathe

accepting the feelings inside.... not holding them tightly

Let the body loosen.... softening the boundaries.... between inside.... and out
allowing.... what is within you.... to breathe.... flow outwards
What rises towards you?
Let each part of the body have its own voice
Listen to what the body needs.... to move.... to be still
Do as much or as little as you wish

accepting whatever is there

Afterwards: *Choose something from what is around you.... a quality.... a colour.... a shape*
***make** a place for it*
Let your body rest quietly nearby
*Take time slowly to **move** in response, then*
***write**.... allow any words to surface.... trust their presence*
Share with a partner
As the partner.... offer a gift for this 'place'

It was a summer afternoon in Devon, exquisitely beautiful, the hedgerows bright with a tapestry of flowers, stitchwort, campion, bluebells, Queen Anne's lace, and swallows swooping in great joyous arcs of movement. I had spent weeks unable to speak, my heart overwhelmed by the grief of my brother's sudden death – to open my mouth was to feel caught in useless words that left me with a sense of utter isolation. A dancer, my body was heavy and numb with pain – I felt unable to move. Wandering listlessly by the river, I noticed a few tall heads of grasses bent by the wind, like broken signals. I do not know why I saw them when so much else passed me as behind glass. I paused, feeling they somehow spoke to me, echoed something. Sitting down by them not sure what I might do I then noticed the dark mound of a mole hill, the soil slightly flatted, no longer fresh. Slowly, I began to shape and gather among the leaves, earth and grasses. And I became absorbed in the details of my making, and something painfully restless inside me seemed to settle, to take root in the small landscape forming between my hands. Later, standing back, it seemed to me I had made or discovered a wayside shrine by the river. And in that absorption in materials in my hands I had, without seeking it, found a place for my brother, and for myself. And for the first time in a long while I felt myself able to breathe and look about me again.
Miranda Tufnell.

Miranda Tufnell, Study for *Wing*, photo: Caroline Lee

The emptiness of the circle – loss – nothing there – a hole – a gap – a wound – even the aching pain of it. The ache of hunger too. But to go down inside to become the emptiness, become even the pain? Then it's no longer emptiness – even no longer pain? But still the question, why not always able to do it? Fearing to become melted down in the Button Moulder's ladle, fearing to become nothing, all form gone, nothing if there is no form? Annihilation. Nobody, no body to be buried. But if one dares risk it, go down to the body's darkness, something does happen, even to one's skin, it begins to burgeon....... And then too, out of the held emptiness, there comes a movement, a gesture, a reaching out to the world again, to the world in which wild flowers grow – and people... Marion Milner, *Eternity's Sunrise.*

Broken

Find something.... that seems broken

Imagine it has a voice

***Make, move and write**.... from its point of view*

Let it go on a journey What/ who.... does it meet?

What happens to it?

At odds

Go out.... wander

Find materials.... that evoke conflict, anger,

frustration.... listen.... explore.... with them

Gradually.... let something form

allow.... questions.... provocations.... rebellions

What happens?

With a partner, speak of what you see

Move** to explore.... then **write

Weighed down

Choose something heavy

feel its quality.... weight.... surface.... shape

What is its voice?

*Gather materials and **make....** in response to it*

What appears?

Move**.... then **write

Dumb

Find something that 'can't speak'....

that seems mute listen to it

Find something else that.... wants to reach it

sense how they affect each other

Gradually.... let something form between them

What appears?.... what happens?

Tended/ untended

Find something.... that seems neglected.... uncared for

listen to it.... what does it need?

choose.... a place for it

Explore what happens as you bring other things to it

Find ways.... to let life in

Loss

Make something for someone you have lost

Listen to it.... what does it speak of?

Seasons of the heart

Romualdas Rakauskas, from the cycle *Blossoming, 1976-85* Photograph

The most ancient festivals mark the seasonal changes of light.
The winter solstice comes at the heart of the year's darkness
and celebrates the moment of change, the return of light.

"We begin with breath" – an account of a project by its initiator, Lucinda Jarrett. Rosetta Life is an artist-led organisation set up to enable people facing life threatening illnesses and their families to move towards a celebration of their life.

We begin with the breath. It is hard to find your way to the heart of someone and their life. By starting with the mirroring of movement, of breath, people feel supported and able to take risks. People risk reaching their active imagination to find what matters in their lives, the living image or the story that wants to be told.... We sit together, taking time gently to breathe, relax and feel each part of the body. Something begins to come together, a connecting of body, emotions, memories and feelings. I listen quietly, without words, following the rhythm and movement of your breath and then I ask you to let your hands move – to express the movement and journey of your breath. And then I too follow, mirroring your movements, the 'story' gently appearing in your hands. Then we pause and rest together, we talk and you tell me of images, memories that surfaced. Our conversation is a dance between you and me, a conversation that grows from the trust of listening and sharing together.... The stories and images offer people a chance to travel from the place of passivity and illness towards a new beginning, a new found confidence that arises from the recognition of images and stories in the active imagination and the shaping of these into works of art that can be shared and celebrated with friends, families and hospice staff. Illness strips away the public sense of personality, takes away career, conventional role models of mother or husband, son or university student. Illness leaves us with only the felt experience of our lived relationships. The role of the artist in Rosetta Life is to be a support and a witness to people stumbling towards the expression of themselves and to be present when they arrive at it. We must strive to catch the expression of the heart and find a shape for it that holds it in the best possible reflection for the person we work with. It is always a dance to navigate another's way of being, to travel with them, to find a renewed sense of connection to self and to life itself. An improvisation based upon risk and trust and the establishment of shared understanding that enables people to answer: Who am I? How do I become me? Together we find a voice and a shape for what wants to be heard – a poem, a video, a drawing, remembering always that whatever emerges comes first from the authenticity of the body and the life movement of the breath.

Andreas Christina, drawing in felt tip

Andreas Christina drew this image in response to his recollections of the coalmining landscapes of his childhood in Italy, where he would spend many hours climbing the slagheaps with friends. Lucinda Jarrett

Emmanuel Joseph, drawing

We ran a project at Marie Curie Centre, Edenhall, London where we invited participants to draw images of the landscapes that mattered to them. Emmanuel Joseph chose to draw images from the landscape of his imagination. He drew prolifically and enjoyed working in pen and ink. He then manipulated these images digitally in Photoshop in order to concentrate on details of his drawings and details of colour grading. Although he had lived in London all his life, as he approached the end of his life he enjoyed drawing rural landscapes, rivers, seas and open spaces. As he lost control of his thinking and became more and more confused he enjoyed the control of his identity that creativity offered him. Lucinda Jarret

The Present Heart

Be still.... breathe.... take time to let your body settle
open the length of your spine.... open the windows of your skin
        widening.... lengthening
let your attention soften.... and spread out into the present moment.... of where you are

opening to your body.... and to what is around you

Let go.... of wanting to do or change anything
let go.... of concerns.... about what is important

be empty.... rest in darkness.... as a plant in winter.... quiet.... stilled
accept.... going nowhere
gently receive the moment.... arriving into you in each breath
trusting whatever is coming.... and going.... letting your attention float

        Many things need darkness to grow

Let the breath come and go.... as waves washing the shore
What rises towards you now?.... as you breathe
follow the unfolding moment

Follow the merest whisper.... or inclination in the body.... to shift and move
turning towards.... or away.... inwards or outwards

Sense the beat of your heart.... sense the horizon
opening.... accepting whatever comes

Gradually.... as you move.... receiving
where.... how.... you are

Sense the temperature.... the weather of the heart
blustery... calm... sparkling... thundery

Sense the light of the heart.... the time of day

evening... the early hours... daybreak... noon

Move to discover the changing season.... of the heart

seeding... budding... ripening... darkening... dying away

Move.... to discover.... the details.... qualities of the heart's land
forest... valley... meadow... sea... harbour

What does this moment offer... give you?
let the heart receive and grow

Each moment a birth.... a creation
Born out of the heart.... meeting.... the touch of the immediate world

***Write** from moving.... discover the words/ stories.... for this time of the heart*

Share with a partner

*Then: gather materials to **make**.... a place for the heart today*

discover, as you make.... moment by moment.... what is needed
a place you could not see.... but was there.... growing within and around you

Explore what you have made with your partner

Pamela Harrison, *Barnacle Geese*, Islay

Songs are thoughts, sung out with the breath when people are moved by great forces and ordinary speech no longer suffices. Man is moved just like the ice floe sailing here and there in the current. His thoughts are driven by a flowing force when he feels joy, when he feels fear, when he feels sorrow. Thoughts can wash over him like a flood, making his breath come in gasps and his heart throb. Something like an abatement in the weather will keep him thawed up. And then it will happen that we, who always think we are small, will feel still smaller. And we will fear to use words. But it will happen that the words we need will come of themselves. When the words we want to use shoot up of themselves - we get a new song.

Orpingalik, Netsilik Eskimo

Glossary of Terms

Body – The body is the means by which we enter experience and feel the world. Descartes, working in the 17th century, conceived of the body as being separate from the mind and his ideas are still deeply embedded in our language and everyday conception of ourselves, the body being regarded simply as a mechanism for carrying us around. In this book we refer to 'body', not simply in terms of its physical parts – skin, bone, muscle, etc. – but as the locus in which all our experiencing – sensation, feeling, instinct, intuition, imagination and memory – is at play. Our tendency is to think of the body as a bounded entity completely enveloped by the skin. Yet, the sensing, perceiving body creates a surface of continual exchange and metamorphosis, each moment improvising its relation and response to what is around it.

Image – An image is the opposite to a generalised and abstract expression – images are tangible and sensuous. We use images all the time in our ways of speaking to express the feel of something – "It was so hot I was melting" ..."his words hit me with the force of a tidal wave". Such expressions have a vitality, and, paradoxically, a precision with regard to feeling, that literal descriptions do not. Expression through images is metaphoric - it communicates indirectly by analogy or suggestion rather than through direct statement. Images are the stuff of dreams, of stories, of gestures – they are the language of the arts. The objects, people, events, places, etc., that surround us provide a reservoir of potential images from which we draw in layers of associative meaning. We come to know more of ourselves through these images we find and create since they articulate some unseen aspect of us. As we work creatively, the relevant images (the ones we need) arrive spontaneously and surprisingly in ways we could never consciously contrive.

Imagination – The word 'imaginary' is used in everyday speech in opposition to the word 'real'. In this everyday sense of the word, when we imagine, we simply depart from reality into disembodied fantasy. But in this book imagination is understood as something essential to perception – our way of getting to know more of what is there through an act of empathy. It is through our imaginations that we 'feel with' what is other than ourselves. In this sense, imagination actually makes the real seem *more* real, because more connected to each of us. And when through an act of imagination we create pictures and stories or dream dreams, something in us is seeking not to escape reality but to throw light upon it, in other words to grasp the real more fully in all its complexity, seen through the lens of metaphor and image.

Improvisation – Improvisation is a way of working spontaneously in response to whatever is happening. It is working with attention to the moment by moment emergence of what is coming to form, rather than aiming towards a preconceived outcome; essentially the end point is unknown until it arrives. All work in the book is approached through improvisation and the same principles apply whatever the art form involved. By abandoning the narrowing focus of a fixed aim, improvisation widens our attention to sensation, feeling and impulse in the process of working. It lends itself to an intuitive approach.

Listening – The word 'listen' is repeatedly used in describing activities throughout the book. Beyond the purely auditory, the word is mainly used to evoke a broadly receptive and open state of attention – 'listening' with all the senses. Being able to be present and open to what is happening in the moment – in our surroundings, or in the body, or coming to us as impulse – is one of the crucial themes of the book, introduced in Ch1 Arriving, but constantly referred to throughout. The whole book could in fact be characterised as a 'listening' approach to living and creating. To both create, in whatever medium, and, simultaneously, to stay 'listening' is a crucial part of all the activities described. Where, in some places, a literal reading of the word is intended – i.e. listening as hearing - this will be clear from the context.

Movement – Whereas, historically, dance forms require an appropriate technical training, 'movement' as a form of expression is something we are all capable of. We move from the moment we are conceived – life is movement. Developing one's capacity to do movement work is based upon informing and refining one's own body sense, mobility, spontaneity, and attentiveness, rather than upon learning prescribed gestures. Dancers traditionally work to prearranged steps, styles and rhythms and aim for a certain external effect or shape in what they do. In contrast, as we simply 'move', we draw upon our innate rhythms – the heart, the breath, the pace that our body needs; movements arise spontaneously from our own sensations and impulses and our awareness of what affects us as we work.

Response – Much of this work is concerned with creating 'in response'...to a place, to a dream, to a chosen object, to something we have just made or done.... And response in this sense of the word is always multi levelled, being both physical, emotional and imaginative. Throughout, we emphasise a spontaneity of response, not trying to know beforehand what we will do. Having absorbed the feel of what it is I am responding to, I in a sense forget it... put it to the back of my mind. Then, I allow whatever impulses arise in the present moment, trusting that whatever I do will be relevant. When I look back, I invariably find that what I did had an extraordinary and rich connection to my starting point – usually in a way that I could not have predicted.

Self – We have conceived of self in this book, not as a closed entity, but as a more fluid and open ended 'place of meetings'. As we engage in the work described, perhaps in any creative work, we let go of the familiar self that we carry with us in daily life. In entering the world of our imaginations, we shed our usual definitions of ourselves in terms of the roles we play, the groups we belong to, our defining problems and limitations. We loosen the iron grip of these characteristics and become at once more permeable to our surroundings and more mutable in ourselves. This can be a marvellous release and adventure, offering us the possibility of coming away from the work with a more diverse and flexible idea of who we are. This is not in the name of 'self improvement' or 'personal growth', nor is it concerned with an idea of returning to some 'essential self', from which we have become alienated. Rather, it is towards a more playful and at the same time a deeper sense of who we are and what is important in our lives, all of which is expressed in our images more precisely than it could ever be described in literal language.

Story – In a broad sense, all the work in this book adds up to a set of stories – the stories we tell of our lives, our account of ourselves and who we are – whether we tell these literally as facts, or, more likely, tell them obliquely as fictions through what we create. This kind of story is a constantly changing narrative which is transformed through what we do and make. We have used the word 'story' in the chapter on this topic partly in its more restricted and usual sense. But we have also applied the word to the loose sense of narrative that may appear in free writing, or in exploring and responding to any kind of image. The key point in all this is that even though we invent a story (or an image), it still tells a truth, even if this truth is couched in metaphor. As has been said in the book, it is in poetic (metaphoric) form that we often come closest to the reality of felt experience.

Selected Bibliography

The Body

Robert O. Becker and Gary Seldon,*The Body Electric: Electromagnetism and the Foundation of Life,* New York: William Morrow, 1998.

Claudia Benthien, (Thomas Dunlop trans.), *Skin: On the Cultural Border between Self and the World,* New York: Columbia University Press, 2002.

Erich Blechschmidt, *The Beginnings of Human Life,* New York: Springer Verlag,1977.

Michael J. Gelb, *Body Learning: An Introduction to the Alexander Technique,* New York: Henry Holt (second edition), 1996. (first published 1981)

David Gorman, *The Body Moveable,* (Available from Ampersand Printing Company, Ontario, Canada).

Philip Whitfield and Susan Greenfield, *How We Work: Understanding the Human Body and Mind,* London: Marshall Publishing, 1997.

Dean Juhan, *Job's Body: A Handbook for Bodywork,* New York: Station Hill Press,1987.

Peter L. Williams, ed., *Gray's Anatomy: The Anatomical Basis of Medicine and Surgery,* New York, London, etc., Churchill Livingstone, 38th British Edition,1995.

Hugh Milne, The *Heart of Listening: A Visionary Approach to Craniosacral work,* Berkeley, Calif.: North Atlantic Books,1995.

Ashley Montagu, *Touching: The Human Significance of The Skin,* (third edition), New York, Harper & Row, 1971.

Frank H. Netter, *Atlas of Human Anatomy,* 3rd ed, New Jersey: Icn Learning Systems, 2003.

Lennart Nilsson, *Behold Man: A Photographic Journey of Discovery Inside the Body,* London: Harrap,1974.

Glen Park,*The Art of Changing: A New Approach to Alexander Technique,* Bath: Ashgrove Press,1989.

Paul Pearsall,*The Heart's Code,* London: Thorsens, 1998.

G. J. Romanes, ed., *Cunningham's Textbook of Anatomy,* 12th edition, Oxford: Oxford Medical Publications,1981.

Franklyn Sills, *Craniosacral Biodynamics,* vols. 1and 2, Berkely: North Atlantic Books, 2001.

Patterns and Processes in Nature

John Bleibtreau, *The Parable of The Beast,* London: Paladin, 1968.

James Gleick, (Photos, Eliot Porter) *Nature's Chaos,* London: Abacus, 1990.

Theodor Schwenk, *Sensitive Chaos:The Creation of Flowing Forms in Water and Air,* London: Rudolf Steiner Press, 1965.

D'Arcy Wentworth Thompson, J.T. Bonner, ed., *On Growth and Form,* Cambridge: Cambridge University Press, 1992. (first published 1942)

Improvised Dance/ Movement

Arts Archive – produced by Arts Documentation Unit, Exeter, UK. (dedicated to documenting the processes at work within contemporary performing arts practice). website: www.arts-archives.org

'Dartington Theatre Papers' available from the above source include:

Mary O'Donnel Fulkerson, *Language of the Axis,* Spring/Summer 1976, Theatre Papers, The First Series, No. 12

Steve Paxton,*The Small Dance,* 1977, Theatre Papers, The First Series, No. 4

Bonnie Bainbridge Cohen, *Sensing, Feeling and Action,* Berkeley, Calif.: North Atlantic Books,

1993. (and Contact Quarterly Editions)
Contact Quarterly Magazine (all issues) from: PO Box 603, Northampton, MA, 01061, USA
Irene Dowd, *Taking Root to Fly: Ten Articles on Functional Anatomy,* New York: Contact Collaborations Inc., 1981.
Simone Forti, *Handbook in Motion,* Press of Nova Scotia College of Art and Design, 1974.
Penny Greenland, *Hopping Home Backwards: Body Intelligence and Movement Play,* Leeds: Jabadao, 2000.
Penny Greenland, ed., *What Dancers Do That Other Health Workers Don't ...,* Leeds: Jabadeo, 2000.
Anna Halprin, *Dance as a Healing Art: Returning to Health with Movement and Imagery,* Mendocino Calif.: Life Rhythms, 2000.
Linda Hartley, *The Wisdom of the Body Moving,* Berkely: North Atlantic Books, 1995.
Michael Huxley and Noel Witts, eds., *The Twentieth Century Performance Reader,* London: Routledge, 1996.
Kalichi, *Dance, Words and Soul: Ways of Moving with Change,* Dublin: Kalichi, 2001 (info@kalichi.com)
Pamela Matt, *A Kinesthetic Legacy: The Life and Works of Barbara Clark,* Tempo, Anz.: 1993.
Cynthia Novack, *Sharing the Dance: Contact Improvisation and American Culture,* Wisconsin: University of Wisconsin Press, 1990.
Andrea Olsen, *Body Stories,* New York: Station Hill Press, 1991.
Andrea Olsen, *Body and Earth,* Hanover, NH.; London: University Press of New England, 2002.
John Rolland, *Inside Motion: An Idiokinetic Basis for Movement Education,* Amsterdam: Rolland String Research Associates, 2nd edition,1987.
Louise Steinman, *The Knowing Body,* Boston; London: Shambhala, 1986.
Mabel E.Todd, *The Thinking Body: A Study in the Balancing Forces of Dynamic Man,* New York: Dance Horizons, 1959.
Mabel E.Todd, *The Hidden You: What You Are and What to Do About it,* New York: Dance Horizons, 1978.
Miranda Tufnell and Chris Crickmay, *Body Space Image: Notes Towards Improvisation and Performance,* Alton, Hampshire: Dance Books, 1993.
Jean Viala, Nourit Masson-Sekine, ed., *Butoh: Shades of Darkness,* Tokyo: Shufunotomo,1988.

Sensory Awareness and Perception

David Abrams, *The Spell of the Sensuous,* New York: Vintage Books,1996.
Frederick Franck, *the Zen of Seeing: Seeing/ Drawing as Meditation,* London: Wildwood House,1973.
James J. Gibson, *Senses Considered as Perceptual Systems,* Westport, Conn.: Greenwood, 1983. (first published 1966)
Jacques Lusseyran, *(Elizabeth Cameron trans.) And There Was Light,* Edinburgh: Floris Classics, 1985. (first published 1953)

Poetry and Literature (with particular reference to body and imagination)

Margaret Atwood, *The Journals of Susanna Moodie,* Toronto: Oxford UP, 1970.
Robert Bly, James Hillman, Michael Meade, eds., *The Rag and Bone Shop of the Heart: Poems for Men,* New York: Harper Perennial, 1993.
Hélène Cixous, *Stigmata, Escaping Texts,* London and New York: Routledge,1998.
T.S. Elliot, *Four Quartets,* London; Boston: Faber & Faber, 1959. (first published 1944)
Louise Erdrich, *Tracks,* London: Flamingo (Harper Collins), 1994. (first published 1988)
Frances Horowitz, *Collected Poems,* Newcastle: Bloodaxe Books, 1985.
Edward Hirsch *How to Read a Poem, and Fall in Love with Poetry,* San Diego, New York; London: Harcourt, 1999.
Ted Hughes, *Poetry in the Making,* London; Boston: Faber and Faber, 1967.

Ted Hughes, *Wodwo,* London; Boston: Faber and Faber, 1972. (first published 1967)
David Malouf, *An Imaginary Life,* London: Pan Books, 1980. (first published 1978)
Anne Michaels, *Fugitive Pieces,* London: Bloomsbury,1998.
Pablo Neruda, *Fully Empowered,* New York: Farrar Strous Giroux, 2001. (first published 1976)
Pablo Neruda, *Residents on Earth,* London: WW Norton, 1973.
Pablo Neruda, *Odes to Common Things,* London: Littlebrown,1994.
Pablo Naruda, (Hardie St Martin trans.) *Memoirs,* London: Penguin, 1978.
Ben Okri, *Mental Fight,* London: Phoenix/Orian Books,1999.
Michael Ondaatje, *In the Skin of the Lion,* London: Picador,1988.
Michael Ondaatje, *Anil's Ghost,* London: Picador, 2000.
Sylvia Plath, Ted Hughes, ed., *Collected Poems,* London: Faber and Faber,1981.
Adrienne Rich,*The Fact of a Door Frame: Poems 1950-2001,* London; New York: WW Norton, 2002.
Adrienne Rich, *On Lies, Secrets, and Silence: Selected Prose 1966-78,* London: Penguin, 1991.
Jerome Rothenberg, ed.,*Technicians of the Sacred,* New York: Anchor Books,1969.
Virginia Woolf,*The Waves,* London: Penguin,1951. (first published 1931)
William Carlos Williams, *Pictures from Breugel and Other Poems,* New York: New Directions,1949.

Art and Materials

James Elkins, *What Painting Is: How to Think About Oil Painting, Using the Language of Alchemy,* New York; London: Routledge, 2000.
Alan Borer, *The Essential Joseph Beuys,* London: Thames and Hudson,1996.
Lucy Lippard, *Eva Hesse,* New York: Da Capo Press,1992.
Frances Morris and Richard Flood, *Zero to Infinity: Art Povera, 1962-1972,* London: Tate Gallery Publications, 2001.

Art and Colour

Judith Collins, *Winifred Nicholson,* London: Tate Gallery Publications,1987.
Derek Jarmen, *Chroma,* London: Vintage, 1995.
Margaret Livingstone,*Vision and Art: The Biology of Seeing,* New York: Harry N. Abrams, 2002.
Winifred Nicholson, *Unknown Colour: Paintings, Letters, Writings by Winifred Nicholson,* London: Faber and Faber.
Andrew Lambeth, *Ken Kiff,* London: Thames and Hudson, 2001.

Art, Performance and the Body

Maria Abramovic, *Artist Body,* Milan: Charter, 1998.
Ric Allsopp and Scott deLahunta, eds.,*The Connected Body?* Amsterdam: Amsterdam School of The Arts, 1996.
Amelia Jones and Andrew Stephenson, eds., *Performing The Body, Performing The Text,* London; New York: Routledge, 1999.

Art, Space and Place

Yves Abrioux, *Ian Hamilton Finlay,* London: Reaktion Books,1985.
Judy Chicago,*Through the Flower,* (Section on the 'Woman House Project' pp.107-132), New York: Anchor/ Doubleday, 1977.
Henri Claude Cousseau (Foreword), *Louise Bourgeois: Recent Works,* London: Serpentine Gallery, 1999.
Lynn Gardner, *'Home is Where the Art is',* The Guardian newspaper, July 7th, 1999.
Lynn Gumpert, *Christian Boltanski,* Paris: Flammarion, 1994.
Carl Haenlein, *Rebecca Horne, The Glance of Infinity,* Zurich; Berlin; New York: Scalo,1997.
Nick Kaye, *Site-Specific Art,* London: Routledge, 2000.
Lucy Lippard, *Overlay: Contemporary Art and the Art of Prehistory,* New York: New Press, 1983.

Bill Viola with Robert Violette, ed., *Reasons for Knocking at an Empty House, Writings 1973-1994*, London: Thames and Hudson with Anthony d'Offay Gallery, 1995.
Edward Wachtel, *'The First Picture Show: Cinematic Aspects of Cave Art'*, Leonardo, Vol 26, No2. pp.135-144.
Jan Wampler, *All Their Own: People and the Places They Build*, Oxford: Oxford University Press,1978.

Place and Identity

Doug Aberley, ed., *Boundaries of Home: Mapping for Local Empowerment*, Gabriola Island; Philadelphia: New Society Publishers, 1993.
Gaston Bachelard, *The Poetics of Space: the classic look at how we experience intimate spaces*, Boston: Beacon Press 1994. (first published 1958)
John Berger, *Pig Earth*, London: Writers and Readers, 1979.
John Berger, *'Field'* pp.192-198 in *About Looking*, London: Writers and Readers, 1980.
John Berger and Jean Mohr, *Another Way of Telling*, New York: Pantheon, 1982.
John Berger, *And Our Faces, My Heart, Brief as Photos*, London: Writers and Readers,1984.
Mihaly Csikszentmihalyi and Eugene Rochberg-Halton,*The Meaning of Things: Domestic Symbols and the Self*, Cambridge: Cambridge University Press, 1981.
Gretel Ehrlich,*The Solace of Open Spaces*, New York, London: Penguin, 1986.
Gretel Ehrlich, *Islands, the Universe, Home*, New York, London: Penguin, 1992.
Mark Francis and Randolf T. Hester Jnr.,*The Meaning of Gardens*, Cambridge, Mass.: MIT Press,1990.
Norman Hallendy, *Inuksuit: Silent Messengers of the Arctic*, Vancouver: Douglas and McIntyre, 2001.
Ian Jeffrey, *Magnum Landscape*, London: Phaedon, 1996. (a collection of images by contemporary photographers)
Neil Leach, ed., *Rethinking Architecture*, London: Routledge, 1997.
Lucy Lippard, *The Lure of the Local: Senses of Place in a Multicentred Society*, New York: New Press, 1997.
Priya Mookerjee, *Pathway Icons: The Wayside Art of india*, London: Thames & Hudson, 1987.
V.S. Naipaul,*The Enigma of Arrival*, London: Penguin, 1987.
Paul Oliver, *Dwellings, The Vernacular House Worldwide*, London: Phaidon, 2003.
Peter D. Osborne, *'Milton Friedman's Smile'*, pp.331-355 in: Erica Carter, Donald James, and Judith Squires, eds., *Space and Place: Theories of Identity and Location*, London: Lawrence and Wishart, 1993.
Luis Poirot, (Alastair Reid trans.), *Pablo Neruda, Absence and Presence*, New York: WW Norton, 1990.
Richard Sennet, *Flesh and Stone: The Body and the City in Western Civilization*, London; Boston: Faber and Faber, 1994.

Image, Imagination, and Creativity

Gaston Bachelard, (Daniel Russel trans.), *The Poetics of Reverie: Childhood, Language, and the Cosmos*, Boston: Beacon Press,1969.
Gaston Bachelard, *'The Poetical Imagination'* pp 88-111 in: Richard Kearney *Poetics of Imagining*, Edinburgh: Edinburgh University Press, 1998.
Christopher Bollas,*The Mystery of Things*, London; New York: Routledge, 1992.
Christopher Bollas, *Being a Character: Psychoanalysis and Self Experience*, London: Farrar, Straus and Giroux, 1992.
Noel Cobb, *Archetypal Psychology's Missing Alchemical Marriage*, pp.129-170, Sphinx 7, 1996.
Camilla Connel, *Something Understood: Art Therapyin Cancer Care*, London: Wrexam Publications, 1998.
James Hillman,*The Thought of the Heart and the Soul of the World*, Dallas: Spring Publications, 1997. (first published 1981)

James Hillman, *Archetypal Psychology*, Dallas: Spring Publications, 1985.
James Hillman, and Michael Ventura, *We've had a Hundred Years of Psychotherapy and the World is Getting Worse*, San Francisco: Harper,1993.
James Hillman,*The Soul's Code: In Search of Character and Calling*, New York: Bantam Books, 1997.
James Hillman, Lectures published in Spring Publications, Dallas:
An Enquiry into Image, Spring 1977, pp. 62-88.
Further Notes on Images, Spring1978, pp. 152-182.
Image Sense, Spring1979, pp. 130-143.
Shaun MacNiff, *Art as Medicine, Creating a Therapy of the Imagination,* London: Piatkus, 1992.
Miller Mair, *Between Psychology and Psychotherapy: A Poetics of Experience,* London: Routledge,1989.
John Maizels, *Raw Creation: Outsider Art and Beyond*, London: Phaidon,1996.
Marion Milner, *Eternity's Sunrise,* London: Virago,1987.
Marion Milner, *On Not Being Able to Paint,* London: Heinemann Educational, 1971. (first published 1950 under pseudonym of Jonna Field)
Michael Parsons, *Marion Milner's 'Answering Activity' and the Question of Psychoanalytic Creativity,* pp413-424, International Review of Psychoanalysis Vol.17, London: Institute of Psychoanalysis, 1990.
Arnold Mindell, *Working on Yourself Alone: Inner Dreambody Work*, London; New York: Penguin,1990.
Thomas Moore, *Care of the Soul: How to Add Depth and Meaning to Your Everyday Life,* London: Piatkus,1992.
Raw Vision, *International Journal of Intuitive and Visionary Art, Outsider Art, Art Brut, Contemporary Folk Art* (all issues). Contactable through website: rawvision.com
Robert Sardello, *Love and the Soul: Creating a Future for Earth,* New York: Harper Perennial,1995.
Robert Sardello, *Facing the World with Soul: The Reimagination of Modern Life,* Hudson, N.Y.: Lindisfarne Press,1992.
Joy Schaverien,*The Revealing Image: Analytical Art Psychotherapy in Theory and Pratice,* London: Jessica Kingsley,1999.
Bani Shorter, *Susceptible to the Sacred: The Psychological Experience of Ritual,* London: Routledge, 1987.
Bani Shorter, *An Image Darkly Forming: Women and Initiation*, London: Routledge,1996.
Martina Thompson, *On Art and Therapy,* London: Virago,1989.
D.W. Winnicott, *Playing and Reality,* London: Routledge,1982. (first published 1971)
D.W. Winnicott, *Therapeutic Consultations in Child Psychiatry,* London: Hogarth Press, 1971.
Marion Woodman,*The Pregnant Virgin: A Process of Psychological Transformation,* Toronto: Inner City Books, 1985.
Marion Woodman, *Leaving my Father's House: A Journey to Conscious Femininity,* Boston; London: Shambhala, 1993.
Marion Woodman, *Bone: Dying into Life,* London, New York: Penguin, 2001.

Myth, Story and Dream

Bruno Bettelheim, *The Uses of Enchantment: The Meaning and Importance of Fairy Tales,* London: Penguin, 1991. (first published 1976)
Hugh Brody, *The Other Side of Eden: Hunter-gatherers, Farmers and the Shaping of the World,* London: Faber and Faber, 2002.
Hugh Brody, *Maps and Dreams: Indians and the British Columbia Frontier,* London: Jill Norman and Hobhouse,1982.
Neil Douglas-Klotz, *The Hidden Gospel: Decoding the Spiritual Message of the Arameic Jesus,* Wheaton, Ill.: Quest Books, 2001.
Mircea Eliade, *Shamanism,* London: Arkana, 1964.
Eduardo Galeano, (Mark Fried trans.)*We Say No,* New York; London: WW Norton, 1992.
Eduardo Galeano, (Cedric Belfrage trans.) *Memory of Fire,* Part 1: *Genesis,* London: Methuen, 1987.

Eduardo Galleano, (Cedric Belfrage trans.) *The Book of Embraces,* New York; London: WW Norton,1991.
Eduardo Galeano, (Judith Brister trans.) *Days and Nights of Love and War,* London: Pluto Press, 1983.
Alida Gersie, *Reflections on Therapeutic Storymaking,* London: Jessica Kingsley, 1997.
Alida Gersie, *Story Making and Bereavement: Dragons Fight in the Meadow,* London: Jessica Kingsley, 1994.
Carl G. Jung et al., *Man and His Symbols,* London: Arkana /Penguin,1990.
Primo Levi, *The Periodic Table,* London: Abacus/ Sphere Books, 1986.
Primo Levi, *Other People's Trades,* London: Abacus/ Sphere Books, 1991.
Brenda Mallon, *Dreams Counselling and Healing,* Dublin: Gill and Macmillan, 2000.
Michael Meade, *Men and the Water of Life: Initiation and the Tempering of Men,* New York: Harper Collins, 1983.
Jill Mellick, *The Natural Artistry of Dreams,* Berkely Calif.: Conari Press, 1996.
Tom Philips, ed., *Africa The Art of a Continent,* London: Royal Academy catalogue, 1996.
Colin Turnbull,*The Forest People,* London: Pimlico, 1994.
Margaret Visser,*'Salt the Edible Rock'* Ch 2, pp56-82, in: *Much Depends on Dinner: The Extraordinary History and Mythology, Allure and Obsessions, Perils and Taboos, of an Ordinary Meal,* London: Penguin 1989.
Marie Louise Von Franz, *Creation Myths,* (revised edition) Boston; London: Shambhala, 1995.

The Arts and People

Patch Adams, *Gesundheit,* Rochester, Vt.: Healing Arts Press, 1993.
Helen Crummy, *Let the People Sing: A Story of Craigmillar,* Newcraighall: H. Crummy, 1992.
Malcolm Dixon, ed., *Art With People,* Sunderland: AN Publications/ Artic Producers,1995.
Albert Hunt, *Hopes for Great Happenings: Learning Through Theatre,* London: Methuen, 1976.
Suzanne Lacy, *Mapping the Terrain: New Genre Public Art,* Seattle: Bay Press,1995.
Alison Stallibrass, *Being Me and Also Us, Lessons from the Peckam Experiment,* Edinburgh: Scottish Academy press, 1989.

Permissions

Quotations

The authors would like to thank the following for permission to reproduce their copyright material:

Extract from *'Wodwo'* by Ted Hughes used with kind permission of Faber & Faber Publishers, London.

Extract from *'Between Psychology and Psychotherapy'* by Dr. Miller Mair used with permission of Taylor & Francis Books Limited.

Extract from 'Looking in a Mirror' from *The Journals of Susanna Moodie* by Margaret Attwood. Copyright © Oxford University Press Canada 1970. Reprinted by permission of Oxford University Press Canada.

Text by Walter Morgenthalter, extracted from *Raw Creation* by John Maizels © 1996 Phaidon Press Ltd. ISBN 0 7148 4009 2. £22.95. *www.phaidon.com*

Extracts from *Eternity's Sunrise* © Marion Milner used with kind permission of Time Warner Books UK.

Floris Books for their kind permission to reproduce extracts from *'And There Was Light'* by Lusseyran, Floris Classic 1985.

With kind permission from Rudolf Steiner Press, to reproduce extracts from *'Sensitive Chaos'* by Theodore Schwenk © 1965.

Reproduced by permission of Hodder and Stoughton Ltd., extract from *'Cold Mountain'* © Charles Frazier.

Extract from *'Lucy Lippard, Eva Hesse'* used with kind permission of the Representative of Eva Hesse Estate .

Quotations used with kind permission from website: *http:/cgee.hamline.edu/see/Goldsworthy/see_an_andy/html* © Andy Goldsworthy.

Extracts from *'The Periodic Table'* (copyright © Primo Levi) used with kind permission of A M Heath & Co. Ltd.

Extract *'Precious Liquids'*, from Louise Bourgeois catalogue, Serpentine Gallery, London 1999 © Louise Bourgeois used with kind permission.

Extract from *'JOURNEY TO IXTLAN'* by Carlos Castaneda published by Jonathan Cape. Used with permission of The Random House Group Limited.

Extract from *'Anil's Ghost'* by Michael Ondaatje used with kind permission of Bloomsbury Publishing plc.

To reproduce extract *'Watching Brief'* by Francesca Turner © The Guardian 16 January 1997.

Extract from *'The Waves'* used with kind permission of The Society of Authors, Literary Representative of the Estate of Virginia Woolf.

Reproduced with kind permission of Cambridge University Press extact from *'The Meaning of Things, Domestic Symbols and the Self'* © Milhaly Csikszentmilhalyi and Eugene Rochberg-Halton.

Extract from *'Space and Place'* by Erica Carter, Donald James and Judith Squires (eds) used with kind permission of Lawrence and Wishart London 1993.

Quotation from *'Duino Elegies'* by R M Rilke Trans. Stephen Cohn used with kind permission of Carcanet Press Limited.

Orpingalik Statement as it appears in *'Technicians of the Sacred'* used with kind permission of the author Jerome Rothenberg.

Illustrations

The authors would like to thank the following for permission to reproduce their copyright material:

Front cover ©Werner Bischof/ Magnum Photos
p2 ©Winifred Nicholson Trustees
p3 photo courtesy of Caroline Lee
p6 Kettle's Yard, University of Cambridge ©ADAGP, Paris and DACS, London 2003
p9 photo included courtesy of Steve Paxton
p10 despite every effort it has not been possible to contact the photographer, Javier Hinojosa
p12 provided courtesy of Kirstie Simson. We regret we have not been able to trace the photographer, Chris Nash
p15 ©Mark Wallinger, courtesy Anthony Reynolds Gallery, London
p16 photos included with kind agreement of Nancy Stark Smith
p17 provided courtesy of Eva Karczag and the photographer Nienke Terpsma
p18 Carmen Thyssen-Bornemisza Collection on loan at the Museo Thyssen-Bornemisza, Madrid
p21 ©Werner Bischof/ Magnum Photos
p24 Reproduced from Netter's Atlas of Anatomy, 2nd ed. Permission of Icon Learning Systems.
p26 ©2003 Museum of Fine Arts, Boston
p27 from an original photo by H.G.F. Spurrell
p28 photo courtesy of Caroline Lee
p30 despite every effort it has not been possible to contact Rabat Musee d'Archaeologie
P39 provided courtesy of Brenda Mallon
p44 ©Werner Bischof/ Magnum Photos
p49 provided courtesy of Min Tanaka – we regret we have been unable to contact Masato Okada
p52 provided courtesy of Min Tanaka, the artist Noriuki Haraguchi and the photographer Toshimi Frusawa
p57 ©ADAGP, Paris and DACS, London 2003 and the Dorothea Tanning Studio and Archive
p60 provided courtesy of Lisa Nelson and David Moss and the photographer Stephen Petegorsky. (©Stephen Petegorsky)
p62 provided courtesy of Malcolm Green
p67 provided courtesy of John Hall
p68 ©State Library of Victoria
p73 provided courtesy of Bobby Cox
p74 reproduced with kind permission of the photographer Anne Lefebre
p76 ©Claes Oldenburg
p79 provided courtesy of Sheila Clayton
p82 provided courtesy of Karen Challis
p84 ©Adolf Wolfli/ Collection de l'Art Brut, Lausanne
p86 ©The Artist's Estate, Courtesy of Marlborough Fine Art (London) Ltd
p92 provided courtesy of Annie Menter and with thanks to Francina Ndimande
pp93/94 reproduced courtesy of Ivor Weeks
p97 ©Winifred Nicholson Trustees
p98 George Rodger/ Magnum Photos
p100 (11-H-2), Sheldon Jackson Museum, Sitka. Photograph by Eberhard Otto.
p102 reproduced courtesy of Rip Cronk and SPARC
p109 reproduced courtesy of Marge Ziius
p111 ©The Artist's Estate, Courtesy of Marlborough Fine Art (London) Ltd
p114 Louisiana Museum of Modern Art, ©ADAGP, Paris and DACS, London 2003
p117 photo courtesy of Gary Fiegehen
p121 photo ©Edward Wachtel
p124 reproduced from Illustrated Encyclopedia of Human Development, Marshall Cavendish
p126 photo courtesy of Caroline Lee
p128 reproduced with kind permission of the photographer Dee Conway
p129 ©Photo RMN - C.Jean. Collection: The Louvre
p130 Collections/©Fay Godwin
p131 ©Tessa Traeger
p132 Courtesy of the Pitt Rivers Museum, University of Oxford (1900.39.70).
p139 ©Bill Viola, digital image provided courtesy of The Bill Viola Studio

p140 Bridgeman Art Library, ©ADAGP, Paris and DACS, London 2003
p142 Reprinted with permission from Gray's Anatomy, ©1974 by Running Press Book Publishers, Philadelphia and London, www.runningpress.com
p143 provided courtesy of Ansuman Biswas
p145 provided courtesy of Miche Fabre Lewin
p149 Masafumi Sakamoto/ Sankai-juku
p151 ©2003:Rebecca Horn/ Rebecca Horn Photo Archive represented by Holzwarth Publications. All rights reserved.
p152 ©Jean Mohr
p153 photo reproduced courtesy of Keith Pattison
p155 ©Janet Cardiff and George Bures Miller
p156 Courtesy The Estate of Eva Hesse. Galerie Hauser & Wirth, Zurich.
p157 photo reproduced courtesy of Roger Bamber and the Natural Theatre Company
p158 provided courtesy of Sheila Clayton
p159 with permission of Cornelia Parker/ ©Tate, London 2003
p160 courtesy of: Library of Congress Prints and Photographs Division, 2.5.03.
p165 provided courtesy of Sadie Spikes
p167 provided courtesy of Karen Rann, photo with kind permission of Simon Fraser
p168 ©Louise Bourgeois/ VAGA, New York/ DACS, London 2003
p169 James Morris/ Axiom
p170 provided courtesy of Ruth Jones
p173 Yu Huei-Hung/ Cloud Gate Dance Theatre
p175 ©Ray Troll
p177 ©Igor Nitoraj
p179 Mary Evans Picture Library
p180 source unknown
p184 ©Graciela Iturbide
p186 reproduced with kind agreement of Koffi Koko, photo with kind permission of Kerstin Feuerstein
p188 provided courtesy of Pep Ramis, photo with kind permission of Jordi Bover
p189 ©Dhruva Mistry/ courtesy of Ulster Museum
p190 Kaiserer/ science and society
p191 Kettle's Yard, University of Cambridge ©ADAGP, Paris and DACS, London 2003
p192 provided courtesy of Bobby Cox
p193 ©Collection: San Francisco Maritime National Historical Park, United States Department of Interior
pp196/197/201/206 Reprinted with permission of Gray's Anatomy, ©1974 by Running Press Book Publishers, Philadelphia and London, www.runningpress.com
p200 provided courtesy of the IOU Theatre Company and the photographer Mike Laye
p203 ©Stuart Franklin/ Magnum Photos
p204 Donation: Ny Carlsbergfondet, Photo: Poul Buchardt, Louisiana Museum of Modern Art
p207 with kind permission of The British Museum (© The British Museum)
p208 provided courtesy of Gaby Agis and the photographer Hugh Glendenning
p212 provided courtesy of Deborah Jones
pp214/218/213/ 220 From Cunningham's Textbook of Anatomy, Reprinted by permission of Oxford University Press
p215 provided courtesy of Ray Chung, photo with kind permission of Theodore Litsios
p217 Pierre Boucher - to be confirmed
p219 ©Winifred Nicholson Trustees
p222 (top) from Hamilton, Textbook of Human Anatomy, Reproduced by permission Macmillan, Oxford
p222 (bottom) from Hamilton, Lockhart, Fife, Anatomy of the Human Body, reproduced by permission Faber & Faber Ltd.
p225 provided courtesy of Karen Rann
p227 ©ADAGP, Paris and DACS, London 2003
p229 From the book "Inuksuit Silent Messengers of the Arctic" published by the British Museum
p230 ©Courtesy Betty and George Woodman, the Estate of Francesca Woodman
p232 ©The Artist's Estate, Courtesy of Marlborough Fine Art (London) Ltd
p233 ©The Artist's Estate

p234 ©Tate, London 2003
p235 The Ronald Grant Cinema Archive/ M.G.M.
p236 Sanda Orgel, Sheet Closet, from Womanhouse, ©Judy Chicago, 1972, ARS, NY and DACS, London, 2003
p237 provided courtesy of IOU Theatre Company and the photographer Mike Laye.
p238 photo ©Jan Wampler
p239 reproduced courtesy of Sara Levart
p240 (top) reproduced courtesy of Alan Boldon
p241 provided courtesy of The Bill Viola Studio
p242 photo by Ray Delvert, with permission of Msr Boigontier
p243 provided courtesy of Simone Forti, and the photographer Isabelle Meister
p244 ©Jake Harvey, Glasgow Library Museums
p245 provided courtesy of Helen Poyner and Annie Pfingst
p247/ 250 Cristina Garcia RODERO/ Agence VU
p248 photo reproduced courtesy of Dan Rack
p249 provided courtesy of Annea Lockwood and Ruth Anderson
p251 provided courtesy of George Wyllie
p252 provided courtesy of Folake Shoga
p253 Magritte, René, The Blank Signature, Collection of Mr. and Mrs. Paul Mellon, Image ©2003 Board of Trustees, National Gallery of Art, Washington
p254 Vivian Russell from her book Edith Wharton's Italian Gardens published by Frances Lincoln Ltd.
p256 From Theodor Schwenk, Sensitive Chaos, reproduced courtesy of Rudolf Steiner Press
p258 Reprinted with permission from Gray's Anatomy, ©1974 by Running Press Book Publishers, Philadelphia and London, www.runningpress.com
p263 provided courtesy of Rosemary Lee and the photographer Pau Ross
p265 ©Janos Vajda, and Akademiai Kiado
p266 reproduced courtesy of AKHE Theatre and with kind permission of the photographer Ken Reynolds (©Ken Reynolds)
p269 provided courtesy of Horse and Bamboo Theatre Company
p272 "Lady with Mushrooms", 1912 Satigny, Switzerland. Photograph by Ernest Bloch. Collection Center for Creative Photography, University of Arizona ©1981 Arizona Board of Regents
p274 ©2003 digital image, The Museum of Modern Art, New York/ Scala, Florence
p276 photo ©John Robertson
p278 ©The Artist Estate, Courtesy of Marlborough Fine Art (London) Ltd
p281 photo courtesy of Caroline Lee
p283 ©Ramualdas Rakauskas, reproduced by kind permission
pp284/5 provided courtesy of Lucinda Jarret
p288 photo reproduced with kind permission of Pamela Harrison

Photographs on the following pages are by Chris Crickmay:
7, 16, 32, 46, 54, 56, 70, 102, 106, 127, 138, 147, 223, 231, 239, 240.
The photograph on p262 is by Miranda Tufnell

Although every attempt has been made to trace and contact copyright holders before publication, in some cases this has not been possible. If contacted, we will be pleased to rectify any errors or omissions at the earliest opportunity.